Experiencing
One-World

Experiencing One-World

Nataraja Guru

DK PRINTWORLD
Publishers of Indian Traditions

Cataloging in Publication Data — DK
[Courtesy: D.K. Agencies (P) Ltd. <docinfo@dkagencies.com>]

Nataraja Guru, 1895-1973, **author.**
Experiencing one-world / Nataraja Guru. – Third impression.
pages cm
Includes bibliographical references and index.
ISBN 9788124605288 (PB)

1. Absolute, The. 2. Metaphysics. I. Title. II. Title: One-world.

BD416.N38 2017 DDC 111.6 23

First published in India in 1996
Second impression in 2009
Third impression in 2017

ISBN 13: 978-81-246-0528-8 (PB)

Printed and published by :
D.K. Printworld (P) Ltd.
Regd. office : *Vedaśrī*, F-395, Sudarshan Park
ESI Metro Station, New Delhi - 110 015
Phones : (011) 2545 3975, 2546 6019
e-mail : indology@dkprintworld.com
Web : www.dkprintworld.com

Foreword

SEEING the parochial and clannish loyalty of the people in India in general and Kerala in particular, Narayana Guru advised his disciple Natarajan to move to a distant place where the mental clime was not infected by the relativistic vested interests of castes and clans. The disciple choose Sorbonne in Paris for the completion of his higher studies and to begin his mission of bringing all the major interests of man to a global appraisal of values and appreciating the collective effort of humanity to live a better life.

Nataraja Guru had the great fortune to have a father who was devoted to Narayana Guru, even before he was born. The Guru gave great attention to steer the mind and spirit of young Natarajan. He evinced his interest in Natarajan's progressive educational formation which came providentially in a graded manner. After his geological studies, he moved to biology especially zoology, and then to educational psychology in which he took his doctorate at the Sorbonne. Up till then, Narayana Guru's guidance and inspiration was with Nataraja Guru. With the one world vision of Narayana Guru, Nataraja Guru familiarized himself with all the great people of his time — poets, philosophers, scientists and educationalists. He came into intimate contact with Henri Bergson and was much influenced by Jean Jaques Rousseau.

After teaching in the International Fellowship School in Geneva, where Rousseau was still considered as 'The citizen of Geneva', the Guru returned to India to share his wisdom with the students of his own country. It was at that time John Spiers came to him as a camp-follower and helped him in all his literary works. The Guru had a programme in his mind of giving a full course in one-world-teaching, beginning with

AN INTEGRATED SCIENCE OF THE ABSOLUTE in which he brought together all the loose ends of the conclusive teachings of religion, science, philosophy, psychology, art and literature.

The foremost need to evolve a one-world-people is to spell out the philosophy of unitive vision, for which Narayana Guru's classic, *Darśana Mālā*, gave him the fundamentals. Based on that, the Guru wrote his *Integrated Science of the Absolute* in three volumes. The major guidelines for thinking in terms on one-world lay dormant in two great areas where human interests are acute. One is the physical needs, so Nataraja Guru saw economics as a basic requirement of understanding and training to meet one's own neighbour as part of the world corporation of sharing the amenities that one gets from nature. That led him to write *Towards an One World Economics.*

To appreciate One-World Economics, seeds of a new attitude is to be sown in children, to look upon the world as his country. A child, like a seed, has to grow on earth, nourished by nature's favours, and his aspirations should be raised to be tall enough to look beyond the trees to the stars. The educational theory of Nataraja Guru therefore touches the alpha point of necessities and the omega point of higher freedom.

Once the young mind is turned on to world fraternity, his natural environment should be a world of socio-political and geographical familiarization with the world where the man at the farthest post is looked upon as a brother. For this, a new manifestation was needed. That made Nararaja Guru turn to World Government, with Garry Davis and his crew as activists in the field as a band of world citizens.

It is at this stage that Nataraja Guru felt the need to have a unified scheme of a common language for scienctists and the bards or spiritual seers. He wanted the ancient and the modern, the physical and the spiritual, and philosophies of all outlooks to be conversant with the language of audiovisual arts and the charm of poetry. He found clearly that the impartial reasoning that brings certitude to all lies in mathematics and the field of its popular application is in the world of architecture and music.

Such was the ambition of Nataraja Guru as an absolute lover of humanity.

I am sure this book will highlight the main features of the well-groomed unitive consciousness of a world citizen who wishes the world to be educated to enhance the dignity of man. Living in the warmth of universal fraternity, we solicit everybody's cooperation in this noble endeavour of restructuring our world.

This book is a compilation of four books and several articles written by Nataraja Guru over a period of about twenty years. Serialized in the English magazine *Values* from Narayana Gurukula, Kaggalipura, Bangalore South, these books and articles are part of a programme of educating the public which began with Narayana Guru's earlier attempts to focus people's attention on evolving a one-world-consciousness.

April 28, 1995 **Guru Nitya Chaitanya Yati**

Contents

Part I

Memorandum on World Government

1

Preamble

THE subject which concerns us here is that of World Government. In the light of Samuel Johnson's statement that politics is the last refuge of scoundrels, and in view of the more than evident nuisance value created by the din of rival politicians at the time of political elections, contemplatives are naturally expected to steer clear of all politics. The question arises then as to why spiritual and contemplative persons like ourselves, speaking of Unitive Understanding (*advaita*) and taking our position on the long spiritual tradition of India, should dabble in such subjects as government and politics at all; and the general reader would be justified in wanting to know the place of *Advaita Vedānta* in such a context.

Vedānta comes into contact with the problem of human welfare only indirectly, and sometimes after prayers there is a sort of ending benediction of *śānti*, which consists of saying, "Let all people in the world be happy". The welfare of humanity is thus not altogether outside the scope of the Vedāntic tradition of India. Suffering anywhere in the world must be considered as belonging to the subject. Every such situation has the subjective side or the self-aspect which might be outside the context of actual suffering, and the objective side or the non-self aspect which is the actual seat or scene of such sufferings.

Advaita Philosophy, which is no other than the way of Unitive Understanding in its essence, must be capable of equating the self and the non-self as interchangeable terms. The suffering of fellow man thus equates itself naturally with the suffering of every true *Vedāntin*. Bliss (*ānanda*) and suffering (*duḥkha*) both take place within the Self, which has the absolute status of cancelling its own subjective and objective prejudices. *Advaita* is a supposition taken between two rival aspects of the same problem. Thus the welfare of humanity and the suffering of even the smallest animal, such as an ant going to be lightly trampled upon by a *Vedāntin*, become subjects of equal concern to him by the two sides of the situation in which he is to be correctly situated.

It is not the suffering as we see it in the headlines of a morning newspaper, glanced at before breakfast in a light-hearted way, that is to be kept in mind here. Headlines big and small reflect disasters major or minor, which take place in this world, and what is read in one daily newspaper is forgotten by the next morning's breakfast. This is the common way of taking casual interest in politics. The difference between this way and the contemplative way that belongs to the Gurukula is that our interest does not fluctuate between morning and evening, or even between weekdays and Sundays.

Newspaper politics has to be reduced to a common numerator or denominator. We get thus a dialectical approach to politics which is, in our case, to be distinguished by two other terms besides **Unitive Understanding**. Firstly, we are interested in **geo-politics**, and not just politics. This implies that we treat of the planet Earth as a unit called *geos*, in which politics is to be discussed under the light of the Sun in terms of **Fus Solice**, the Justice of the Sun. We are thus interested in world politics, and not just local or even national party politics. Secondly, our politics is based on a **dialectical approach**, the essence of which can be stated by the formula inscribed on the shields of the two female figures in the monument of the Swiss Confederation in Geneva, Switzerland. One tall female figure holds a shield bearing the inscription, **One for All**; the other corresponding counterpart of the same tall woman holds another shield, though placed on the ground, with the reciprocal part of the formula, **All for One.** Thus between the **General Good** and the **Good of All** there is a dialectical interplay of values. Politics emerges into view, as amply proved in the *Social Contract* of Jean-Jacques Rousseau, when two factors, one standing for the **General Good** and the other for the **Good of All**, come into interplay.

These subtleties require much more elaboration than what we can make in these short preliminary remarks. Geo-politics, thus understood geo-dialectically, is a special branch of discipline. We cannot go into all the detailed aspects here, but we can refer to some of the salient features of the geo-dialectical approach to World Government, by way of indicating some of the highlights and by way of underlining some of the characteristics of this kind of politics, to show that such a subject is not outside the scope of a contemplative or spiritual way of life, especially at the present-day, when mass communication portends a time when humanity will receive messages which cannot be distinguished from the medium, nor the medium from the message.

Humanity is One

This is the *a priori* given basis of the World Government outlined in this Memorandum. The recognition of the unity and solidarity of mankind follows from the correct application of the scientific or unitive approach to the problems of humanity. Just as belief in many gods is incorrect, so when humanity is considered relativistically as consisting of closed groups, however big, or justified in the name of power or practicability, such a view violates this first and fundamental principle of the indivisible unity of Man. Humanity is one by its common origin, one in its common interests and motives of happiness here on earth in everyday living, and one in its relation to the aspirations and ideals which bind human beings together by bonds of sympathy for each other. A

Unitive and Absolute Value is at the basis of human life. This High Human Value knows no frontier either actual or ideological. It makes no discrimination between rich and poor, high and low, civilized and backward. Sympathy for suffering and indignation against injustice to fellow men transcends time and clime, and reaches out evenly or pointedly, as the case may deserve, to the uttermost recesses of the one world which man inhabits.

Human Nature, 'Good' and 'Bad' at Once

To say that evil does not exist and that God created all men good will sound unrealistic to modern ears after all the experience of humanity which historians have recorded. To state, on the contrary, that evil is the basis of human life, leaves us equally unconvinced. The wary man would back out of the paradox involved by saying that the verdict would depend on the particular case and refuse to generalize. He might even go further and say sophistically that the possibility of error or evil in human nature is what makes man human at all; and by the same token it could be argued that even evil must have a basis of goodness. Such arguments have brought human affairs up against impasses again and again. We are no nearer to the right answers to such questions than we were thousands of years ago. General scepticism drives people to sit on the fence.

Irrespective of time or clime, wise men have repeatedly tried to teach us a way out of these dilemmas. There is a method and a theory of knowledge proper to wisdom which is not the same as that of logic, ratiocination or even 'objective' or mechanistic intelligence.

A New Yet Time-honoured Approach

Such an approach should be scientifically formulated. It will then resolve conflicting counterparts of a given situation or problem, unitively, without conflict. Just as One Humanity is true, so One Absolute justice for all mankind, One Goodness applicable to all mankind, and One God or Ideal of Human Happiness could be stated to be at the basis of common human existence. The ordering of human life on unitive lines is the function of the World Government as envisaged in the present Memorandum.

The Science of Dialectics

Whether human life is fundamentally good or bad does not concern us here so directly as whether it is possible to cancel out evil by the good residing in human nature itself, i.e., whether there is still hope for humanity to overcome ignorance by wisdom. The static verity of human goodness or badness should be viewed dynamically as belonging to the flow of human life shaping itself in time. Living unitive thinking is concerned with the progressive shaping of human life based on values which fuse into an ever newly integrated flux which is subject to a constant process of becoming. The old order changes giving place to new. It is in this sense that wisdom is a perennial way of contemplation. This wisdom forms part of a science which could be called dialectics. The Truth that makes men Free and the Knowledge that gives Power are open and dynamic human values to be understood in the light of dialectics. The 'evil' that is necessarily present in human nature when viewed unitively according to dialectics, is as true as the 'goodness' inherent in human nature when viewed in a similar way. All values, positive or negative, when unitively understood, belong to a vertical scale of values which man must recognize, and every moment he has to choose between opposite alternatives. At each step here a constant process of dialectical revaluation is involved, whether in the life of each man, each unit group, or of humanity as a whole. Such an approach to world affairs is what this Memorandum recommends, and it is this which makes it so unique as legitimately to claim the attention of all lovers of humanity who are interested in a World Government which for the first time is scientifically conceived. This newly formulated science, wherein pure dialectical reasoning is applied to problems of the world, may be called the 'Science of Geo-Dialectics'.

The Geo-Dialectical Method

The geo-dialectical method consists of clearly recognizing the two counterparts which belong together in any given situation or problem to be eased or resolved in human affairs. Man is caught in necessity or bondage on the one hand, and, one the other, reaches out towards the contingent factor of freedom. If we could say that his necesssity is symbolized either by the need for bread or by common hunger, contingency is symbolized by the need to live and breathe freely, and in fulfilling one's life according to the inner urges within each man. Man has to fulfil life according to his own nature without being stifled or suffocated. Bread and freedom resolved into unitive terms of a central value spell Happiness. When each man is happy, all mankind is happy. When there is a general happiness of mankind as a whole, each man has his happiness most secure. No mother is happy unless the child also is happy, and no ruler is happy unless the subjects too are happy. To recognize and deal with the dialetical counterparts, while respecting fully the nature of the individual or the integrated personality of normal units called nations, in such a manner as to cancel out counterparts in unitivie terms of positive human values conducive to human happiness, is the basis of the geo-dialectical method. Being an applied part of pure dialectics, the full implications of this statement can be clarified only after studying dialectics.[1]

Anomalies, Absurdities and Dangers of the Mechanistic Approach

The non-dialectical, non-unitive, mechanistic or unilateral approach which does not respect the integrated personality of nations or individual citizens gives rise to many anomalies, absurdities and disasters. If the case of a mother is taken up without including with it the case of the child, if the case of a ruler is taken without considering the ruled, or the master's case without the servant's, and even if we should forget to take into account that the one and the many are interdependent or reciprocally interrelated in a subtle dialectical manner, we invoke disasters large or small and sow the seeds of injustice and consequent suffering. Each man consists of what he is subjectively, and what he holds as dear as life itself, such as his money, his family, or even his faith. These adhere closely to and result in the happiness that each person craves for. National and cultural groups also have integrated personalities of their own which cannot be subjected to a mechanistic treatment which is merely based on quantitative statistics or facts, without injury. Such roots of integration lie deeply buried in history. The partitioning of nations has resulted in genocidal tragedies.

Operating through decades or centuries, historical necessity gives the *raison d'être* to the jigsaw puzzle patterns of the differently coloured patches on the mapped surface of the globe which school children are taught to distinguish as self-contained or autonomous political units, entities, states, countries or notions. Sometimes such patches tend to mark merely an area where an amorphous mass of people live who are dictated by external forces. Even while the child is being taught political geography, the patches change their outline or encroach on each other with a strange irrationality. These patches are not the result of any scientific ordering of the world, but are arbitrary and haphazard in their origin and growth. They have been traced by wars old or recent, whether just or unjust, and *de facto* status of certain units do not correspond to their *de jure* status in the present set-up of nations. The status of member nations in present-day international bodies such as the United Nations depends on the veto or whim of the powers that be. No public or objective noms prevail here. Neither the natural law of the jungle nor any law consciously formulated in any manner in keeping with the much-vaunted dignity of man regulates internationalism at present.

The Zero Hour for the Declaration of a World Government is Past

In the days of chivalry willing combatants fought duets in strict accordance with certain codes of honour consistent with human dignity as understood in those olden days. But the day has now come when a brave general is reported to be proudly contemplating the extermination of 'whole sections of people' by the latest weapons which human intelligence itself has placed at the service of irresponsible adventurers. Instead of the knight errant helping women and children in distress, humanity today hears of threats against the innocent and the unarmed. We hear of war criminals punished after wars have ceased, when we are not sure whether the punishment or the crime violates human codes of honour or justice. While their children wait for the horrible news outside the prison, parents get the electric chair for not keeping their own intelligence from helping those whom one nation or other suspects for the time being. Politics too strangely keeps changing its own complexion from day-to-day. Concentration camps and the lot of millions of displaced families who are denied 'papers' year after year, making illegal even their right to work and earn a living, and thus in effect taking away their *de facto* status as fellow human beings, prove that the days of barbarity and slavery are not over. Exposed to fear and insecurity, humanity knows not which way to turn for consolation. Helplessly, it looks on with impotence when the dignity of humanity itself is at stake. The zero hour for the declaration of a World Government, at least in principle, is long past. Such a Government must voice human honour and self-respect. It must preserve the wisdom-heritage of humanity and hand it down to coming generations. Those who love humanity and absolute human values at every level and department of life must be protected. Those who hate their fellow men for reasons that are not universally valid are as good as not existing. Those who adhere to rival relativist values are bound, in any case, to cancel out one another. There is no real need to name the enemies of humanity because their days are numbered if humanity has any hope of survival at all. That humanity will survive, the supporters of World Government do firmly and solemnly believe. Therefore the time has come for all lovers of humanity to take a definite stand, avoiding double-talk, duplicity, compromise and doubt.

Note

1. See the *Dialectical Methodology, An Integrated Science of the Absolute* and other allied works by the present author.

2

Genesis

The World Government is an Accomplished Fact

THE World Government came into being (in principle at least) at Long. 63° 25' West, Lat. 44° 32' North on Sept. 4, 1953. Utter Necessity was its justification. Very special states of stress, both personal and global, ushered it into being when a stateless person was forced into a closed territory against his own will or consent. Even a *de facto* citizen of the world already, with a fine record of service to the same closed territory or 'nation', was denied the right to make a living or pursue his own happiness. There was no Government to represent him or stand by him. The World Government had therefore to be conceived as though **immaculately**, though neither illegitimately, disloyally, nor dishonourably, born. Time waits for no man. Better now than never. Necessity knows no law. All is fair in love and war. These are some of the sayings that hold good here. It takes only two to start a quarrel or sign a pact, and only one to tell the truth. It is not numbers that can justify a government, but its instrinsic quality based on Absolute Truth or Justice. It takes but one to steer the ship to safety, though hundreds may weep and wail in vain.

The Validity of the World Government is not Questionable

If even today the simple accident of being born in a so-called royal family can justify the formation of an absolute monarchy, it can be seen that no principle of geo-dialectics is violated by the formation of a World Government. The World Government has no territory other than the surface of the globe. It is not conceived as a rival to any existing government. It does not intend to duplicate any of their functions. Neither does it wish to be a parallel government, nor has it ambitions to be a super-state. On the other hand, it has no wish to occupy a second place among nation states. It has an absolute status of its own as understood in the light of the science of geo-dialectics already referred to. In the usually understood sense the World Government has no programme of action or territorial ambition. It does not rule by threat, force, or the power of the magistrate or the police. Knowledge is its power and, instead of threats or punishments, it relies on the truth of the dictum that a word to the wise will suffice. Just as a ball of iron can be made white-hot without the ball itself suffering division, change, or control from outside, so the World Government proposes to influence humanity in and through humanity for humanity. Nothing is to be disrupted in the process. A certain type of truth which has been called 'the pearl of great price', the 'little leaven that leaveneth the whole lump' or that '*dharma* (right way of life), even a little of which will save from great fear' is the pinch of Absolutist Wisdom which is to be added to the chaotic world-situation so as help us to reorientate and re-integrate and regulate human affairs. In other words, the World Government applies a subtle form of **vertical pressure** corresponding to spiritual heat or electricity. Order then emerges as with magnetized iron filings from non-magnetized chaos.

Confirmation of the World Government

A second step forward in the formation of the World

Government was taken at Long. 77° 38 East, Lat. 12° 58' North, on May 15, 1956. A recessive part of the world, never even to be suspected of any intention to dominate the world through its power, has been chosen this time as the location from where to confirm and sanction the first formation of the World Government at a dominant part of the world. To rise above suspicion, World Government has to be established neutrally between the dominant and the recessive aspects of world political life. No one carrying the threat of the atom bomb in one hand and a message of peace in the other can be trusted by others who sail in the same boat. Relativism breeds rivals while the correctly dialectical or Absolutist approach unites and frees men in the name of a humanity which is understood unitively.

Between the initial formation of the World Government and its later more precise formulation and confirmation, nearly three years of experimentation, meditation and study have been undertaken. This second time, as stricter geo-dialectics would require, there were two sides represented by two men, in the solemn pact before the declaration of the World Government. One of these contracting parties represented the **Good of All** and the other represented the **General Good**. This subtle dialectical contract sets the pattern for the growth of the World Government. Such a formation of an actual government, at least in a nuclear form, has been duly announced. More conferences could be contemplated in the near future in different parts of the world, of those who represent the General Good or the Good of All, or both. The nuclear yet actual government will gather momentum by the good will of the people of the world from day-to-day so as to become an efficient and effective instrument for the reorientation and regulation of human affairs under the aegis of the Most High Principle of Goodness, or the Most Supreme Value of Happiness that humanity can accept to regulate its life. This Memorandum hereby greets all lovers of humanity with the happy news of the birth of the World Government. Its presence is to be felt, not especially in any fixed locality or centre, but all over or in every part of the world or wherever it can best serve its supreme purpose which is the political happiness of humanity. It is however the global, unitive one-world politics of all mankind with which we are concerned here. Because of its Absolutist character, this can be called both politics and no-politics at once, or a politics that gets rid of politics. In other words, the World Government is based on the pure politics to be known as geo-politics.

3

Other Partial Approaches

All Approaches Hitherto are either Negative or Relativistic

To the natural question why we should not join hands with other organizations working already in the field of internationalism, we have to answer that there is the fundamental drawback that all of them are vitiated by either a **negative** or a **relativistic** approach. What we mean by these two expressions must be somewhat clear from what we have already said.

By negativism we mean that proposals for peace or disarmament have been based on a regret or a fear connected with wars just fought or wars expected. At such moments there is great volume of collective emotion available, and those who offer quick results get nations to pay large sums for preserving peace or in the name of security. The regret, however, passes, as also the fear. Positive attitudes take their places, and one organization which failed to fulfil its contract is succeeded by another in a modified form. This is how the League of Nations was displaced by the United

Nations. The latter may be expected to go the way of its predecessor as soon as its impotency in the matter of securing peace becomes evident to all. It is patent that in spite of its declared intentions, the U.N. has not been able to make its member nations reduce their armaments, nor has it been able to mitigate the national excesses of its member nations. Of course in some matters it is better than nothing, but in other matters it is worse than nothing. Representatives of major nations get the chance of calling each other names at the glorified debates held under these bodies. With points of order, explanations of votes, amendments, counter-amendments and arbitrary powers of veto or methods of filibustering or blocking through satellite members, the U.N. has no power to implement even the smallest item in its own Declaration of Human Rights, not to speak of objecting to the dangers of atomic tests. Actually, it is used by power groupings to sling mud at each other. At best it is a glorified debating society employing thousands of interpreters, stenographers and clerks who live and move in a beehive of modern buildings. They are obliged to keep the powers that be in good humour. Every effort has been made already to try and work through the U.N. by the sponsors of the present World Government. The story is too long to relate here. Suffice it to say that it has been a signal failure.

By relativism we mean that some sort of duality as between **free nations** and others who are not so is still retained in the structure of the organization. The organization is not unitively conceived according to any science of Absolutism. Representation, admission, or expulsion are based on no uniform norms of any science universally or publicly formulated.

Private, Partial or Party Organizations with World Programmes

There are various religious, political or even commercial bodies which influence world affairs. There is the Communist Party which shapes the trend of world politics. Then there is the Catholic Church and various other bodies which have world programmes. Commercial combines and banking agencies fulfil openly or secretly many functions which properly should belong to a World Government. These serve humanity in good, bad or indifferent ways, but as long as a correctly formulated World Government is not there, no one has any right to find fault with whatever service they render or even with whatever exploitation they consciously or unconsciously excercise in world affairs. International organizations exist in many departments such as the Universal Postal Union, etc. Member nations may or may not ratify their resolutions, and even when they do so, the limitations of their own arbitrary sovereignty or nationalism are not wholly discarded. The approach to such problems is not based at present on any exact science such as we claim to be at the basis of the World Government as envisaged in this Memorandum. This class of organizations can be almost good or the next best, but just as one cannot jump a chasm in two leaps or expect a prize for the number nearest to the one that wins the prize, so the wholesale scientific basis of the World Government is all-important. The science of geo-dialectics is based on a rare and precious way of higher reasoning without which no World Government can be expected to succeed. Such undertakings would not be justified even if they should obtain a large measure of success. Here almost true is not good enough. This same verity is couched in the old word that 'good government is no substitute for self-government'. **The mandate for any government has to be derived from the people who are to be governed on the one pole and, from another pole, derived from the Absolute Justice implicit in any such government**. Like religion or morality, there are two different sources to World Government. It has to be the resultant of ascending and descending dialectical counterparts. Such principles, however, can be made clear only in the light of general dialectics, which has still to be formulated and taught in the proposed Institute of Dialectics. Meanwhile we are here obliged to state with seeming dogmatism that partial and unscientific approaches to the problem of World Government are not valid.

4

Unique and Positive Qualities

What the World Government is not

We have already stated in passing that the World Government is not based on power with the weapon of threats of punishment. Its authority is derived from humanity's need for it and from its rightness and justice. It has been mentioned also that it has no territorial ambitions or designs. It does not propose to arrogate to itself any functions that are being fulfilled already correctly by existing governments. No overlapping or duplication of functions is in the scheme presented here. Neither is diarchy or a parallel form of government contemplated. However, in spite of this position, the World Government will not be second to any other government. It will consciously avoid functioning even as a supra-state in the usual sense. If we should want to think of the political theory on which it is to be based, it can be said here in advance that it does not subscribe to the *laissez faire* doctrine. Much less does it adhere to the doctrine of 'might is right', which, though more positive, is still outmoded. The Benthamian doctrine of 'the greatest happiness of the greatest number' is also not in keeping with the principles of the present Government. It does not think quantitatively at all. That would make it fall into the capital error of being mechanistic or relativistic in its approach, which we have stated to be the very drawback we wish to avoid. It is based on a dialectical approach to world problems. What this implies we shall clarify as much as possible below.

Based on a Solemn Pact

The World Government is based on a solemn pact between the people of the world and their own dialectical counterpart in the form of a wise lover of humanity representing the general good of humanity as a whole. Although stated in the form of two aspects, these counterparts form the obverse and reverse of the same coin called Absolute Happiness, Goodness, or Justice of Humanity. This is a unitive central Value whatever the word-stimulus employed may be. Moreover, it is essentially a human value in keeping with the dignity of the human species. Bread and freedom will be provided for all when such a Government comes into its full swing of effective and efficient working, by the conscious co-operation and understanding of the people of the world. Stated in the most general terms, the task of the World Government will be the intelligent ordering of human life activities in a manner normal and natural to man, without violating his own innate dispositions, legitimate interests, or aspirations.

The World Government must Govern its Subjects Actively or Positively

It must be practical and effective in its functioning. Mere pious hopes like that of waiting to establish the kingdom of heaven on earth will not improve matters. A government worth the name must deliver the goods or benefits belonging to the domain of politics. It must make human life on earth less full of humiliation, helplessness or suffering. While this is right, the World Government must guard itself from falling into the opposite error of getting involved in a maze of overt actions which will fan feelings of rivalry and create more warring camps than ever. To avoid war, to guarantee **collective security**, to make **co-existence** possible or to practise the virtues of the *pañca-śīla* of non-interference, or to cultivate an attitude of **positive neutrality**, have been the recommendations of some of the world's politicians for improving human affairs. These recommendations, though good as far as they go, embody the negative side of the virtue of international life. **To leave matters well alone** and not to make more rules than are necessary, are cardinal virtues for the World Government to cultivate. Stopping at harmless virtues which are still relative will not make a World Government function normally. The positive programme of the World Government has at every stage to balance or cancel out the negative, so as to strike the just mean between war and peace, activity and passivity, hot and cold attitudes, co-operation and competition. A constant pressure has to be maintained between these opposing tendencies so as to throw up constantly a higher value as an ideal for humanity.

Positive Pressure and Vertical Ascent

A man becomes a better man by intensely and consciously wanting to be good. When he is good he should mind his own business and not interfere with others. His own inner urges as a man, insofar as they are in keeping with human nature as understood scientifically in all its bearings, have to get the full play of expansion and expression normally, without clashing with others who want to have the same chances. Those deep-seated specific qualities which distinguish man and make him unique and unrivalled, must be brought out into creative expression instead of lying dormant or unfulfilled. If virtues such as these apply to the individual, they could apply equally to families as normal human life units. Rural or urban units could have personalities cultivating the same virtues or moral principles in keeping with a science or philosophy of human life. Bloated amorphous political units must also attempt to conform to the requirements of this geo-dialectical absolutist morality. When all formations follow the same laws, the order which constitutes World Government can be expected. No feverish horizontal activity is here involved. A certain positive pressure resulting in a vertical ascent is what needs to be constantly maintained in human life. This pressure can also be compared to a moral or spiritual heat or to the magnetizing influence of a current of electricity. The principle of double negation and double assertion as known to scholastic philosophy in Europe should be understood as implicit here. Only a fuller treatise on geo-dialectics itself can clarify such matters more completely or elaborately.

5

Active Programme

What the World Government Actually Proposes to do

WHAT the World Government actually proposes to do is first and foremost to bring to bear a new and total world outlook upon world problems. It will help to turn out more and more World Citizens. They will be human beings who have attained the full status of persons who represent the General Good and the Good of All. While making themselves happy according to the light of dialectical wisdom, they will constantly strive for the happiness of their fellow men in a manner consistent with the same wisdom. Such a balanced life between two interests unitively treated, will enhance the value of the individual in society. He will carry with him a subtle influence or presence. Such a man would be a modern version of a knight errant seeking the right kind of adventure to face in the name of his love of humanity. He would soon be appraised of innumerable opportunities presenting themselves to him where he can render signal service to his fellow men without going at all out of his way. Many such functions might lie outside the scope of geo-politics proper, with which alone we are concerned primarily in this Memorandum. However, this should not deter such a man or woman from placing his or her high personal credit at the service of the cause of World Citizenship and World Government. To call oneself a sovereign citizen of the world and consciously to affiliate oneself wholeheartedly to the noble ideal, reveals in one who does so the true human value which a lover of humanity must carry with him, thus enhancing his value at once with reference to himself and with all others with whom his lot is to live on earth. These are the rights and duties that such an affiliation at once confers.

As such a status comes from an understanding of the science involved, there is no danger of groups of such men considering themselves as belonging to any **superior caste** or group. The danger of such a contingency need not, however, be ruled out. On the contrary all such World Citizens should be taught to keep this danger constantly in their minds, to correct themselves consciously, and to help fellow world citizens to do the same. The danger, however, should not deter humanity from launching the undertaking, just in the same way that burst boilers or air crashes do not deter man from navigation or flying. Moreover, by the overall unitive approach, which is the basis of the whole new outlook involved in the World Citizenship Movement, the danger of clannishness or caste-mindedness can always be counteracted consciously even when the tendency is there. This unitive outlook is more deeply rooted than at that level of life where World Citizenship has to express itself, which at most, is the waking world of the conscious ego. The unitive approach to reality will permeate the sub-conscious, the infra-conscious, and the fourth stratum of transparent or direct awareness in the individual, so that the danger of exclusiveness as an individual will be countered very effectively. This is the definite advantage of the approach to world problems being actually a particular branch of the general science of Wisdom dialectics. This will further guarantee proportion, balance, normality, wholesomeness, harmony, and humane grace or correctness to World Citizenship.

The success of the World Government depends on its

ability to produce the right kind of World Citizens as its champions in different parts of the world. They could be described as the most important single asset on the side of the undertaking.

Political programmes can be made effective from inside or outside, from above or below, the present formation

Once the reorientation of the spirit or the change of heart in regard to world problems has taken place in a given individual, and he feels keenly that he has to **do** something for the furtherance of his ideal, it is possible for him to do it from where he happens to be naturally. If he is a legislator he can stand for election on a World Government ticket. The immense popularity of the One World idea will only enhance his chances of success. According to qualitative geo-dialectical principles it would not be wrong of him to enter any given council, big or small, national or local, urban or rural, swearing allegiance to the head of that group or the head of several groups for the time being; for in doing so he would be recognizing only the symbolic absolutism implicit or inherent in the person (president or monarch) who happens to be at the head. Moreover, in terms of universal human values for which he is a politician, there is no contradiction or conflict between the interests of that particular political unit and in the human interests of the world itself taken as a unit. There is a geo-dialectical secret involved here which could be brought out by a homely example. If an old well should be hidden by a flood which covered it later, the water that quenches the thirst is the same water whether it comes from the hidden well part or from the lake overcovering it. There is no conflict possible between two concentric circles. This is the ancient wisdom found in the *Bhagavad Gītā*, which comes to the rescue of world politics by which all the walls of the Jerichos in the world must fall. The blast of absolutism from inside or outside the wall, or both together, by those placed superiorly above, or in, as it were, helpless positions below, dominant or recessive men or women the world over, have only to want real solemn earnestness to make the World

Government effective. Thus the World Government work will become most practicable, positive, and irresistible.

How to Practise World Politics from Inside

When once elected to a local or national body on a World Government ticket, the man or woman concerned takes a course of action in keeping with the principles of humanity and world morality or value comprised between the two poles of bread and freedom. Taking his stand on the norms and standards of geo-dialectics the World Citizen generally takes a middle-of-the-road position in respect of leftist or rightist parties, and generally supports the president when Absolute Justice, Morality or the Ideal are not violated by his position. When resolutions are moved or voting is explained he gets a chance of placing before those who are politically minded a new approach based on global human interests. He can bring token cut-motions on armament budgets when disproportionate, and the people's sense of justice can be appealed to. If he should be ousted from the Council the people will follow him into the street if his cause is just and in the name of the interests of the common man and humanity at once. Here, for the present, the possibilities of such action from inside must be left to imagination. When permanent support to the world approach is certain, 'mondialization' within such units is not impossible. Symbolic acts in keeping with the code of honour or morals proper to the World Citizen could be resorted to, resembling Tolstoyan or Gandhian methods as revised in the light of a stricter geo-dialectical science.

The Practice of World Politics from Above

Men, and more especially women, who occupy positions of influence or who have resources at their command, can study the plans of World Government and bring their weight to bear on the side of supporting human rights and preserving the best in the heritage of mankind, whether in art, culture, or wisdom, Dante, Shakespeare, and Kālidāsa belong to humanity first, and the claims of particular nations for them are only incidental. There is also the one perennial contemplative tradition based on a science of the Absolute which is the common property of humanity. In preserving these and in protecting the common wisdom heritage of mankind the best interests of the common man will be secured also.

Poor men, who have to make a living wherever it is at present available to them, are kept from freely reaching out to their God-given opportunities by artificial man-made rules. These rules must be broken down. Travel becomes more and more difficult and rules are piled upon rules by nations big and small for no valid or justifiable reason except to retaliate in the name of national pride or exclusiveness. Parochialism, tribalism, casteism, and nationalism have much in common with fanaticism or blind orthodoxy. A world philosophy and religion critically and scientifically ordered will help to relieve the existing asphyxiating conditions wherein miserable men and women have to live in the prison of criss-cross rules which is the present world. All modern people are keenly aware of this stifling atmosphere. The well-to-do, the influential, or at least their wives, must take interest in the poor, not to disrupt anything or anybody, but to bring just that kind of legitimate pressure which will ease the trouble of the common man. There can be a World Order of Ladies or Knights who could function as supervisors, permission authorities, world guards or witnesses of natural integrity, peacemakers or arbitrating advisers in the numerous walks of life in all matters ranging between the gaining of bread and the gaining of personal or spiritual freedom. Premarital, post-marital, and familial arbitration or advice, helping juveniles and children from possible maladjustments, the re-education of delinquents, psychological guidance, a pedagogy which respects the personality of the child, co-operative centres for the reclamation and relaxation of persons caught in the stress of life or in conditions of tension, and occupational guidance or treatment — these are only a few of the fields in which the World Citizen could help the lot of humanity from wherever he or she might be living. A complete philosophy and a way of life shaped on unitive and absolutist lines is of course presupposed here. It will be the task of the World Institute of Human Affairs to elaborate, formulate, and make this available in the different languages of the world.

The Practice of World Politics from Below

Individual men and women are caught in the barbed wire frontiers, both ideological and actual, of rules and interdictions against freedom to pursue happiness freely and peacefully on the surface of the God-or-Nature-given earth. There has been no way hitherto for the articulation of their grievances. Not content with enforcing the rules of his own country, police belonging to stranger countries have begun to help the other country in enforcing wrong rules in the name of internationalism. There is thus a double barrage of many absurd rules which themselves are multiplied beyond reason or necessity. The clever ones get away with every restriction somehow, but the lot of the ordinary man becomes difficult. One has to linger only for a few minutes at passport or permit offices to be convinced of the large volume of suffering to which men and women are subjected. To refer even to a few typical cases would be outside the scope of this Memorandum and would mar the sobriety of style which we wish to preserve here as far as possible. In one of his works Ruskin got a paragraph from a daily newspaper printed in red ink, because the subject was shocking to all decent human sentiments. The untold sufferings of the common man because of red-tape and regulations would have to be printed in some other ink if it is to find a place in a Memorandum such as this is intended to be.

What the common man could do is to register with the World Government as a World Citizen and try to bring a vertically conceived pressure to bear on the situation. He has to rely on numbers here to cope with the machinery of governments which have a great deal of inertia in them. All shoulders have to be applied to the wheel to set affairs going normally. The trumpet blasts for absolute fairness from outside the walls of Jericho have to resound in consonance with the trumpet blasts from above or inside.

The Overall Functioning of the World Government

The inarticulated feelings of the soul of humanity or the emergent personality of the people of the world has to find its voice in the World Government. The point of view of the World Government has to be broadcast unhesitatingly in no uncertain terms and even with authority. Truth must be given a chance to prevail. Relativistic compromise is what makes humanity at present weak. These are facts which need no repetition here. As the World Government emerges more and more to public view, it will represent the conscience of humanity and will spotlight from day to day the errors detrimental to humanity's interests. In such a task it must keep clear from tacitly or openly becoming a tool in the hands of any existing power block. Even if help should be obtained from someone quarter more than another, the World Government must be above suspicion in pointing out mistakes. The cheap headline world of propaganda must be avoided. A **Voice of Humanity** and a **World News Agency** may be started to serve the cause of the World Government.

The Issuance of World Passports

The issuance of World Passports has already commenced. This would ease the situation arising in the cases of millions of persons who have no national status within nations. The response of nations is already there. Such persons will henceforth belong to the World Government. Their combined voice will and must be heard through the instrumentality of the World Government.

Proclamation of the Universal Declaration of Human Rights

Proclamation of the Universal Declaration of Human Rights made by the United Nations at Paris 1948 gives a legitimate overall function covering many points so far remaining unimplemented. Many major and minor nations are already committed to the thirty articles in this Declaration. In bringing vertical pressure to bear on this matter of implementation of that Declaration, the World Government would be in fact only helping the great number of nations to be true to their avowed undertakings.

To Have a World Committee

To have a World Committee to give assent to the World Government and its functions from time to time and hold World Conferences to compare notes and do all that is incidental to the formation and correct functioning of the Government, are also matters which are naturally to be provided for as normal to the programme of the Government as it is expected to unfold and expand quickly or gradually as the outside conditions and innate forces warrant. Powers of supervision and assent may be vested in a **Representative Select Committee** of those who are wise normally or who have received proper training in the **Institute of Dialectics** connected with the World Government.

6

Jurisdiction, Revenue, Resources, etc.

Territorial Jurisdiction

THE territorial jurisdiction of the World Government is the surface of the Earth. It does not think about owning any limited area to run its own primary Government with land taxes, frontiers to protect, and defence arrangements. Overweighted with these items, present governments are in many ways outmoded remnants of the past which must all be subjected to drastic revision. These revisions will take place automatically when the World Government as envisaged here begins to be more and more effective. Mondialization of select units of administration is not to be ruled out.

Revenue

Revenue is to be derived from the principle of indirect taxation as it prevails even now. Though indirect, the revenue will be by mutual consent. Service rendered by the Government could be charged for and, while prime necessities will be exempt even from such taxation as far as possible, items of luxury could be freely taxed. Such matters will be attended to by the World Service Authority under the World Government. Indirect taxation is a form of profit which it is open for the World Government to make against services rendered. In fact trade combines and banking corporations — not to speak of religious bodies — even now exist, which have enormous assets sometimes as large and general as that of many existing governments. Economic and financial experts can see through the irregularities of some of the present monetary and other arrangements in which, by words such as 'going off the gold standard' or in dividing the world into 'hard' and 'soft' currency areas, wealth is conserved in pockets which when examined by standards of absolute justice, do not belong to them. Gold is stored in vaults without use for the artificially inflated credit of power blocks, and various book adjustments are made behind the back of the common man to whom the money really belongs. World banks and world currencies exist already without the regular consent of the people of the world and what is called a loan to one country from another is not really a loan, but a long term commercial deal. It would not be impossible for the World Government to have its own credit and currency valid the world over, and planned on some rational human basis such as one day's labour equals one day's food and shelter in a 30 or 40 hour week (or even less) in a world where competition has been counteracted by cooperation, and where labour-saving devices are employed for more human conditions.

As we have already said, the most valuable single asset of the World Government is the World Citizen. Since World Citizens can be found by virtue of the rightness of the cause in any part of the world in unlimited numbers, the assets of all well-intending people anywhere in the world are already in effect those of the World Government. A revised living and organic system of accounting and budgetting has to be devised. There being no duality of ends and means in this work, receipts and disbursements need not necessarily show large figures. After all, on final analysis, large-scale banking is nothing but book-keeping.

7

World Law

WHEN we think of World Law, and of somebody who is able to conceive it on concrete lines, we are at once confronted with two rival aspects of the same question. A law is made to benefit a group of people; such a group of people, whether in a particular state or country or political unit, geographically understood or merely ideological in status, must consist of individuals. Each individual is likely to differ from another individual, in some detail or other at least. Temperaments and tastes have to tally with what each man receives or deserves to receive. One man's meat could be another man's poison. What a man needs may not be the same as what a woman needs, nor what a child might need. Thus, what is called the **General Good** can never be the same as what is conceived as the good of each individual, or the **Good of All**. One has necessarily to bring in the mathematical notion of the greatest common multiple or the least common measure when thinking of any one item that caters to the needs of a group treated as comprising individuals, or else as a general totality treated as one unit.

To give a concrete example, a municipality might have Rs. 10,000 to be distributed generously. This amount might be spent in two ways: it could be used for giving a prize or scholarship to the best student at school, or else it could be evenly distributed to buy books or slates for every student in the municipality. In the latter case, it is the **Good of All** that is behind the motive for the benefit conferred. On the other hand, in the first case of helping the best student, it is through the satisfaction of the individual that the benefit is supposed to be conferred on all the students. Thus, in formulating beneficial laws for any group, one could think in only one of these two alternative ways. But law has to be conceived for the benefit of the **General Good** primarily, and it should harmonize within its scope the **Good of All** secondarily.

Between these rival claims of the general and the individual, there is a subtle dialectical formula which has always to be respected. This formula could be stated in the words, "**One for All and All for One**." We thus arrive at the famous formula on which Rousseau's *Contrat Social* is based, and on which the Swiss Confederation has been conceived. A socialistically conceived law respects the same dialectical formula when it lays down the maxim, "From each according to his ability and to each according to his need."

Thus, the lawmaker can take his stand on the **General Good** or on the **Good of All** when he formulates his laws. Just as an umpire cannot be a player in the game, it is not possible for one and the same person to fulfil these two roles which are necessarily dialectical counterparts. It is therefore that Rousseau says that the man who lays down the law should be "oceans removed" from the problems of the group itself, so that the **General Good** and **Good of All** might have a healthy interaction. What could be good for a small group might not be good for a big country, although the overall structure of both might conform to the same pattern. Good government or law is the resultant of an equilibrium established between what represents the **Good of All** individuals in it, and what is conducive to the **General Good** of the group taken as a whole.

Global Structural Perspective

Keeping this dialectical secret in one's mind, World Law must conform to an abstract structural pattern within which these two rival considerations can have a full and free scope for attaining a harmonious equilibrium, where individual interests cancel out against collective interests in every walk of life coming within the scope of government.

Thus, World Government and World Law need not necessarily be thought of in terms of a world that is only geographically true. Whatever the extent of the population or government, the same structural pattern and the same dialectical counterparts are found to prevail within its total frame of reference. A World State has therefore to be conceived first as a structural abstraction, while the functions of the state and its head — who is always a singular person — with all the other ramifications constituting the functions of a government, whether *de jure* or *de facto*, have to be thought of as Rousseau has been able to do masterfully in his *Contrat Social*. But Rousseau remains even to this day a much-misunderstood man. Let us therefore briefly turn our eyes elsewhere to see if this same dialectical approach is found acceptable to any other tradition or civilization.

Here we are confronted with a surprising coincidence. In ancient Sanskrit literature, there are revealed norms and patterns of behaviour attributed to celebrated kings such as those of the Solar Dynasty descended from Manu, the first lawgiver. Kālidāsa's *Raghuvaṁśa* is an epic of nineteen Cantos, each of which depicts a king who conforms to this same dialectically conceived and structurally balanced pattern of hehaviour. Economics, ethics, aesthetics and education are all woven into this general political fabric inextricably in the works of Kālidāsa. The King, who is a ruler of earth, is treated as a replica of Indra, the ruler of heaven and its denizens, the only difference being that of levels of value systems, each having its centre in a scale of a vertical series of points. Politics and law are thus conceived under the aegis of what is called an absolute pattern of principles as well as of behaviour. Any World Law has thus to be formulated with due respect for these relational aspects.

Besides the masterpiece on such a subject from Rousseau, it would be profitable for the modern student of

World Law to scrutinize in great detail the implications of a unified World Government as revealed in the writings of such great poets as Kālidāsa, more especially as such matters are brought into relief successively with reference to a long line of model monarchs in whose praise the immortal epic *Raghuvaṁśa* has itself been conceived. World Law is likely to receive a valuable original impetus when studied on the broad basis of a two-sided or dialectical interaction between the **General Good** and the **Good of All**, especially in India where holy tradition seems already to be in favour of such an approach. Rousseau's name, supplementing such a view from the Western world, would be sure to give it additional confirmation and support, even in the light of the most modern political theories. World Law thus becomes one that is unwritten, as well as being easily given to a common sense of justice in human relations. It is thus in this double perspective that we invite the attention of students to this all-important subject.

8

Conclusion

Unitive Approach

WHEN it is said that wars begin in the minds of men, it is already conversely admitted by even full-fledged politicians that the solution to world problems are of a spiritual order. The doctrine of Dialectical Materialism, which puts necessity and hunger first, follows another line of approach. Both these approaches can be reconciled in a unitive approach to world problems as implied in the present Memorandum.

Let us consider the armaments race which is due to mistrust and fear of other nations. A serious proposal from the World Government is sure to have an almost magical effect in easing the tension of mistrust between nations. The dehypnotization of the mentality of mutual suspicion will save every nation, large or small, from the lop-sided provisions at present made in their budgets. Let world opinion merely support the idea of the World Government and a tangible relaxation will be felt at the poles in the personality of nations which breeds mistrust, and even theoretically respected authority can avoid the waste of billions of dollars for the world as a whole.

Various Incidental Items

Let the World Government honour the farmer instead of vexing him with ever more items of taxation; let it start co-operative colonies to ease the tension of competitive life, such as those known as the Kibbutz now working successfully in Israel, where there is no money exchanged at all; let it start fair-price shops, taking a percentage in the place of a tax and so effectively eliminate the middle man, the black-marketeer and those who corner the necessities of life and make great and disproportionate profits at the expense of the common man; let it create clubs or pensions for persons obliged to pass their lives in eternal boredom, by means of colonies which will give them natural outlet for expression and opportunity for light occupation without competition for the young, the old and the weak; let it confer titles or honours on people who render signal service to the needy and thus give them a legitimately deserved chance to shine in the eyes of their fellow men. Such are some of the miscellaneous ways — too numerous to list completely — by which the World Government can justify its existence while it gathers momentum to be finally effective.

Decentralization and the Cancelling out of Problems

Another method full of possibilities for the World Government, is decentralization and the method of cancellation of the plus and minus of a given situation. For instance, capital is the cause of the sufferings of labour. Large mills are responsible for slums. Promiscuous religious charity is responsible for begging. These pairs that are interdependent could be cancelled out one against the other without punishment or reform coming from the centre. The head and the tail aspects can be cancelled out dialectically without central interference. The World Government can help in the ordering of such matters, taking into consideration the counterparts involved in each problem.

New States

There are many new states which require a new and fresh constitution. They could be guided by the World Government so that their new constitution would be framed in the spirit of World Government itself. This would save their disruption when world-mindedness in politics becomes a fully accomplished fact.

Need for Sacrifice on the part of World Government Sponsors

The sponsors of World Government have ever to keep before their minds that only through sacrifice and renunciation can such a noble idea be ushered into being. Human unity is an idea which is valid in theory at present. For people to adhere to the idea earnestly, they have to be sure that those who stand for it are not themselves lovers of power or grabbers of goods with unholy greed. Such a detachment should not be merely superficial, taking only the outward form of abstinence or even austerity. Happiness in the contemplation of the Self in its Absolute sense alone brings that blissful self-sufficiency which belongs to one who is able to be an exemplar of Wisdom. This contented state of happiness is induced by knowledge of the Science of the Absolute. A human being attains to his full stature as man when he is happy with himself, and thus in himself represents this high human Value. Such an ideal is within the reach of every human being without distinction of race, religion, nationality, sex, or even station in life. Even the humblest can walk in the way of the Absolute. A bad man who has taken the decision to regulate his life with reference to this final Absolute Norm of human life becomes by that mere decision equal in spiritual status to the greatest of wise men.

Thus having referred finally to the fountain-source of Wisdom from which one has to drink if one is to become a World Citizen in the fullest sense of the term, we hereby commend this Menorandum with all its imperfection to the attention of those generous spirits who are favourably disposed to examine it with sympathy and earnest understaning. Let those who are not of this category at least spare the sponsors of the Memorandum from their disadoption of it and consequent disparagement of its contents. Such is the prayer with which this document goes out to lovers of Wisdom and of humanity.

Part II
One-World Economics

9

Introduction

Economics deals with wealth as a value in life. Political economics as talked about in our times, whatever it might really be in itself, is confined to such subjects as would tend to make a chancellor of the exchequer act more intelligently than he might have done had he not studied them. The subject of economics has been laughed at by most serious thinkers, and been dubbed a 'dismal science'. It is based on a chronic desire in man to become richer and richer. In this sense economics is not a science at all, but reflects the diseased condition of an individual who thinks of the wealth of nations, or of one nation, from the ego-centric standpoint of self-aggrandizement.

The conflict involved in economics is paradoxical: one is to love one's neighbour as oneself, but at the same time Britannia must rule the waves. Between such rival positions, economics textbooks range in endless variety, wherein so-called wise people indulge themselves in notions such as those of supply and demand, production and distribution, or communication, transport and exchange. The token value of a coin should not be mixed up with its precious metallic content, and an unintelligent change in the proportion of silver added to minted coins in a state can make all the coins disappear from the country in the twinkling of an eye. Such are some of the dangers that economics textbooks warn the chancellor of the exchequer about.

The spiralling of prices, increase of rent-value, pressures of population, the efficacy of tariff walls — unjust and immoral in themselves, in which crag barons rob bag barons, as Ruskin would put it — give us an endless variety of textbook subjects as taught in colleges and universities of the present-day all over the world. One hears of possible explosion of population, and control of displaced persons to keep them from seeking livelihoods beyond national frontiers. Liberty is flaunted at every step of what passes for good economics.

Vague Theories and Questionable Practices

Subjects like inflation are as vague in the minds of economists as in the most ancient days, when economics was not taught in schools as a science as it is at present. We are told that it is good to have a high standard of life in a country, while at the same time there are economic experts who ascribe the spiralling of prices to too much planning. Quantities of edible products are known to be buried, burned or thrown into the sea so that the height of prices could be maintained, without respect for the hunger of people who might be starving.

Every market woman knows that demand and supply have to balance each other, but the relation between production and exchange is still a mysterious factor. One hears of countries like England going off the gold standard at a given moment — when it is their turn to pay their debts — while they themselves respected it at the time that the standard was favourable to them. Whether this is honest dealing has been questioned by eminent authorities, irrespective of the side they took in economics.

There is a recognition of such factors as sterile and fecund wealth, as also of the possibility of 'creating credit' to help nations in special kinds of economic distress, who could be allowed time to recover by long-term credit adjustments arranged by financial magnates who meet in secret to have questionable dealings. A bank can function with only one-tenth of its capital inside its coffers and carry on ten times the volume of business, without anyone knowing whether the assets are really in the vault or not. It is the "Big Ten" — whether in Wall Street, Lombard Street, La Bourse, or in Bonn or Tokyo — who decide the fate of other people's money without their consent, and without telling them what they are doing in their names.

Insurance companies gain enormous profit by maintaining account books in big buildings like the Empire State Building. Their article of trade is the natural fear or anxiety among the generality of their clients, which they exploit on the basis of their gullibility, promising security from fire or fear, etc. 'World Banks' seem to lend money to help borrowers, while actually being primarily interested in promoting their own exports. Dumping of condemned goods from 'advanced' to 'backward' countries contains a snag which only now people like Chavan (the then Finance Minister of India) are opening their eyes to. 'Hard' and 'soft' currencies are discriminated without justice in respect of the membership fees of so-called World Banks.

Scarcity economics has created an impasse which has climaxed into what is now understood as a joke under the name of Parkinsonianism. Maintain the price line; don't let the dollar wobble; keep the pound steady; these are slogans referring to economic malaises which come to evidence in various countries, the remedies for which are equally vague and have to be guessed at from the graphs of such bodies as the Chase Manhatten Bank, whose experts know everything. The 'iron law of necessity' regulates the relationship between labour and capital, but there is a more complicated Surplus Value Theory which has come into the picture of economics and for the clarification of which one has to read Engels' *Anti-Duhring* where he discovers the subtle relationship between production and exchange — more difficult to understand than the graphs of infinitesimal calculus — where parameters cut curves marking ups and downs in the economic progress or regression of a given country.

Lastly, nobody speaks of a World Economics at all. There

is no textbook of World Economics, though economics as a science — if it really is a science — should necessarily be most directly concerned with the happiness of humanity as a whole. Instead, economists visualize a world consisting of differently coloured Hitlerish patches of territories, from within which each man is thinking hard economically so as to defeat his neighbour. Such is this dismal or sombre science, which is not a science at all.

Statistics and Scarcity Economics

The greatest prop of this science is statistics, about which Mark Twain said that there are three kinds of lies: lies, damned lies and statistics. Statistics can prove anything, and one can easily rob a neighbouring country by using high finance based on false statistics. Statistics about population are the worst of them all. They say that God protects his creation, but there are international agencies at present which kill human progeny before they are even born. All textbooks declare that the Malthusian theory of population is an exploded one, but castration of men and women based on the most garrish of inducements rudely violates and circumvents the law of the individual, in a manner that could only be described in mild terms as questionable.

Opulence and abundance are not distinguished sufficiently clearly. Creating scarcity can raise the standard of life, but living in plenty is said to be a backward condition, only because such backward countries do not buy transistor radios or refrigerators, and because the women take care of their wealth by keeping some gold ornaments in thier boxes. Why they are wrong is not clear to any intelligent man.

Combines and monopolies are a menace to those who have no shares in such concerns, and at whose expense they become rich. A 'limited liability company', which is respected in the eyes of the law, amounts to pooling the funds of several capitalists so that the power of the bag could weigh more heavily on the poor people who are not able to pool their resources in the same way. Ruskin stated this truth most pithily in his *Crown of Wild Olives*, when he said, "bags and crags have the same effect on rags."

The same applies to politics when economic blocs are formed between countries, and 'common markets' instituted so that their bargaining power against others could be strengthened. Paper money is not always supported by tangible wealth within the vaults of big banks. Even world currencies are being floated by big companies cutting across the currencies of nations in circulation, the moral justification of which is still to be clarified. Indefinite credit can be created by financial experts meeting together now and then, giving them enormous power over the inarticulate masses who are always the sufferers at the hands of the more clever ones in the world. Paper currency cannot be eaten instead of rice or wheat, and its value has to reflect those aspects of wealth which are not just paper but which touch human well-being more directly and actually. The great discrepancy between the two spells grave disasters underneath the visible level, and no power is trying to balance them, and no textbook tells us how to make the correspondence between them more compatible, just or even barely honest.

All economists cry hoarse against unemployment. The present writer is unemployed, but has never been sorry for it all his life. Economists sometimes create problems which really don't exist, or at best exist only in their imagination, propped up by that master lie called statistics.

Laissez Faire

In short, what we wish to point out is that whatever measure an economic authority might consider applying to a situation in a country, whether advanced or backward, mercantilist or agriculturalist, in an opulencist or abundancist context, whether standards there are high or low, where demand and supply are not balanced, and where inequality is the prevailing given datum in whatever branch of economics, it would be better to leave affairs well alone to let them find a natural balance between the rival prevailing forces. Don't control population, lest the balance of nature should be disturbed. This is a dictum which has been proved with rabbits in

Australia. The lopping of a tree makes that part of the tree proliferate all the more. Shaving too often only increases the growth of beard. Such subtle factors have all to be taken into consideration before a complete theory of economics could be developed, more especially, as we have said in respect of the one world of tomorrow.

The *laissez faire* policy of Bentham must have been suggested by such a line of thought, but who takes it seriously? Planning, on the other hand, and even over-planning, is the order of the day, in spite of such ideas as Parkinsonianism becoming equally credible side by side with it. One might ask, what is the remedy. The answer is simple, but will surely not receive the approbation of professional economists because it would imply indirectly that they should put themselves out of commission.

An Absolutist Approach Required

Relativistic theories of economic happiness must give place to an economics based on norms and constants derived from an absolutist standpoint Slogans like "Liberty, Equality, Fraternity", "The greatest good of the greatest number", "*laissez faire*", "Equality of opportunity for all" and all the varieties of socialistic dicta such as "Dictatorship of the proletariat", "Classless society", etc., have all of them the needle pointing in the same direction towards the need for a normalized form of economic theory based on first principles, rather than one which serves as a basis for further fanning into flames rivalries that lurk within the relativistic set up, however good they might be from utilitarian standards. Lukewarm economics favours the fecund proliferation of injustices which keep creeping up from its hotbed. Such an economics can create more problems than what it can solve.

Voices in the Wilderness

We have to turn away from formulating further economic theories in which relativism is allowed to vitiate our approach even at its very inception. There are no textbooks at present which seem to fulfil this requirement, except in the voices of protest against modern economics raised by such lovers of humanity as Plato, Rousseau, Tolstoy, Ruskin, Carlyle, Quesnay, Compte, St. Simon, Gandhi, Thoreau, Emerson and others. These voices are hardly audible above the clamour contained in other literature, and they are put into shade by not being taken sufficiently seriously. We have, therefore, to turn our eyes elsewhere for any consolation in such an important question which touches the happiness of humanity intimately.

If we look over the utopian pictures that have been painted in various books describing a perfect state of economy prevailing in any country — which by the very meaning of the term 'utopia' as applied to them stand self-condemned — we have only a very thin and negligible quantity of literature left which could be said to describe a normal viewpoint. It is that part of economic theory which stems out of the totality of values in the world that can relate the subject correctly to that very zone of general happiness from which alone an axiologically based subject could derive its origin.

There are starting postulates and premises for every precise science. Literature often tries to portray perfect conditions to serve as a model or basis for further discussions on the subject. It was because such a model was needed that Gandhi often alluded to *Rāmarājya* for expressing his own special ideas. One could substitute this term with another equally good, which we could call *Dharmarājya*, which would however have a Buddhistic flavour of Aśoka's time. Constantine's empire and the days of Akbar and of Aśoka have left impressions recorded in literature with economic theories directly or indirectly stated in them. Mahābali and Dilīpa were also just rulers in whom absolutist standards of ethics, economics and aesthetics were supposed to have prevailed. Their stories continue to inspire generations of humanity even to the present-day. Although in their approach to value-judgments, economics is treated together with other subjects as being only one among many of them, it is not impossible to derive the purest of guiding principles from such writings. There is the whole of Kālidāsa's *Raghuvaṁśa* which affords us ample ground for searching for normative guidelines in formulating a new theory of economics in the absence of any at present, as we have said, which could be called normalized at all.

Candide

Before recommending that we should turn our eyes to the wisdom of the 'Golden Period' of Indian history for gleaning guidelines on this subject, which might itself be said to be a product of Western civilization, we have to establish sufficiently clearly that economics in the West has proved itself to be a complete failure so far. It might be suspected that such a sweeping statement could be due to some old-fashioned mode of thinking not at all acceptable to the ways of the Age of Enlightenment of which men of the twentieth century are unquestionably proud. How could backward countries even think of criticizing advanced countries to say that they are wrong?

In such a predicament, one has the unstinting support of a writer and thinker of unquestionable status, who could himself be said to be one of the representatives and fore-runners of what we call the Age of Enlightenment. Between him and Rousseau, we have two great names in the history of modern thought who could be said to be the harbingers of modernism itself, leaving behind the mentality belonging to the so-called Middle Ages. One has only to mention ***Candide*** to modern enthusiasts of Western economy with their contempt for anything old or oriental to see how the very name itself succeeds in turning the tables against their stand. "Have you read ***Candide***?" is all that needs to be said to see the retroactive effect on the face of an enthusiast of the economics of the West. Opulencist economics, mercantilism, the 'gold rush', the South Sea bubble that burst and Eldorado with the edventurous search for the Golden Fleece are all satirized in this classic by Voltaire,

The Normative Frame of Reference in Kālidāsa

Indian scholars did not compartmentalize disciplines

unnecessarily. Thus, valuable theories of ethics, aesthetics and economics find unitive treatment in the vast body of classical Sanskrit literature — particularly in the works of Kālidāsa, the uncrowned king among poets of the Indian soil. Vikramāditya's empire must, as scholars think, have been a model of economic success. The theories which contributed to such a success must have influenced Kālidāsa's own theories. There are many precious passages from which the ground-work of economic theorization itself could be collected. Even the verses of the *Kumārasambhava*, when carefully examined, reveal their own economic theory studied at a point where all human values stem out of the context of the *ātman* or Self. Man is the measure of all things, and the proper study of mankind is man. One must first know oneself, and be true to oneself, and one cannot then be wrong. The normative reference for wisdom was seen to be located and rooted in Self-knowledge, and was fully schematically and structurally analyzed by the Upaniṣadic seers conforming to a fully scientific and sound methodology, epistemology and axiology.

It is true that Sanskrit literature is clothed in the cryptic ideograms and favourite cliches of its own peculiar *lingua mystica*. This does not detract, however, from the fundamental postulates and sound starting premises of the economics envisaged therein. It has to be treated as a study in itself, before the contributions could be analyzed and enumerated so as to reveal their great value in acting as a corrective to modern economic theorization.

10

Gold in Wisdom's Language

GOLD is the God of the world of finance. It occupies a central position among things that men, and women more especially, wish to possess and keep. The value of all other things is determined mostly with gold as the **norm** or standard. Although it is a thing, when related to man it has more of a perceptual status than a mere outside object. Its utility is often a theoretical and negligible factor. It is by the intimacy that gold is able to establish in a personal sense with human beings, that it gets its value. It thus reflects a state of mind of which the businessman knows how to take advantage.

If we should toss a gold dollar and handle it we are struck by its weight and its sound quality, revealing its superlative materiality. In addition, it has a dull gleam resembling the subdued brilliance of some of the distinct stars. Of the earth most earthy, it has yet about it something celestial. Its radiance embellishes the glory of the scepter or the crown of kings, and the spires of temple towers shine with its lustre. It is thus more than a mere piece of inert matter, and this must be the reason why the *Tarka Śāstra* (the Indian science of categories, relations of things, analogies, etc.) brings it under the mite of *tejas* (fire, light) rather than under the category of 'earth'. It is thus lifted hypostatically and glorfied in the philosophical thought of India. Its mysterious role in human affairs, dating from antiquity to the present-day, seems only to justify this status.

In Matter-of-Fact Language

When gold is yet in its raw or natural setting in the womb of the earth, it is hardly more than a virtuality or a potentiality. Once brought to the surface after good luck in prospecting, speculative investment and many man-hours of labour, it might be made into ornaments, plates to stagnate in the form of treasures or relics. Its main role is to pamper vanity. The newly rich and the more ancient nobles, through gold get an ostentatious satisfaction of shining in contrast to the ragged poor around them. These 'bag barons', as Ruskin would call them, like the 'crag barons' as the same writer nicknames them, who were not other than highway robbers hiding in places of vantage against unwary travellers, had the same effect on 'rags' who were the poor. Thus he developed the famous aphorism: "Bags and crags have the same effect on rags".

When gold does circulate from hand to hand, it happens more often secretly, sluggishly or slyly avoiding the public gaze. It takes the form of a gratification, a personal consideraton or a mark of favour. Even at times of inflation, which is a form of modern economic malaise, gold value is not affected much and gold is not scattered about in the same way as paper currency. There is a steady dignity in its 'buoyancy' or 'shyness' in the money market.

The Dragon of Finance

When once outside the personal or domestic context, gold has the elusive way of hiding in safes or vaults. In national capitals like Moscow, Paris, London or Washington, gold exists in built-in safe vaults, more by supposition in the form of a credit which can be abstract or concrete or both. Even there it is an elusive presence. Mutually protected against rival officers themselves who may represent business or government interests or both, it has a way, as has been reported recently, of being just 'found missing'. Later, when nobody is the wiser, book adjustments can set right matters and neither business nor government are visibly worse off for it. Regeneration and recovery apply to money as well as to life or health. Whether the actual gold is in the mine or buried somewhere by a miser or still in the forty acres of London's Banking District, it makes no perceptual difference to the actual individual human, whose meal reaches his mouth by the resultant interaction of multifarious life factors and circumstances both man-made and natural.

Credit can be created at the head-end of the dragon of finance while the debit is a virtuality residing at the dragon's tail where gold-prospecting might be in progress. Irrespective of the amount of gold and in spite of more and more being dug up, human life in its most vitally necessary aspects goes flowing on, the same as ever. Gold makes itself evident through the newspapers now and then as a customs' haul as a contraband article in the most unforeseen places, or as a treasure-trove unearthed thousands of miles away from its origin and thousands of years later, making men ashamed or proud under varying circumstances. Gold infatuation also comes into evidence in human affairs now and then as a fecund cause of culpable homicide.

Normative Principle of Possession

We read in the *Don Bell Reports* the following interesting commentary:

> Throughout the Babylonian Empire, temples were built to worship false gods. Within the temples were strong rooms presided over by priests (later to be called bankers). The priests exhorted the people to bring their gold and other precious items to the strong-rooms for safe keeping. Customers were handed little clay tablets as receipts (paper not yet being invented). The people paid interest to the priests (20%) for guarding their gold. And since it was inconvenient 'to go to the bank' for every transaction involving use of gold, the clay tablets began circulating

> as a 'medium of exchange'. The clay tablets were backed by gold supposedly deposited in the local 'Fort Knox'. So nobody questioned the use of clay tablets instead of gold.
>
> But the priests of the strong-room made a startling and history-shaking discovery. People seldom called for their stored gold. Less than ten per cent of the gold was ever called for in a single day. Therefore, clay tablets, representing **ten times the amount of the gold on hand could be issued**, and no one but the bankers themselves would ever be the wiser. The banker could loan out ten times the value of the actual deposits and remain solvent. So instead of making twenty cents on each dollar in hand he could issue **credit money** and make ten times twenty cents on each dollar in hand — or make two dollars profit for each dollar actually deposited in the bank.[1]

Gold thus enters into human life as finance. The possessive instinct of human beings and the advantage of one dealing with the possession of many by proxy, as it were, in a thing like gold, is at the basis of this kind of financial relationship which works to the mutual advantage of both borrower and lender. 'Interest' and 'discount' which vary only in the time of actual use of value, makes for the thriving of banking. The modern bank-rate may be juster and better founded, but the reference of finance to gold and the constant of ten per cent chance in favour of the banker are features that have not changed and cannot. The 'inverted pyramid' of the credit system thus becomes erected, with which the common man who cashes a cheque or buys a meal is unconcerned or ignores.

World Credit System's Need of a Golden Rule

Nimrod who founded the city of Babel at the dawn of history, is said to have started to use gold as a norm in state affairs. Nebuchadnezzar, fifteen hundred years later, established the gold standard publicly. Although Britain went off the gold standard as early as 1931, it holds on to gold as tenaciously as in days of antiquity for the sake of regulating its international commitments through the Bank of International Settlements at Basle, Switzerland, or the 'World Bank'. The Governors of the Federal Reserve Bank of America or of the Bank of England are the architects of what is called 'sound finance' for their respective areas, or for world finance generally, which they might be doing in the interests both of governments and of business at once.

There are lurking contradictions at the core of financial policies which are of a secret dialectical order wherever the interests of one comes into relation with the interests of the many, whether at the social, national or international levels. The laws which might hold good in regulating the 'Credit of Nations' will not hold good the same way in dealing with 'One-World Economics' which transcends national interests. Private or limited liability-finance is thus different from public unlimited liability-finance, which makes all the difference to the justice or validity of the transactions. Without any unitive wisdom principle being consciously introduced here, chaos in world credit is bound to prevail. A golden rule based on the virtues of integrity, trustworthiness, parsimony in the interests of one and all, and just use of the power of credit, is involved here, which is still to be properly formulated.

Spirituality and Gold-Value

Saints or spiritually inclined men generally have despised gold (with wine and women) as filthy lucre. The worship of false gods or Mammon is associated also with the worship of the golden calf in Mediterranean religious history. Even a coin placed under the bed of Sri Ramakrishna of Bengal is said to have shocked him in a strange way; and it is written of him also, may be rather imaginatively, that he used to throw lumps of gold and mud into the river Ganges to prove to himself and others the truth of the dictum, otherwise familiar to many Indians, that the man of wisdom considers a lump of clay, a pebble and a piece of gold with the same equanimity of mental attitude (*Gītā*, VI.8). A saint generally wishes to live outside the world of high finance. The plain living and the parsimonious economical virtue that they generally cultivate for the emulation of their immediate followers, makes them consciously or instinctively recognize the truth of the saying of the American philosopher Thoreau, "Superfluous wealth can buy superfluities only. Money is not required to buy one necessary of the soul." (*Walden, Conclusion*)

The Guru Narayana was once offered some natural flowers with a few gold ones thrown among them, by way of a pious birthday offering by a rich devotee who thought of surprising him and pleasing him by such a gift. The Guru picked a flower made of gold and, smelling it, remarked disappointedly that it had no scent. This was a gentle way of teaching the difference between the real value represented by a fresh blossom and the false value implied in the gold of the rich man. On another occasion, on the contrary, the Guru was known to have himself presented a gold coin to a disciple who was starting on a long voyage. He had questioned the same disciple already about his attitude to money and, on his telling the Guru that it was superfluity for a spiritual person, had remarked also that it was natural for one to keep money and use it, if only for purchasing a railway ticket.

Pastoral communities that might survive in mountain seclusions like the Nagaland where salt still takes the place of gold, may be supposed to live in a more or less self-sufficient economy of their own, in which currency in our sense may not hold good. Money, like everything else, is right in its proper place when used with proper human intelligence or wisdom. Economists like Adam Smith have also voted on the side of saints when they wrote such words as these:

> A rich country in the same manner as a rich man, is supposed to be abounding in money; and to heap up gold and silver in any country is supposed to be the readiest way to enrich it . . . . Among the Tartars as among all other nations of shepherds who are generally ignorant of the use of money, cattle are the instruments of commerce and the measure of value. Wealth therefore according to them consisted of cattle as

according to the Spaniards it consisted of gold and silver. Of the two, the Tartar notion, was the nearest to the truth.[2]

Wisdom from Myth and Fable

Much wisdom about gold is enshrined in mythology, fables and parables. The gold disc that is said to hide the face of Truth is mentioned in the *Īśa Upaniṣad*. It refers to the false relativistic value which can hider the vision of the Absolute Value behind it.

The *Hiraṇya-Garbha* (gold-germ) which represents the supreme value of the Vedic hedonistic context, is the ontological and hierophantic counterpart of the disc of gold hypostatically referred to above. Between them they may be said to touch the two poles of value in the world of gold.

The golden ladder of Jacob's dream in the *Bible* (Gen. 28. 12) which touches heaven and earth and where angels with wings, who are supposed to be wiser and holier than ordinary men, go up and down the ladder, refers to the same two aspects of values, as in the *Gītā* (XV. 2) where branches of the great fig tree turn up and down also.

The language of myth is not meant to be realistic or logical. Myths are to be understood with the help of intuitive imagination which can enter into the spirit of the situation, which even the shrewdest of financiers are not usually capable of doing in any thoroughgoing sense. In the Indian legend Prahlāda suffered because he would not worship Hiraṇya (Gold personified). There is the famous fable of king Midas whose object is to bring out the difference between the gold to be possessed as a thing and the gold that is a mere symbol of possession. The boon of the golden touch became a curse because of the *adhyāsa* or false attribution of reality to the wrong aspect of gold in the mind of the king. Normal human relations with his own daughter were thereby frustrated. It is the distinction between the real fatted calf and the golden calf set up for worship, which annoyed Moses.

This confusion between the perceptual and the actual

object is a fecund cause of error by which even very worldly wise financiers can make grave mistakes in calculations which concern the everyday happiness of millions of human beings who come under their money-power. False and true credits are hard to distinguish except through the highest kind of dialectical wisdom. Even such wisdom is not for its own sake, but for the real happiness of mankind which is the resultant of the correct dialectical treatment of human values which refer to the good of all and the general good at once.

The Two Worlds of Gold

The Midas mystery of gold is that economists recognize as Gresham's Law by which it becomes important to balance the exchange and utility values of coins put into the open market. The slightest tilt in favour of the utility side of value in a coin can make it disappear from view altogether into the unknown domain of financial virtuality.

Thus possessions can belong to two mutually exclusive worlds of value, which, when wrongly handled, can spell double gain or double loss to the persons concerned. When carefully studied between the lines, the parables of the *Bible* reveal this subtle reciprocity between the two worlds, placed between which the 'certain rich man' of the various parables touching gold or coin teaches this wisdom in the name of Christ. Whether dealing with the wages for the workers of the rich man's vineyard, the good and faithful servant who used gold rightly, or the prodigal son who was dead to one world of economics in favour of another, and was found again by a parsimonious father who feted his return to the first world of economics, or of the rich man who was the rival of Lazarus who suffered in the 'other world' while the latter suffered only in the world here, we have rare dialectical wisdom secrets involving property values recorded for human guidance. To this day however, humanity remains deaf to such wisdom teaching.

Lack of Wisdom about Gold in Economic Statistics

Modern economic investigation has fallen back on the normative method of statistical studies in arriving at laws, rules and controls to be applied to gold and economic policies. Here, however, the great drawback is that economics has not yet been brought properly under a normative science. The picture of a wealthy or prosperous state or individual, which should be the norm in economic thought, has not been clearly stated. The two worlds of wealth and gold, one of which aims at **abundance** and the other which has mere **opulence** as its ideal, have not been treated with any correct methodology.

While parables and fables guided the older generations in these matters, the modern man relies on statistics which have no better status in reliability. That statistics prove nothing and, if at all they did prove anything, they could prove either side of a question that involved the 'pro' or 'con' of a proposition indifferently, has become a modern joke. F.H. Le Guardia as early as 1933 observed: "Statistics are like alienists — they will testify for either side. (*Liberty*, May, 1933). Then there is the famous pleasantry about statistics attributed to Disraeli by Mark Twain which says, "There are three kinds of lies: lies, damned lies, and statistics".

Even if these sweeping statements are not to be taken seriously, we have in the official publication of the Chase Manhattan Bank of New York, perhaps one of the biggest financial houses of America, the following on "Economic Statistics" with the subtitle "Economic Pulse-Takers Need Better Information" :

> Mark Twain, having listened to widely varying estimates of the length of the Mississippi river once marvelled 'at the fascination of a science where one gets such wholesale returns of conjecture out of such trifling investment of fact.'
>
> . . . . only a quarter of a century ago, the same could be said of economics. The subject dealt heavily in abstraction and was short on actual facts against

> which to check the theories. Economists often disagreed because they had no accurate measurements.
>
> Economists have devised new and better methods for measuring the trends of our economy. As a result the Federal Government spends about $ 40 million a year on compiling economic statistics today.[3]

It is not clear to the laymen of common sense who scrutinizes the above paragraphs, whether facts or statistics are given primacy to prove what is vaguely referred to as "trends of our economy". Textbooks on economics openly declare that there is no agreed explanation as to the cause of fluctuations, and that five theories have been put forward, namely: (1) the Over-Production Theory, (2) the Under-Consumption Theory, (3) the Monetary Theory, (4) the Psychological Theory, and (5) the Climatic Theory; up to 1940.[4]

Whether more statistics will tend to prove the validity of any one of these theories or help to make more theories instead, is not certain. The same statistics may be used to prove the sides of both the parties concerned in a controversy. The proper use of statistics in such matters is itself to be questioned, because many generalizations based on statistics like those of Malthus have signally failed. Thus proof, the fact which is to be proved and the theory on which actual data are to be collected and interpreted, leave room for so much vagueness and conjecture, that the common man stands confused in regard to the correct way of applying economy to his own personal life. Men have to be clear first about what they want before theorizing or proving.

The Best Use of Gold

The fraction of gold implied in a penny is a principle that we recognize through dialectical reasoning, as when we say that the value of the gold dollar inheres in the cent and *vice versa*. The unit copper coin of any country, like the bad penny that turns up again and again in everyday human affairs, has only a negligible practical value in human terms.

Gold thus enters human life more as a figure of speech than as an actuality and, when it does enter mentally in this manner, it has two distinct aspects. One of these is usually that of Mammon, and the other that of God's kingdom. The gold at the tip of a fountain pen or in its cap is valuable only to the extent that something sensible is written with it. Again, we are called upon to distinguish likewise between what is to be rendered as a tribute to Caesar and what is due to God. The worship of the golden calf also refers to some wrong attitude to gold which ancient writings have condemned. Gold representing true or false value has entered into wisdom literature in various ways and forms of rhetoric. Eternal values are compared to the phoenix which burns itself at the altar to be reborn with its golden plumes at once. The fattened calf may be contrasted with the golden calf, which latter is associated with Mammon worship which is the same as what Washington Irving called "the almighty dollar, that great object of universal devotion".

High finance is known to be a gamble in which the loss of both cash and credit makes speculators jump out of the skyscraper window. To see through the contradictions involved requires high common sense or rare wisdom. The virtue of the Golden Mean recommended by King Cleobulos of Rhodes and developed later by Aristotle really implies a man with gold or goodness in his heart. Economists recommend frugality of a certain kind which can be tilted in favour of stinginess on the one side or prodigality on the other. A golden rule or line may be imagined also to separate the world of abundance from the world of opulence. The most important matter for one to make up his mind about is whether he wants one or the other of these, because as a rule they are mutually exclusive by their very nature. Rousseau, in his famous essay on the Government of Poland, presents two types of states to choose from. One he describes with the following epithets: "noisy, brilliant, redoubtable, influential over other nations"; and the other he describes with the epithets "free, peaceful, wise, fearless of anyone, self-sufficient and happy". Then he gives us the unequivocal warning against trying to combine the two in any single state. He writes:

> Above all do not try to combine these two projects: they are too contradictory; and wanting to be related to both by a composite way of progression is to want to miss both.[5]

Gold and Goodness Interchangeable

Between the language of myth, fable or parable and the graphs or pictorial representations of economic trends or situations found in modern magazines or books, whereby the common man is called upon to wade his way through such concepts as 'surplus value', 'trade cycle', 'economic equilibrium', 'sound finance', 'stable exchange', 'conditions in the foreign market', 'currency restrictions', 'creation of credit', and 'the inverted pyramid of credit', in order to live his life in the light of common sense or wisdom, a more direct and simple way has to be found at the present stage of man's education or progress.

Of the three schools in economic theory distinguished as the classical, the neo-classical and the dialectical, the last-mentioned has at present succeeded in catching the imagination of the masses in many countries. Meanwhile great controversy and polemics rage on such questions as the theory of rent value, interest, capital, and even on the initial definition of wealth. National wealth and international wealth have not yet been clearly distinguished. Every professor of university who writes a textbook on this highly abstract subject starts with a different intellectual formation nurtured on academic soils which differ widely from country to country, and as between the Old World and the New. Each develops a set of anecdotes or examples in his mind for the use of teaching and, as between Adam Smith, Karl Marx or Marshall, the variety of rival theorization is so great that one has to cry halt and begin to think for oneself with the help of common sense and general information.

The first dictum we can arrive at immediately is that economics is for man and not man for economics. If it yields general satisfaction and works in experience, it must be acceptable, and if it reaches out vainly from one theory to another, it has to be discarded. As a science it is not an 'experimental' one or no experiments are needed here, as common experience contains the elements of experiment.

If it is to be treated as 'normative' science rather than as an experimental one, the norm of human happiness has first to be fixed in terms of economics. As neither of these seem to be done at present, we make bold to adopt a method where intuitive imagination is brought in to help us to see more clearly what economists are talking about.

A Simple Economic Situation

Here the time-honoured wisdom language is being admitted by the front door only to save us from the confusion of tongues in which we find ourselves at present. It will be seen that this unitive way of approach is the same as what has been called the **dialectical approach** though not in the limited sense of post-Hegelian dialectics, but in a sense with what is known as perennial wisdom the world over. It has ever had an apodictic quality which humanity has always recognized whether in the Chinese, Indian or the pre-Socratic context.

With gold as a symbol of wealth and as a central notion of value, we shall try now to focus our attention on a simplified economic situation, in order to see the subtle aspects which have contributed to make gold a mystery. A simple question may be asked by the layman as to why gold should not be left in mines if it is only brought out to be **reserved** in the banking areas of the great capitals, buried again in vaults, as an elusive presence. Could not hoarded gold elsewhere be treated at least as eqaully respectable and justified?

Let us then enter intuitively and freely into a simple economic situation which will serve as a pattern for the understanding of other value-factors involved in economics, both in its static and dynamic aspects. Closed and open economic situations may also be distinguished with the help of this simplified pattern of everyday life in our minds.

An absent-minded professor of economics goes for a walk

towards the country side and comes to a crossing of roads fringing on a forest reserve where a monkey happens to live. On the diagonally opposite corner of the road crossing is a vendor of bananas and peanuts exposing his wares for sale. The professor being a frugal and kind-hearted man, living apart and alone from the busy world of getting and spending, just happens to have an old unit coin of small change in his pocket. Seeing the monkey eyeing the nuts hungrily, he wishes to make the best of the situation by offering his coin to the vendor to induce him to give a handful of nuts to the hungry monkey. Before accepting it, the vendor examines the coin. He hesitates, first because that coinage was one officially withdrawn from circulation but, having been minted when gold reserve covered credit better, it thus had a price-value which is to his advantage in spite of its low exchange value and no face value. He therefore gives the nuts to the monkey and the professor returns to his room as a satisfied representative of the human race.

The various aspects of gold value involved here can be schematically represented in the diagram (on p. 67).

Conclusion

Here the abstract regulating economic norm or principle of gold value is the central notion to be kept in mind. We can readily distinguish four aspects of gold value which meet at the central point where values change over or interact in a subtle dialectical manner. The vertical axis represents transactions where time is the primary consideration. Interest and discount rates which are always balanced in any country, operate along this vertical axis.

The horizontal axis would represent actual exchange as between price and commodity. These take place in the present but have the two sides of actuality or virtuality involved. The price value of a banana is virtual, while the banana as an actual product of labour is an actuality which is more specific and presents a more contingent verity. Need is hidden in the man, like hunger in the monkey, and is a virtual instinctive disposition from which man suffers in the

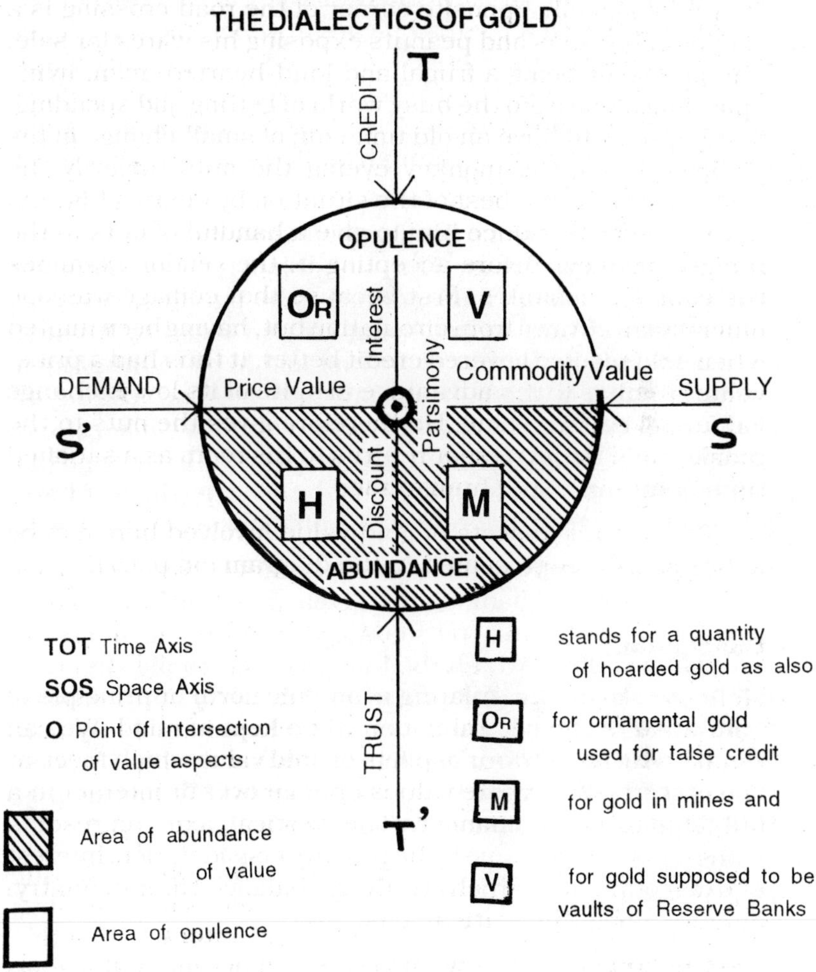
THE DIALECTICS OF GOLD
T
CREDIT
OPULENCE
OR
V
Interest
Parsimony
Commodity Value
DEMAND
Price Value
SUPPLY
S'
S
Discount
H
M
ABUNDANCE
TRUST
T'
TOT Time Axis
SOS Space Axis
O Point of Intersection of value aspects
Area of abundance of value
Area of opulence
H stands for a quantity of hoarded gold as also
OR for ornamental gold used for talse credit
M for gold in mines and
V for gold supposed to be vaults of Reserve Banks

*Fig.*10.1

present or the eternal present. The price we pay for getting rid of hunger, which itself is a necessary suffering, is negative as compared with a positive pleasure which money or gold might command. Thus price value meets commodity value from opposite sides in this situation. The horizontal world of events, things, movements or activities has to be distinguished from paper transactions through bankers, which belong to a world of tokens or symbols.

Here again credit and debit, interest and discount, interact to make business thrive. The banker has to be trustworthy and stable. The bank manager has to be parsimonious and has certain virtues of not being carried away by outside events too easily. He has to be just and keep to the golden mean of value without being involved in false lending or borrowing. He must have credit *vis-a-vis* other bankers, and clearing houses must honour his cheques and to that end his accounting and book-keeping must be on sound lines. Above all he must have an address in his official capacity at least.

The gold reserve somewhere in a vault is the nominal or actual credit for all bankers in a given area. This thin golden line of credit value may be said to go past human affairs as a vital line of life in which the kind man has to play his role in the name of the happiness of humanity as a whole. Reputation, goodwill, kindness, integrity and stability and sound credit are all involved here. They are qualities whose fund man must increase by all means for his happiness. It is thus important for man to have a heart of gold.

To revert to our example. We have to remember above all that there are distinct sectors which represent economic compartments or worlds which cannot interact directly. There is no use having the monkey borrow the bad penny from the professor. The vendor has behind him the plantation and the labourers, while the monkey has behind it, at best, living regions of fruits and leaves. The mercantile nation and the pastoral nation cannot thus be correctly related except through a very wise arrangement of economic interdependence. And finally, it is important to see how money must circulate, if it is to serve life at all. Hoarded gold might increase the wages of mining labour, as Professor Jevons says, but it would not be playing its legitimate role in human affairs, because as we have said, money is meant for man and not man for money. Similarly, the burning of food products for the sake of better prices, as we hear of sometimes, is an absurdity of wrong economics. The contrast between opulence and abundance is also a matter for the imagination of man to visualize as belonging to one or other of the sectors represented in our diagram. As Rousseau points out, it would be unfair to ask a poor hardworking peasant to pay his tribute of tax or rent to the money-lender or to the government in the form of money which does not belong to his economic sector or world at all. The farmer belongs to the world of abundant actual produce, while the money-lender belongs to the opposite world where wealth is merely a symbolic token. Increase of tokens may not agree with the produce in hand, and might produce economic crises which experts are still explaining. Caesar's domain and that of God should not be mixed up.

Notes

1. *Dan Bell Reports* (Florida, USA, Aug. 10, 1956).
2. p. 324, *Wealth of Nations*.
3. Manhattan Bank of New York, *Official Reports*, No. 10 of 1956.
4. cf. pp. 276-82, Silverman : *The Substance Economics*, London.
5. Translated from the *Contrat Social*, p. 384, Edition Garnier, Paris.

11

Towards a One-World Economics

I

ECONOMICS is a modern substitute for religion. While religion holds out promises for the hereafter economics refers to the betterment of life here. Both can have questionable enthusiasts as leaders or blind believers in outmoded ideologies. The mass-mind can be swayed in the name of the one or the other into holding exaggerated or distorted notions against the General Good and the Good of All. Economic creeds can be as fanatic as religious ones, and claim as much toll of human life as the other at times of trouble. Both can join hands with politics and work havoc among peaceful inhabitants. Whether it is doomsday or perfect equality of opportunity, simplified pictures of felicity or suffering hold the imagination of either ideologist to fill him with much misplaced fervour at times. Between the ends and means visualized in either of these groups of believers, who insist on having nothing to do with the other, the visible common event that takes place is that, somehow, what is in one man's pocket is transferred into another's without usual commodities being exchanged. One who writes a book on the best method to abolish poverty proves his case best by becoming himself rich at the expense of his admirers. In the name of being saved from sin or suffering the same phenomenon can be seen in the camp of orthodox religion. Much vague talk might intervene while the transfer is taking place which lacks apodictic precision that distinguishes either science or common sense. Both thrive in the twilight atmosphere of a pseudo-science. Vain verbosity prevails in the name of both religion and economics at present.

Nature of Economics

Economics is common sense claiming to be science. It invloves Value-Wisdom. It deals with wealth and aims at welfare, starting from scarcity, poverty or want as its basic assumption. This assumption is not unlike the assumption of sin or suffering in the catechisms of religions. Scarcity of good or goods is to be overcome by dealings or arrangements involving **long term** or **short term** measures from simple ones as when ants store grain against winter to international monetary adjustments.

It calls for certain types of virtues such as parsimony, abstention or shrewdness for intelligent getting and spending which should not err on the side of penny-wise or pound-foolish. It is in the midst of a modern state that economic wisdom sits with grace, and the sum total of its contrivances, whether conducive to wealth, welfare or both, is vaguely called 'good economics'. The success or failure is not measureable except by measuring rods whose validity itself is questionable. Raising standards of life need not tally with the degree of satisfaction of a people. Between maximum, minimum and optimum standards, calculations can vary or go wrong. From the family budget to the national one the special sagacity or wisdom called for, in the heads of families or states, is a very elusive one based on varied schools of theorization.

It has now become common to read strong and impassioned condemnation of one economics by another rival school. Respectable writers of one group are humbugs for others and *vice-versa*, which are making economists themselves wonder if the claim of a scientific status for their subject is not mere wishfulfilment. Universal elements in economics are sadly lacking at present.

The Fragmentary, Closed or Static Approach Prevailing

Adam Smith's *Wealth of Nations* by its very title reveals one of the chief drawbacks of the so-called science of economics. He did not dare to write a book on a science of Wealth or even of Value, but carefully limited himself to 'An Inquiry into the Nature and Causes of the Wealth of **Nations**'. The nations that he had in mind were surely those that resemble England, where the Lord Chancellor of the Exchequer, sitting on his wool sack in London, exercised his economic wisdom in favour of his country, just the same way as those in Rotterdam or the Hague decided on wise economic policies to bring gold into their own treasuries.

John Stuart Mill who was employed in the East India Company, wrote the next standard work in which he was honest enough to avow that political economy was a subject bound to be in favour of aggrandising itself. Jevons pinned on the word 'utility' to fix the nature of wealth, and theories of Value have been put forward by others which involve almost metaphysical notions of the reality of what is called wealth, value or goods. At present it is not the fashion any more to define economics or wealth. It is even stated that 'Political Economy is said to have strangled itself with definitions' (Keynes). Meeting man's physical needs is the aim of economics stated in its most scientific form in some modern articles, and it is becoming the fashion to say that there is no need to define economics at all. It is not hard to see from all these that the central notion of economics is not a normative notion at all. It is not conceived in universal or unitive terms. Each writer has his own closed, static or fragmentary notion of what constitutes the core of economics as a branch of knowledge. How could a science emerge without the basic notion being clearly defined?

Scope and Limits of Economics

Exchangeable value factors interest the economist rather

than non-exchangeable ones, although they may hold a high place as a personal value. Father and mother are not precious to the extent they are not values of the market place. When we think of such subjects we transcend the limits of conventional economics. A rare painting for which a rich man might be willing to pay a high price touches another limit in the world of economics. A film star carries his or her value in the person only indirectly contractible and treatable as an economic factor. Edible fruit in the thick of a forest is not an economic product although it might satisfy human or animal hunger. Natural resources such as springs or watersheds are factors contributing to economic immaturity rather than signs of economic assets, because from the 'home-market' point of view they are only negative economic factors.

Capital and wealth are poles apart according to textbook notions of economics on which generations of modern experts are nourished. Maturity and backwardness in economics are myths that have developed in the days of the gold rush, mercantilism and colonialism which are fast getting outmoded. Before a normal one-world economics can come into full view many of the old lessons will have to be forgotten. What is more, trusted advisers of the old school are likely to conceal attitudes which deserve to be suspected rather than respected in the new set up. Charlatanism can be hidden under the cloak of economic advice. Countries once under colonialist economists will find it not so easy to unlearn what they have imbibed from their old exploiters who might pretend to be their advisers still in the interest of states which have changed their self-interest from one side to the other.

A discerning eye can discover many anomalies in the matter of economic policies. The London School of Economics has still its disciples seated in key positions in India and in the far-flung dominions of the Empire that once flourished at their expense, still safeguarding the same interests of the 'home-market' which is no more at home. Scarcity-based economics with its emphasis laid on exchangeable goods and built on the notion of capital has many elements which are pernicious in their effect to human happiness, and what concerns us more at present is that they do not represent the whole or even a good part of scientific economics. Closed, static and curtailed in its applicability and its power to spell general happiness, or even the happiness of all, it is high time that one-world economics sheds its limitations and expanded into its proper proportions.

Scarcity economics has its natural counterpart in the economy of abundance. Before we can visualize the implications of these two mutually exclusive worlds in economics we have to focus our attention on possible worlds of value.

Possible Worlds of Value

When men have different goals in their minds as most desirable for themselves or their fellow beings and visualize corresponding means for accomplishing them, they may be said to live in different worlds of their own. Just as purgatories and paradises can be piled in graded fashion one above the other in a vast possible series, the world of economics can present a series of value-worlds.

Utopia and **the *Republic*** were ideal worlds painted with political as well as economic factors. In England itself we have had mercantilist adventures side by side with highly humanitarian authors like Ruskin and Carlyle, whose economic worlds were different. When Ruskin was once asked by a London Association of Architects for some suggestions, he outlined for them the statue of what he called the Britannia of the Market Place as a goddess that would correspond to the world of money and selling, in which they lived. Carlyle was no less vehement and protested strongly against the economic trends of his times. Even now the London School of Economics represents a body of economic thought which pertains to a world of its own.

If conservatism dies hard in actual politics, its ideological shadow in the world of economics persists longer still, and works through believers who continue through generations lisping the same jargon as their predecessors, and public schools and colleges continue this pattern of thought when actual conditions belong to another world altogether. Through

Adam Smith, Mill, Ricardo, Marshall and Marx we have graded worlds of possible value within the four walls and with whose frames of reference they outlined their economic theories. From scarcity at one end of the scale of values their worlds can all be visualized as ranging higher and higher into the world of gilt-edged notions of wealth or of capital.

Pure credit as an abstract value is now emerging as an internationally acceptable economic factor, and in the name of scarcity or abstinence, economics at present includes measures of large scale castration of healthy men and women so that some optimum equilibrium of population, long discarded by regular thinkers, can be attained. The human touch is now leaving economic thinking altogether, and we do not know if respectable looking economic advisers are not wolves in sheep's clothing. The contemplative background of economics has been long left behind. The possible worlds in which an honest economist hides himself ranges from the cell of a hermit to that in which the economist is becoming more and more suspect dangerous to public life.

From the Gold Rush to Das Capital

Gold and capital are overlapping values. Credit is another economic term that is becoming more and more used. When credit is not covered by gold reserves it attains the status of a pure abstraction in the world of values and when this point of recognition of credit is attained, the concept of credit begins to resemble that of God in theology.

Economics started with the wisdom of the wool-sack of the Chancellor of the Exchequer in London, and has ended at present in the surplus and labour value theories conceived by Marx is his *Das Capital.* An impartial thinker brought up far away from the home-markets of Amsterdam, Rotterdam or the Hague and free from prejudices of gilt-edged notions of value will find that, when we begin to forget the one-sidedness that has been recognized in respect of values all through, from the wool-sack economists to that of the Capital of Marx, we are at the same time called upon to think of economics with a revised frame of reference altogether, with differently conceived four walls within the limits of which economic life is to live and move if it is to make sense.

Opulence is not the only point of view from which economics can be envisaged. Opulence is only the visible portion of the iceberg of what has to be recognized as the total situation on which a unitive, global and scientific theory of economics has to be based. While one-eyed or lame economics progress lop-sidedly, a healthy economics has to progress normally on both the aspects of abundance and opulence. Scarcity economics implies capital, but the economics of abundance adds another new world to the whole matter. Economics must comprise both its natural counterparts of what refers to gold and to its negative aspect.

Non-Mercantilist Notion of Wealth

Gold in relation to scarcity of marketable goods has a meaning that is quite different from gold in the context of abundance. The relation between the external shining thing called gold and its different aspects, virtual and actual, deserves special examination. Economics as a science of values must recognize that virtual and actual gold can be considered economic values by any philosophically minded economist. We read in Plato's *Republic* the following interesting passage:

> They (the Guardians) must be told that they have no need for mortal or material gold and silver, because they have in their hearts the heavenly gold and silver given them by the gods as a permanent possession, and it would be wicked to pollute the heavenly gold in their possession by mixing it with earthly, for theirs is without impurity, while that in currency among men is a common source of wickedness.[1]

Gold as a value in economics is a notion far more complicated than at first sight might appear. If one should object and say that Platonic notions do not apply to modern economics we would turn to Marshall whose name commands respect among those who have put order into economic principles. He emphasised both the sides that go into making economics a wholesale science when he said:

> Economics on one side is a study of wealth; and on the other, the more important side, a part of the study of man.[2]

Even before Marshall thus reluctantly, as it were, admitted that economics was for man as much as man for economics, many honest Englishmen had recorded their protest against the tendency for economics to lose its human element. Chapman referred to two possible aspects of wealth when he said: "External goods are goods only in relation to internal goods." Ruskin unequivocally declared:

> There is no wealth but life: Life including all its powers of love, of joy and of admiration. That country is the richest which nourishes the greatest number of noble and happy human beings.[3]

If all these statements are not to be treated as merely poetic or philosophical effusions, how is it to be explained that the professional or official economist still thinks of wealth in terms of money? This question could best be answered in the words of a modern textbook writer who says:

> Wealth is studied simply and solely because in this world of ours, wealth is the only convenient measure of the intensity of human motives. Other motives like love, friendship, family affection, charity, etc. too exert their influence, but the fact is that the steadiest and strongest motive behind economic activity is the desire to get 'money income'.[4]

Even with money as measure, Moore further admitted:

> There is no convenient yardstick by which to measure the currents of business affairs for these are subject to gusts of fear or perhaps fantastic optimism as unpredictable as earthquakes.

Money-mindedness or mammon worship is thus, by such admissions, a charge from which economists even of the present-day cannot claim full absolution.

It is Time to Lament for Economics

If by their own admission economics remains still money-dominated in its attitude to problems and ignores non-mercantilist values in life, it will be admitted that the time to lament for economics has come. In fact, economics has in our day become patently recognizable as a kind of die-hard religion to which, like a drowning man, the man who once began to speak its language, willfully clings, while fully aware that his arguments hold water no more. We have heard, besides being charged with mammon worship and often suspected of charlatanism over and above the standing charge of economics as a dismal science, that the claim of this branch of knowledge to be included among sciences has been questioned.

August Compte could not include it among the positive sciences. Its aspirations in this direction have been described by some eminent economic authority as a form of wishfulfilment. Wooten in his book on *Lament for Economics* puts, as it were, the grave stone on this economics that we are asked to lament:

> Whenever six economists are gathered there are seven opinions . . . . Economists are under the suspicion of being charlatans and they cannot afford to arrogate honourable titles to themselves . . . . in the increasing common application of theoretical economics of the term science to their studies, there is an element of wishfulfilment . . . . the zealous student of economic science would do well from time to time to remind himself that, of all the demand and supply schedules, cost curves and difference curves that give so formidable appearance to his textbooks, not one (unless by accident) is founded upon fact. . . . . The reader would search far and wide through the works of analytical economists before he came upon a single prediction endorsed by the weight of authoritative opinion of the course of events to be anticipated in any concrete historical situation.[5]

When even Dr. J.N. Keynes deplores, "Political Economy is

said to have strangled itself with definitions", it would be permissible for the layman to lament officially the death of old time economics. Textbooks now begin by apologising for not being able to give a definition of the subject, and even if they try to do so, make the definition so banal and insipid that it almost tells us nothing. The Columbia Cyclopaedia contents itself with somewhat the following: "Economics deals with supplying man's physical needs."

The Mechanistic Approach to the Vital Problem

Travelling in trains or returing from the West in ships, as the present writer has had occasion to do, one of the most distressing sights that he has been exposed to has been the meeting of young men and women who are still living in the ideologies that have long been outmoded or dead, especially in what pertains to economic matters. Many off-hand statements are made by those who have had training in schools of economic thought. They would talk of poverty in India as if Indians themselves were responsible for it and not their age long exploiters from outside. They would then speak of over-population as if Malthusian theories of population were still valid. A statement like, "there is hardly standing space in India for the present population", is taken for granted by most of them. But if one happens to travel with any one of them in a Trunk Express from Madras to Delhi, for days and nights one sees outside windows, as they pass, vacant lands fit for cultivation as evidenced by similar bits already cultivated in thousands of miles.

They are more ready to believe literally the machanistically conceived mercantilist economists than what they can verify with their own eyes. If you happen to speak of family planning, the same mechanistic attitude may be seen to colour their arguments to the point of childishness. They would state, as if very evident, that when there are too many members in a certain family they will begin to starve, and if one mentions that birds migrate to places where it is favourable to life such a biological verity too is unthought of in the domain of mechanistically conceived economics that their teachers might have spoken to them about.

When speaking of over-population they often forget that **maximum** population and **minimum** population mathematically understood have between them what is called an **optimum** population which the very textbooks mention. The optimum has to be determined not by any mechanistic thumb rule but depending on the economic unit that is the basis of study. Rural and urban units differ and standards of living have very variable factors entering into their makeup. The luxury of one generation can become the necessity of another, and units in society are not static specimens in a museum to be studied *in situ* megascopically or microscopically. They have to be examined in their living setting. Standards of living measured in terms of money must make allowance for many factors of incertitude. High prices might raise the figure without raising the amenities of life involved. The Engel's Law that enters into regulating the standard of living is often overlooked by second-hand economists. The tendencies of the market place are changeful with every gust of wind in market conditions and it is next to impossible to visualize any rigid standard of life as prevailing. What appears as a favourable figure from the opulence side of economics might in reality be just the opposite judged from the abundance side of the same economics, when viewed in a perspective of a full-fledged science. The whole question is vitiated by what might be called the mechanistic approach which is a kind of religion of the modern man.

Anything that comes within the scope of a brass instrument passes as civilized, and there are among us still disciples of Western pragmatists and behaviourists who are directly descended from the days of Cortes and Clive, who put on the air of Sir Oracles, and who talk down the common man or woman with a superior air. Ancient civilizations and their wisdom of the ages do not count any more. Economics has become, in short, the enemy of the best in an ancient heritage like that of India; yet it is a pity that India's own best sons who wish to see their country free from the shackles of colonialism still live in ignorance of the evils of wrong economics as mechanistically conceived by Western fortune hunters of old.

Let us therefore lament for old economics and try to rethink this whole subject from a new and global standpoint.

II

The tradition that has been handed down to our times in economic thinking having its origin and basis in the mercantilist adventures of early colonialists, and conceived as it was in the interests of the wool-sack Chancellors of the Exchequer or their counterparts in the West, has to be given a decent burial before even the outlines of a one-world economics can clearly emerge to view. Economics has to get rid of the inhuman and immoral background in which it had its origin. Even in the days when mercantilist economics was in full swing, in Elizabethan England and Europe generally, there were heard some honest voices who protested against the inhuman and immoral aspects of self-aggrandizing principles tacitly taken for granted by its partisans and thoreticians. The French School of Economics, who may be said to be the founders of modern economic theory, could not make themselves heard over the clamour for gold and capital which was the main incentive with the majority.

The Physiocrats* of France had many fundamental principles to enunciate which indirectly influenced the author of the *Wealth of Nations*. The thoroughgoing statements of the Physiocrats were watered down by Adam Smith and comprised into an economic theory which still retained its closed and static character as against the fully free and human attitude implied in the position of the Physiocrats. Adam Smith's book became a sort of Bible for the English and those others who thought in terms of a home-market as against the colonies, for making select nations in the North of Europe wealthy at the expense of the 'underdeveloped', whatever this term applied to far-flung dominions might strictly mean.

---

* Followers of Quesnay a Frenchman who, in the 18th century founded a system of political and economic doctrines based on the supremacy of natural order, and making the powers of nature the only proper source of public revenue.

The immoral and inhuman elements that vitiated the origins of European economic thought were connived at or condoned in the name of practical economic shrewdness which did not lay much stress on morality or just human relations between man and man. Thus it is that we find their disciples, that have been produced generation after generation, still tutoring the administrators of those dominions which have now become nominally independent except in the matter of that other ideological domination which in effect is worse than physical servitude.

The same pernicious habits of thought that go against the interests of the larger humanity involved in economics are lurking here, and there are canker blossoms within secret brain-trusts and academic advisers who are still behind the policy-makers and planners for larger countries. When, as we have seen in the first section that the very nature of economics as a science applicable to all men anywhere is questionable, it is not hard to imagine the dangers to which the people of the world are exposed by **advisers**, who are already inside the countries or visit them from time to time under the respectable front of guides or guardians of good economics. In these days when cartels exist on an international scale, and trust-busting is in vogue, such a suspicion would be seen to be only normal.

Lack of Yardstick for Economic Measurement

A science is sometimes described as something that depends on precise measurements. There is always a unit of measurement in all branches of exact sciences. If we now ask the economist, what his unit of measurement is, he will say he is obliged to fall back on money as the measure of wealth, because wealth as a pure welfare value does not lend itself to measurement. We have already seen textbook economists bewailing this lack and openly suggesting that money itself could be used as the yardstick for economic measurements. We know too well that both the token and exchange values of money are not firm enough to be used as a measuring rod in economics. The measuring rod has to conform to some sort of stable **norm** before it can measure another factor subject to many forms of fluctuations or variations. If it could be otherwise, each piece of cloth could be measured by another piece of its own kind, instead of by a yardstick which has a standard or normalized prototype determined absolutely by outside considerations independent of the object to be measured and free from change itself.

Writers on economics have been frank enough to admit themselves, that a money-standard of measurement is adopted by them because there is no other substitute available. Prof. Dewett whom we have already cited on this point openly admits:

> There is no convenient yardstick by which to measure the currents of business affairs for these are subject to gusts of fear or perhaps fantastic optimism as unpredictable as earthquakes.[6]

A measurement in terms of money is wholly untenable when the measuring unit itself is subject to various fluctuations. Economists speak of comparative standards of living in countries such as India or England, in spite of the fact that they involve so many uncertainties and fluctuating factors. Yet it is surprising that we read of raising the standard of life whose effect is not directly visible or measurable and which is not unlike trying to read a writing on water. When even decent men take such matters seriously, we cannot but help thinking that, as in religion, there are certain favourite notions which cling to otherwise intelligent minds and which persist as superstitions that die very hard. The myth-making instinct in man finds consolation in such.

Economics vainly claims to be a normative science and one of its greatest drawbacks is that it lacks a yardstick or even a central normative notion altogether. This can be pointed at as the one single defect of the subject taken as a whole.

Value, Wealth and Money

From the token value of a coin gone into disuse, to credit that can be created by bankers or states, we have a whole series of notions of wealth, value or money which have confounded economists for generations. Exchange Value and Utility Value besides Marginal Value exist as defined in textbooks. Price can fluctuate but it is said that, "There cannot be a general rise of values although there can be a general rise of prices." Rent is another of the notions of value which has subtle theorization implied in it, and clouds of subtle theorization on the part of authors have added to the vagueness of the notion. Whether interest is moral or usury fair is still an open question.

There is then the famous Labour Theory of Value which has involved writers in polemical duels and battles in recent years. The Surplus Value Theory is one of the masterpieces of theorizations about value that has come down to our times. All these values must refer to some sort of good or goods that have relation to the happiness of man. Then there are inner and outer values.

Economics must be for man at least as much as man is for economics. When economics becomes more important than man it ends in absurdities. Economics derived from ethics is becoming more and more absurd in our days. The latest of such absurdities is when people think that future progeny must be eliminated for the economic welfare of mankind. No other species of animal would be so ultra-intelligent as to think of its own extermination! Value, wealth and money in relation to human welfare is a matter still only vaguely understood.

The Economic Value of Man

Economics will recognize the value of goods of all kinds from frogs to monkeys, when they are marketable and have a money value. In days of slave trade human beings were bought and sold, and were goods of the market place. As soon as this was declared immoral by public opinion and equality of all men became recognized, there began to prevail the opposite tendency to consider man, except for forced labour, as a superfluity. A monkey cannot read or post a letter, but a human child can run very intelligent errands. Why should such a difference be of no value in human life? When there is too much fish caught and people cannot eat all, they use it as manure, but when it comes to the value of the human body or the living human being, the same intelligence seems frustrated and driven into abnormal and absurd directions. An intelligent boy can run away from home as Clive or Robinson Crusoe are said to have done..

Man is capable of many exploits and adventures that few animals are capable of, and finding food and shelter for him is not a problem. As long as there is any vacant space left in the surface of the earth it would be nonsense to think of exterminating populations, potential or actual. Even to think in these terms must normally be repugnant to a sensitive human mind with its natural interest in its own kind.

Although every textbook of economics now devotes a paragraph at least on how the calculations of Malthus have been proved false, there are men and women who claim to be intelligent and who put on a superior air of civilized persons, who think they know more than what God could ever know and make statements about over-population, long rejected and thrown overboard. Science has now come to a stage in which sex determination mechanisms in biology are even vaguely understood, but it would, with impugnity, dare to interfere mechanistically with what nature orders with its own balance and justice. The consequences of tampering with the balance of nature is known to biologists in the domain of rabbits in Australia and with other animals both favourable and nuisible to man. Society and governments even tolerate methods that are suspect, not to speak of motives that are actually involved in this question of what is respectably labelled '**family planning**'. What passes for persuasion can often hide subtle subjugation against the will of individuals, in special circumstances that prevail in interior localities with innocent villagers. Those who cannot create human life must not think of taking it.

Although the days of slavery in physical chains are over, there are questionable methods of propaganda and persuasion, which, judged by their large scale adverse effects, are more detrimental to man. The Eichman trial has revealed that castration of women had been practised by Hitler to exterminate the Jews whom he did not like as a community. When foreign foundations of a different civilization who have once spoken of the dangers of the yellow or the black perils which multiply fast, why should it be over-suspicious to think that rival interests in the matter of population control can be operative?

A child that may be white, brown, black or yellow is precious masterpiece of nature or God's creation. Anyone who has watched the growth of intelligence of a human child cannot help to consider it as the dearest of goods. Slaves in the market place in chains could be angels instead of mere gun fodder as the moderns might tend to treat them. The omission to recognize the value of man and to give him his legitimate central place in the world of economics, is the sin of the present mechanistic age of technocracy. It is high time that contemplatives of the world joined with the voices of those fathers of modern economic thought in England and in France, men like Carlyle and Ruskin and the well-known Physiocrats, who have been hitherto mentioned with mixed approval, such as Quesnay, Turgot and others, to raise a protest against this degradation of the value of man in the prevailing picture of economic progress in the mind of the average man.

Man is the Veritable Measuring Rod

From the time of Plato we have heard of men having, "in their hearts the heavenly gold and silver given to them by the gods." In the light of such a view of the value of man himself, is it hard to accept that economics must be as much for man as man is for economics? There are modern writers who belong to the mechanistic and technocratic age who still recognize at least two kinds of goods, those within and those without, which together spell human welfare or happiness, which is the very purpose of economy. Ethics and economics have, in our days, become so divorced that they spoil the case of both at present instead of enhancing the teaching of each other. This is a tragic state of affairs and it is a shame that some economic books go so far in the name of matter-of-fact modernity in market place economics, as barefacedly and blatantly to assert that economics has nothing to do with ethics. Even culture and art would be outside its scope according to such uncivilized writers, whose ideas are still steeped in the ideas of the search for the Golden Fleece.

The normative notion that every science needs to build its theorization or practice round, is naturally the happy human being himself, and there is no need to seek all over the warehouse for a yardstick for economics which, as we have seen, has ended up in the setting up of money-standards for measuring wealth. Man is the greatest of values and the best of goods available for man. The proper study of mankind, whether in philosophy or science, is man, and he is, as the ancient dictum puts it most pointedly, the measure of all things, even in economics. No man, no economics!

'Bags and Crags Have the Same Effect on Rags'

Adam Smith was influenced by the continental Physiocrats of Europe in his own time. With Ruskin, Carlyle and Emerson we had even among the colonialists and mercantilists of that Elizabethan age of adventure and expansion, honest men who thought right in economic matters. Their voices have been stifled by the louder clamour for money bags, and it was Ruskin who put the whole protest in poignant and pithy terms when he declared: "Bags and crags have the same effect on rags." Clothed in figurative language, it is not hard to expand his words fully and state that capital, as represented by **money bags**, has an adverse effect on the interests of the poor, who are referred to as **rags**. Capital gives to the man of **bags** the same unfair advantage as a highway robber who sits on the **crags** which stand for points of vantage from where unwary innocent passersby could be attacked. This pithy slogan contains all the lesson that we have once again to learn in bringing proper one-world or globally human economics to prevail for civilizing human life once more after the abolition of slavery.

The whole economic thinking in recent centuries has been sadly vitiated by one dominating factor, symbolized by the **bag** referred to by Ruskin above. The **bag** represents some kind of undue advantage taken against the common fellow-man who is willing to be in **rags** or to work for wages as a slave. The subtle upward sucking power of money in the form of credit in banks and in the form of capital has first to be clearly visualized in economic theory, and in this matter much credit must go to Karl Marx who in his two formidable volumes called *Das Capital* has put his finger on just that single factor which has been the bane of true economic prosperity ever since the days of the gold rush.

The Limits of Free Enterprise

In recent years especially in the economic life of the more 'mature' countries like America and Europe the dangerous extent to which money bags or capital could go in the direction of what is known as free enterprise, has come into evidence as it were with a bang. Cartels and questionable trusts exist which have required the enactment of 'trust-busting' laws by states without which the large scale mergers of big companies would make them so powerful as to dictate terms indirectly to Government purchasers themselves on such a scale that laws are now being dramatically enforced against hitherto rich and respectable businessmen drawing salaries up to $ 125,000 a year, and directors of important concerns. Some of these have been put under handcuff and guard. A peep behind the curtains of such a development could be got from the following extracts taken from the *Time Magazine*:

> What merger-minded U.S. Bankers regard as malicious harassment continued to be the Department of Justice policy last week. Unfettered by the refusal of a Federal court, a fortnight ago to bar absorption of Chicago's City National Bank and Trust Co. by the Continental Illinois National Bank, Attorney General Robert Kennedy's trustbusters raced into New York in an attempt to block the merger of the Hanover Bank (assets $ 2 billion) and the Manufacturers Trust Co. (assets $ 37 billion).[7]

The background on which the above news item would become more understandable are from the following extracts from an earlier report entitled *The Great Conspiracy* in the same magazine.

> In tense and packed Philadelphia court-room last week, a dramma took place that U.S. business will long remember to its shame. The case before him, said Federal District Judge J. Ollen Ganey, were "a shocking indictment of a vast section of our economy. They were more than that. They showed clearly that the executives of a mighty industry, publicly devoted to the concept of competition, had privately conspired to rig prices to the detriment of their customers on a scale so vast that it embraced everything from the Tennessee Valley Authority to the private utilities that supply the nation's light and power.[8]

Later in the report we read:

> What aroused Judge Ganey's indignation was not only the conspiracy but also the efforts of almost everyone involved to justify his misdeeds as part of a prevailing business morality. "What is really at stake here", said the judge, "is the survival of the kind of economy under which America has grown to greatness, the free enterprise system".

The conflict involved between the offenders and justice comes into clearer perspective as we read the following continuation of the same report:

> F.F. Lock, president and general sales manager of Milkwaukee's Allen Bradley Co., who was slapped with a $ 7,500 fine and whose company was fined $ 40,000 maintained that, "no one attending the (business) gatherings was so stupid, he didn't know they were in violation of the law." Then he added in a suprising non sequitur: "But it is the only way business can run. It is free enterprise."

Free enterprise thus has come to mean the opposite in the

mouths of the judge and the hitherto respectable businessman. Capital, competition and free enterprise have thus arrived at a blind alley in our own days.

The Double Reference of the Economic Man

Although it is not in fashion with modern economists to think of the economic man as an abstraction, relying more now as he does on cobweb charts of equilibrium analysis, even of which he is beginning to be more proud because of its factual emptiness and lack of effective predictability in economic trends, we revert to the ideal economic man here not in terms of man as a self-seeking monster of the money bag epoch in economic history, but in order that man may yield the central normative notion for this branch of knowledge which has been wishfully rather than legitimately laying claims for a place among the regular sciences.

Man can be a monster and a menace to mankind itself, or he can be a beneficial human as created by Nature. The power of the money bag often distorts his personality with its pride, and greed makes him tamper with the beauty of nature spoiling the surface of the green planet in which man is destined to seek his happiness.

Money or capital is only one aspect of the double reference that applies to the economic man at one and the same time. Opulence and abundance have to find a healthy equilibrium in the normative notion of the economic man conceived in generalized abstraction. Through Protagoras and Socrates down to the time of the writing of Pope's *Essay on Man*, this need for a norm of thought has been sufficiently recognized in wisdom lirterature the world over. Between Natural abundance and money-bag opulence man must find a middle of good economic living.

The Economic Man at the Crossroads

Economics resides as a double-sided virtue in the golden heart of the man placed in this two-sided economic environment. Like two immiscible liquids in the same bottle, there are two polarised ambivalent factors involved which rarely live together in the same man. The miser and the man of natural generosity do not live together. In this virtue it is that economics can participate its value content with aesthetics and ethics.

The exchange of values, whether horizontal as between prices and goods, or vertical between plus and minus sides of abstract value, takes place according to certain fundamental given laws in the normative world of economics which tallies with economic man on one side and his proper economic environment on the other. It is true that such a theoretical picture is getting outmoded because in pragmatic terms it has not yielded practical guidence for policy-makers of recent years. In spite of this fact, of which we are fully conscious, it must be stated that any economics that mixes up the polarities involved is worse than no economics at all.

We should divide the **haves** and the **have-nots** so that economic programmes for the advantage of one or the other, or for regaining equilibrium in times of crisis or economic malaise, could have some intelligible meaning at least. Instead of giving up methods developed so far in this direction and abandoning the normative idea of the economic man, we here suggest that we should make a fresh and revised effort, from a global background this time, instead of in a partial fashion as hitherto. The two polarised worlds of abundance and opulence have to find equal place in this new normative scheme of economic life.

Private and Public Happiness

There are certain aspects of wealth and consequent happiness that we cannot share or exchange. Love of son by a father or wife by husband refer to vertical happiness of this order and the use of a good public road or bridge belongs to another order. A millionaire who might be living with a wife who has filed a suit against him and is not on speaking terms, can feel more keenly his state of unhappiness than a happily wedded poor peasant and his wife who might be living in a hovel and half-starved but endowed with love.

There are some commonsense banalities that need not be repeated if it is not to show that one-sided welfare economic programmes have lurking factors of uncertainty that might be hiding in the very heart of the problem which experts often miss. The planners in offices who sit with statistics and calculations, predicting varied good or bad results of large scale measures, often do so looking at life quantitatively and mechanistically which can be absurd as the superstitions in the age of the witch-hunt and sorcery. Between the Scylla and Charybdis of the situation, *laissez faire* and *laissez passer* economy would be more safe than trusting to wrong experts who might turn out to be charlatans. There is ample room for suspicion and clash of interest in the modern world.

On the very day I am writing this article we have the tragic news of the death of the Secretary General of the United Nations which has economic and colonialist implications, as strong and as barbarous as in any of the bygone days, still alive in the world and manifesting in the broad daylight of modern public opinion which prides itself on being progressive.

The Uncertainty in Economics

When Shylock says in the last scene of *The Merchant of Venice* that taking away his property would amount to killing him, he is speaking the language of dialectical wisdom by which a man and his property are related in bipolar verticality as a private or personal means of happiness and freedom, which are matters that are guaranteed by every free constitution all over the world. To seek his own happiness freely would mean nothing other than the liberty to have happiness according to one's own private individual notions, whether right or wrong from public standards. There are two worlds each of freedom and happiness involved here, which cross the paths of one the other contradicting, compromising, or counteracting the ways and means of one by the ways and means of the other. The human values involved can be frustrated and foiled for man or for mankind generally when mistakes are made involving violations of dialectical verities.

Paradoxes present themselves in almost every question of the happiness and conflicting means to be adopted make of a life a net-work-tangle of criss-cross problems. These are the domains where fools walk non-chalantly where angels fear to tread.

The whole matter of economics has to be viewed in the light of a revised dialectical point of view in which private and public interests of yielding negative results would on the contrary give double gain. One-World Economics must head in this direction if it is not to flounder altogether and get lost.

Factors of Malaise and Disequilibrium

Economics is a four-cornered game, in which we lose or gain or suffer disequilibrium of maladjustments in various ways that are subtle and gross. Time enters into this as well as quality. Credit and debit, and demand and supply mark the four aspects and when the game is played the ball goes from one side to the other, horizontally or vertically, within the limits of a mathematically conceived vectorial space where various stresses and pressures act and interact. The periods of deflation and inflation that come into evidence now and then within economic areas, limited or general, affecting large and small groups of people at a time, or the whole of humanity when general hard times prevail, have various factors that enter into their composition as unpredictable as the wind that blows where it lists. In accepted language the four corners of the game are known to be the **land**, the **capital**, the **labourer**, and the **entrepreneur**, but these factors are to be understood as more generic and symbolic than specific or literally fixed in meaning. They are only symbols in a larger mathematically extrapolated or elaborated abstract economic world involving higher or lower, greater or lesser values as they touch human life in particular or in general.

We come to face here the mystery of economics as a whole in which the virtues of the economic man come up against the whole of the economic situation, possible, actual or intentional, in any place at any time. This is the theoretical picture tacitly kept in the mind of economic theoreticians while the lesser spirits only played with one or another aspect of this global picture-board in their minds, their own game of checkers. A world of abundance often formed one side of the court, and the world of opulence interacted within it with movements of manoeuvre and contrivance which comprised the expert game which has always been going on. In spite of all these contrivances, human problems are only on the increase both in number, scale of extent, complexity and intensity. To separate, in our minds, the two main factors involved so that we could at least see the sides to which the players or pieces belong in such a game, is that first desideratum without which economic insight should for ever remain a closed mystery.

The economic man, who, within his heart carries that double-sided streak of golden virtue which makes for good economics of any one generation, in this human world of getting and spending, falls broadly into two distinct types. One is represented by the peasant who tills the soil and the other is represented by the man who multiplies his money by lending interest. Although the latter practice has been condemned by the *Koran* and the *Bible* as disreputable, these two types have existed from time immemorial and are likely to exist hereafter. Any picture of prevailing economic climate in which humans are likely to eke their livelihood must count on the world of the peasant and that of the usurer, who belong to two rival worlds and carry their own virtues in their hearts. A generous usurer and peasant miser are possible but rare. They represent, respectively, the world of abundance and opulence.

Only intuitive insight can open the doors to these respective worlds, and in order at least to have a rough idea of what they import, it is necessary here to lapse into a kind of biblical pictorial language.

The World of Abundance

What lies spread before the natural man with all its varied intentional, possible or actual opportunities for a happy life, of birth, living, and multiplication of kind, with the food and shelter that it implies, is the Garden of Eden of the *Bible*. A spring on fertile ground situated at the higher level of gentle slopes is not at once an economic wealth, but in the course of natural living by a normal human family unit, translates itself into wealth by slow imperceptible degrees, by a progression subtler than the arithmetical or geometric one. Perhaps the law of squares holds good here and a logarithmic spiral might mark ascent of this apparently wasteland in terms of wealth. This can happen with different peasants living their own separate lives of Adam-Eves in their own particular and closed economic Edens or paradises. These monad-like closed worlds as in Leibnizian philosophy are units with doors only and no windows.

A happy family unit, as found in natural conditions, is one in which individual, personal and intimate values prevail vertically as it were in self-sufficient independence. Collective economy is repugnant to the spirit of such a windowless universe in which human happiness is secured. An infinite number of monads can coexist in a happy economic whole.

Happiness of All and General Happiness

There are inner goods which yield individual happiness for all and outer goods which contribute to the **general** happiness. Happiness of **all** must not be confused with **general** happiness. If so confused, the outcome would be uncertainty of value results. This in principle is not unlike the modern notion of uncertainty known to physics and associated with Heisenberg. Inner happiness has to be individual and for oneself while outer happiness could be shared. This innate law of reality has to be recognized properly before an integrated body of scientific economic thought can emerge as applicable to the whole of humanity.

The money value of a trickling spring on the grounds of a peasant in the fringe of the forest in some inaccessible mountain district in any part of the world would mean zero to the eyes of the shrewd banker-economist. But the eye of the peasant is guided by quite other considerations. The trickling waters of the spring, though a negligible factor in short-spanned economic valuation, is one that can endure through generations when his children and grandchildren might be expected to live in the same place. The totality of the value that the apparently negligible spring has, in reality, would represent, vertically viewed, enormous wealth whose exchange value at a given moment might be negligible in the valuation of the money-bag economist or bag-Baron. Thus, there are values to be appraised vertically with the long time-span units and values that are to be estimated horizontally as money in exchangeable market place contexts. These might present a law of direct or indirect logarithmic proportions between them. The calculus of real value thus becomes a complicated affair because of the double uncertainty principle involved. There are thus two sets of values to be distinguished which are vertical or real values and their reflections in the market place where horizontal values are exchanged by token or exchange money by means of coins or currency.

The Ascending Pyramid of Opulence or Credit

Credit is an abstract value in economics, that could be created by common consent, and the high-priests of the credit system live in Wall Street or in Lombard Street and are votaries at the altar of the Dollar or the Sterling which at present is distinguished and treated with favouritism as key currency by them, whether covered by gold or not. When public confidence is withdrawn which can happen, theoretically at least, at any moment, and actually only by the will of God or the whim of Chance, this high citadel of the temple of credit might crumble and a new money will have to be devised that will have a more broad based liquidity or exchange value. Funds might flow from the Dollar to the Sterling, or in the reverse direction to stabilize one or the other by short term recovery programmes in the hope of full recovery of these key currencies. Credit, after the Sterling was off the gold standard in September 1941, became a purer abstraction than before.

These two aspects of credit, one more abstract and independent of prices of things than the other, would be clear from the following paragraph from J.S. Mill quoted in Thompson's *Elements of Economics*:

> When credit comes into play as a means of purchasing distinct from money in hand we shall hereafter find that the connection betwen the prices and the amount of calculating medium, is much less direct and intimate and that such connection as does exist no longer admits of so simple a mode of expression.[9]

The notion of credit is thus seen to be one that need not be directly connected with gold or other coins on hand. When England came off the gold standard, this aspect of pure credit came into evidence more clearly than ever before in economic history. After this momentous event, the ethical implications of which remain questionable still, there has been further ascent of the notion of credit into higher and purer altitudes. In fact when we come to the International Monetary Fund and the conventions, adjustments and common tacit understandings between countries, whether of the key currency areas or the areas which come under the European Common Market, the status of credit as an abstract value rises one degree higher in the ascending pyramid of credit which we have to imagine. The arrangements and contrivances, both short-term and long-term, by which the credit system is at present propped up by agreements between Governments and bankers, American, British and Continental, hold many mysteries for the common man who has not had a peep behind the scenes where these stabilizing or recovery measures are worked out and applied.

Financial wizards alone know or pretend to know all that is going on. What is more important is the question whether all that is accepted by expert advisers is really tenable from universal ethical standards. The crag-barons of the money-bag world know how to hide their egocentric closed and static interests by putting on what they call the facade or big front of respectability, while in actuality painted tombs might worms unfold.

It is not considered respectable in such matters to speak bare-facedly the whole of the truth because we are supposed to live dreamily in the best of possible worlds. I shall therefore content myself by quoting excerpts from two recent articles written by two of the latest authorities of England who have put the matter in the proper BBC language clothed in respectable phrases now acceptable. The keen man of common sense can discern here and there gaps and lacunae which violate normal notions, moral, economic and even aesthetic, which ought to be expected to prevail when the wealth and welfare of the peoples of the world, mature or immature, advanced or backward, developed or under-developed, are equally involved. The cause of equal justice to all will be seen to be violated in a subtle way by the very statements which a scrutiny of these passages will reveal to any one who retains some degree of common sense and common interest in the future of mankind.

Under the caption 'Death of A System' *The Listener* of July 27, 1961 contains an article by Robert Triffin, a leading economic expert:

> Among the millions of corpses strewn among the battlefields of the first world war, lies one which we have vainly tried for a half century now to dig up, dust off, and put back on its feet: the corpse is the nineteenth century gold standard.

The gist of the plea of Triffin is contained in the following extracts (Mr. Triffin himself explains):

> The so called Triffin plan is merely an attempt to couch this broad vision of my President and your Prime Minister into concrete and negotiable terms. It remains far short of the admittedly distant ideal of a free world central bank.

Explaining that the sovereign rights of individual states to create credit within their own frontiers would not easily be given up, Mr. Triffin goes on to indicate the way and extent to which international money could be created by a kind of half-consent, by **interpretation** of what has been tacitly accepted by a sufficiently large group of parties whose common interests are already involved. He goes on:

> I would, as a minimum, authorize some international body — let us say the International Monetary Fund — to hold international, gold guaranteed reserve deposits for the central banks of the member countries which wish to take advantage of this facility. It is generally felt that this could be done through some mere interpretation of the present status of the International Monetary Fund and would not therefore require re-negotiation and parliamentary approvals etc. . . .

What is in the back of the mind of this expert will come into unmistakable relief when we read the concluding paragraphs of Mr. Triffin, where he refers to "**A Godsent Channel**" for **Britain**, the title of which itself is sufficient proof that Mr. Triffin is thinking still in terms of the closed prosperity of his own group or country without being strictly a One-World Economist, as we envisage it here. He says:

> Finally, speaking to a British audience, I hardly need stress the relationship between this problem and the prospective move toward unification of the six or seven of the European Economic Community, Britain and its other European Free Trade Association partners.

The Moral Aspect of Creating Credit

The accent on the word 'interpretation' above involves the question whether moral considerations should come into this picture of a Godsent opportunity to create credit as if by the back door.

Another expert, Alan Day, writing in *The Listener* of August 3, 1961 explains and proposes the following way out:

> We are in the middle of a rescue operation for the Sterling which is probably of far greater magnitude than is generally realized; the steps being taken and likely to be taken, could, by a small diversion of their direction lead to the creation of a new world currency which would safely supplement the use of gold.

Once the new world currency is thus established by the small diversion mentioned above (instead of the interpretation that Mr. Triffin relied on) Mr. Alan Day opines:

> We can go on to the third stage of creating more of this currency in accordance with our needs.

The British Prime Minister's Conscience

The ethical consideration involved in creating world currency without a proper world government is a matter that is not faced in these two expert opinions which seem to think in terms of back-door and short-cut terms, with the continued prosperity of only Britain in their minds. Others can use the money thus created if it is good for them or not. The Prime Minister of the United Kingdom is the only person who seems to have any qualms of conscience in this matter as may be seen from his words quoted in Mr. Triffin's article. He is quoted as saying:

> All sorts of remedies are being suggested. The main difficulty about many of them is what I might call the mental hurdles that they might present . . . there seems to be something immoral in increasing the credit base by mutual agreement. Just as each individual country painfully acquired a central banking system, so there ought — ideally — to be a central banking system for all countries of the free world.[10]

Whether the British Prime Minister is going to be an idealist or one of the rank and file of shrewd economists of the wool-sack or money-bag tradition is a matter to be seen. In the meanwhile we can only say that if the problems are not faced frontally and honestly without relying on back-door, patch-work or short-cut methods along adventurous 'Godsent' channels, for the saving of Britain first and the rest of the world next, economic problems and maladies may be warded off temporarily but never be solved on an enduring and true foundation. In 'trustbusting' and the collapse of the Sterling there are signs of the end of the old capitalist tradition. There is need for a wholesale and absolutist answer based on a thorough-going One-World Economics which also is yet to be scientifically formulated.

III

World Economics is More Than a Treasure Hunt

We have noticed at the end of the previous section that free enterprise, as understood in a scarcity-based and money-centred economics, is facing, at the present moment, a critical phase. There is reason to think that the whole economic endeavour of the Western World is heading towards a blind alley. The very realization of the dream of big-business success on the lines of free enterprise is having the paradoxical effect of putting the present heroes of enterprise under government guards and in handcuffs to be marched off to prisons. Anti-trust law is by itself a bad sign of the reversal of the course of economic progress.

Further, the crisis in which the key currencies are caught at present is making financiers think of creating new credit and new money. They have to take this bold step or face further grave deterioration of the situation. Borrowing by governments has reached some kind of limit of elasticity of long-term recovery arrangements. Tariff walls do not keep out the smuggler any more than this gives further room for economic anxiety on a world scale as the crime itself has attained to large international proportions which have broken through the frontiers of countries. What are called 'silent ships' cross constantly the high seas with contraband cargo reaching from coast to coast, while mountain frontiers themselves are becoming increasingly vulnerable to this international crime. Flouting of tariff walls, trust-busting and credit-creation are new problems that face the economy of opulence. Soaring prices too point to inflationary tendencies. These, together with the rumblings of a possible war, cold or hot, give us a somber picture indeed of the world of present-day economics. The end of the chapter of this 'dismal science' which has had its own course to run since the days of the fortune-hunters, may be said to be in sight. It is time that all informed minds think in terms of One-World Economics instead of dividing it up to confine it within rival, hard or soft, key or sundry, currency areas in any relativistic or piecemeal fashion.

A Unitive and Normative Approach

The Physiocrats under Quesnay's leadership represented a school of thought in economics, who looked at the question from another pole altogether. They gave primacy to the world of the farmer and the circulation of wealth, whether in kind or in coin, that took place between the farmer and the landlord who received rents from him. According to this school which thought in terms of natural abundance of nature's products as against the money value, as between the three main classes, the farmer, the commercial and industrial class and the landlord class, wealth had to circulate freely from one pole to the other, for economics to be healthy and conducive to welfare of the given area of populated land such as France. The circulation of wealth in the form of money, agricultural produce, or raw material, within one stratum or sector only of the three, was not considered economically significant at all by them, and even when two strata or sectors were involved in the circulation, such a movement of wealth in the world of economics was called '**imperfect**' still, by Quesnay and his followers. When wealth passed in one form or another, cutting throguh the stratifications to reach all who were involved in the economic endeavour of any country, now changing from the farmer's hands to the wage earner and the businessman, and reaching the landlord or whoever received the benefit of the rent in money, and now returning to the farmer in a certain annual cyclic alternation and succession, that was a circumstance that spelt real economic progress of any country.

We have over-simplified and pesented this matter of changing hands and circulation of wealth so as to be able to clearly visualize the underlying scheme and the mode of operation of this subtle process of economic circulation, visualized by the Physiocrats who are generally accepted to be the real founders of economic theory outside the old

English School. These latter were glaringly economists of 'opulence' rather than of 'abundance' which latter label would more correctly apply to the Physiocrats. In order to show that in so oversimplifying the fundamentals of the circulation of wealth within the main economic classes we have not deflected materially from the authentic position of Quesnay's school, it will not be out of place to quote one paragraph from Engels' essays entitled *Anti Duhring* where he masterfully summarises Quesnay's *Tableau Economique* as follows:

> The whole process is certainly 'fairly simple'. There enters into circulation: from the farmers, two milliards of money for the payment of rent, and three milliards in products, of which two-thirds are means of subsistence and one-third, raw materials; from the sterile class, two milliards in manufactured commodities. Of the means of subsistence amounting to two milliards, one-half is consumed by the landlords and their retainers, the other half by the sterile class in payment for its labour. The raw materials to the value of one milliard replace the working capital of the latter class. Of the manufactured goods in circulation amounting to two milliards, one-half to the landlords and the other to the farmers, for whom it is also a converted form of the interest, which arises at first hand out of agricultural reproduction, on their invested capital. The money thrown into circulation by the farmer in payment of rent, however, flows back to him through the sale of his products, and thus the same process can take place again the next economic year.[11]

This summary of the *Analyse du Tableau Economique* of Quesnay, the father of modern economic theory, is described as 'fairly simple' to understand by Engels in the above paragraph that we have just quoted. Engels himself admits elsewhere in the same essay:

> The *Physiocratic school* left us in Quesnay's *Tableau Economique*, as everyone knows, a riddle of which all

former critics and historians of political economy have up to now broken their teeth in vain. This *Tableau* which is intended to bring out clearly the physiocrat's conception of the production and circulation of a country's total wealth remained obscure enough for the economic world that which succeeded it.[12]

Quesnay's Tableau Further Scrutinized

A lay man of commonsense can read, with all the attention he can muster and scrutinize even now, the above quoted paragraph in which a master economist, Engels, states in 'fairly simple' fashion the gist of what happens in a given unit, in any part of the world, when wealth is produced and is allowed to circulate under normal and normative conditions. We have to underline ourselves here certain key notions involved in the *Tableau* thus presented, before it can become meaningful to an ordinary reader of the present-day.

1. Quesnay here attempts a **normative notion** in respect of the production and the circulation of wealth in the most general and mathematically precise terms as such a subject will admit. Taking his own France as the normative example, he speaks of milliards or livers as the unit of measurement, *grosso modo* considered for purposes of discussion. He relies here as usual on a monetary yardstick even when he includes to the value of raw produce or consumer goods within its meaning. The abstract and elusive notion of wealth is thus arbitrarily brought under a **common value reference**, independently of its actual exchange or commodity value prejudices. The milliards here refer to an **intermediate kind of generalized and abstracted value** notion measurable in terms of pounds or livers, which as we shall see, is not fully satisfactory.

2. After thus selecting France as his unit of a populated area, to an economic unit and fixing the yardstick with which to measure value in the abstract, he goes

on to divide the stratifications that normally exist in any normal society, comprising three main divisions, where again the other sub-divisions of economic, religious or political classes or groups, if any, have to be fitted by us, as secondary items that belong to the same picture. There is the farmer who tills the soil and cultivates. They are the real producers of wealth in any country. Industrialists and commercial people only transport, exchange or modify goods, without affecting the real production or circulation of wealth. These form the second class, and the landlord who represents the modern capitalist represents the third class whose main function is to receive the rent paid by the farming class. The state and the church too have a share in this rent which have all to be understood **inclusively in generalized abstraction** if we want to have a simple living and vivid notion of how wealth originates and circulates in a given community. Labelled generically, for the sake of simplicity, we have to think of the **'Farming'**, the **'Commercial'** and the **'Capitalist'** classes as forming the three successive strata cutting through which wealth in the abstract, whether in kind or coin, changes hands. Another rule that Quesnay has laid down is that true circulation of wealth is only what takes place between the three stratifications of the farmer, commercial world and the world of the receiver of rents. The other **horizontal circulation that is absorbed, as it were, within the stratum of one class itself is not counted as wealth at all of any economic import in the interests of the country as a whole. Just change of form or of pocket is not to be counted**. When circulation cuts across all **three** stratifications of the society, we have, according to Quesnay, a **perfect** circulation. If **two** strata are involved the circulation is **imperfect** and the wealth which is absorbed **in the same class like stagnant water within a bed of sand not available for drinking purposes** for the general good, although it might benefit individuals within the group or class and only indirectly contribute to the good of the All.

3. In addition to these key indications we have to remember that Quesnay treats the whole matter *grosso modo* and takes for granted that prices remain constant and that individual exchanges and transactions that actually take place in instalments are all added up into a total for the purpose of visualizing the total wealth in circulation.
4. During the course of any one economic year, the money paid by the farmer **who belongs, as it were, to the negative pole of the situation**, to the landlord or capitalist who receives it, circulates, cutting through the successive class stratifications and comes back to the source where it started. It, in other words, flows back to the farmers, after going through changes as commodities or exchange values in a very abstract and complicated fashion which we have to visualize through much intuitive understanding. Thus from the actual producers, the farmers, wealth may be said to pass through the sterile and unproductive class of the industrial and commercial stratum to reach the rent-receiving class, whether in cash or as means of subsistence, for each class, **as it rises to the surface like a spring** of net product or surplus value. Thus, to separate the net or surplus value that results from economic endeavour in any country, is the whole purpose of the *Tableau Economique* of Quesnay, which has puzzled generations of expert economists, but yet remains simple to imaginative minds, like that of an Engels, as he himself says.

In underlining the key notions implicit in Quesnay's normative picture, which is both simple and most elusive, we have in the numbered paragraphs above tried to add our own contributions to the thought in those parts which have been in **bold type**. The reader would do well to scrutinize them again and also to take a look at the paragraph from Engels finally. He would then be able to form in his own mind, however vaguely, the outlines of a normative notion for economic thought which he should retain in his mind in reading the rest of what we have to say ourselves.

The Notion of Value in Economics

Next to Leibnizian Monadology or Indian *Vedānta*, there is no subject that is given to theoretical speculations of hair-splitting as modern economics. The one word 'Value' under its different aspects and complexions, has been the subject of volumes of literature filling many shelves in modern libraries. If we should pick any book on advanced economic theory and turn to the letter 'V' in the subject index, we are invariably likely to find a long list of items there, referring to parts of the work devoted to terms such as **token value**, **price value**, **use value**, **net value**, **surplus value** and the like under direct reference to value and indirectly to the discussion such questions as **rent value**, **interest** or **discount value**, **profit**, **product**, **commodity** or individual '**good**' or '**goods**' seen in the perspective of a particular social context or of a particular **time** as a **necessary** or **luxury** item of value. In fact, in the first section of this series we have tried to describe economics itself as pertaining to '**Value-wisdom**', and then we see that others like Engels have referred to the theory of Value in economics as, 'the touchstone of the genuineness of economic systems'. If we should further delimit the scope of this value-science, if we may call it so, as pertaining, not so much to happiness in after-life as to **life here** in an earthy sense, we would have fully given to the notion of Value the central place in this branch of knowledge. When we remember here also that some eminent economists refer to **inner** and **outer** values, **quantitative** and **qualitative** values, **long-term** or **short-term** values, **positive** or **negative** values, the ramifications of the notion of values of the economic world of our day becomes a tangled cluster, well, ill or indifferently understood.

There are values of the market place and intimate personal values. Extended notions of value that trace its necessary evolutionary origins from the biceps of a monkey to that of man, as Engels traces it in great detail, brings into this confusion more complications. Can we ever expect that a day will by itself arrive when this kind of subtle theorization would attain to its final term to leave behind it some simpler over-all outlines of the coherence of fundamental concepts in economics? The prospects seem to be bleak at present. On the contrary, rival theories are on the increase as departmentalization and specialization of branches of Value-wisdom tend more and more to disintegrate economic thought, dispersing individual notions instead of making them hang together by a single central normative concept. This applies not only to the so-called science of economics, but to all knowledge which are tending to fall apart for want of one common integrative and normative notion which alone could give to subtler aspects of knowledge that unity, without which they must remain pieces of information without attaining to the full status of a science or wisdom.

The Complex Net-Work of Possible Human Values

The notion of pure or absolute Value which is important for us to fix for normative purposes of economic thinking, extends from good or goods that refer to life here to those that go beyond such limits into the hereafter and even to the 'here-before'. An old curiosity shop can have much money and market value, but the commodities exchanged therein might have little reference to physical life here at all. Books of antique import, souvenirs and heirlooms, old paintings and the section in which religious articles can be included, all refer to a past which has gone into disuse and left behind by life here as such. There are other articles of prospective import which refer to the latest vogue, pointing to a tomorrow that can invade the fashion-market which sometimes has fabulous money values involved. These might refer to a flimsy feather or fur that is just coming into use in high-life. The price of a toy is not regulated by the congealed man-hour labour or the scarcity of the material that enters its composition. As opposed to milk which might be normal food for a newborn child and which might go bad in a day, we can have diamonds or medicines which do not refer to any simple necessary or general life interest here and now. The value of these vary with individuals and with the time they are most needed. The value of a beautiful tree in your home lawn is not exchangeable nor could it be replaced by so many man-hour units which might represent a high value in itself. You might be willing to pay an enormous sum to see it left alone, without any other article in exchange for it at all.

Life insurance has many kinds of theoretical values that enter into the economic world without commodities that correspond to them. Human fear, worry or anxiety is the negative wealth involved which can be cleverly exploited. Likewise, religious charlatans can exploit the gullibility of women or other simple and superstitious people, and this too can loom large into the economic life as a factor. How drugs and patent medicines can play havoc with healthy economic getting and spending, and go against welfare is also evident in modern days. There is thus negative wealth and positive wealth which can both yield capital or profit. The way of value in human life is more mysterious than what most economists make out. They offer us simple pictures of the promised land of gold which is not unlike the promise of paradise by their counterparts in the rival group of persons who deal with goods of the life to come. Whether life here or hereafter is involved, whether freedom from fear is the only commodity in question or happiness and plenty for progeny still unborn for whom misers might hoard money normally, the world of values presents a complex picture. Between human nature and what it might want for its inner or outer satisfactions here and now or hereafter, clinging to things of the past, or when looking for a prospective world of values, some orderly organically conceived normative way of relating all of them into a unitive whole, must first be devised before we can answer simple questions of economic import such as whether a well-bound and gilt-edged Bible would be better to give away than an equal weight of bread for a hungry man at the door. The cow might die when the grass is being grown is a familiar proverb which faces the opposite way to the sense of the other similar saying that man does not live by bread alone. Problems of Value-wisdom are many and varied.

One has to feed the inner and the outer man, and food at one time for a person can be poison for another or even the same man at a different moment. In such a domain of indeterminism and incertitude, where time and space as components to determine value, it is sheer childishness to think that value can be visualized in the abstract in mathematically generalized terms without any normative notion to hold together the different aspects of the reality implied. Whether we like it or not or whether modern thought sanctions such or not, unitive One-World Economics would be impossible if no normative notion is supplied as a basis for proper economic theory to be raised on its foundations, as a lasting superstructure.

Protolinguism to the Rescue

Profit, interest, rent, net product, marginal value or surplus value have been variously understood and defined from Ricardo to Marx and a host of others too have left behind a heritage of confused economic definitions, based on theories which give primacy to one or another economic factor such as utility, consumer, producer, labour etc. At the present-day there is a forest of rival ideas. If we will only interpose that law that economics must be for man at least as much as man is for economics, and think in terms of a double-sided relationship between the interests of man and corresponding outer values, we will be able to arrive at a psycho-physical normative double-sided notion which will represent the relation-relata complex in which economic life may be said to live, move and have its being. The normative notion has to be simple. We can follow the lines indicated by the founder of modern economic theory, Quesnay, who has in his *Tableau*, which we have examined, simplified for us, the economic picture common to any country.

A living picture of the economic forces or factors in a normative economic unit anywhere in the world is what we should first visualize. Here, instead of relying on verbosity, as most books do in bringing clarity and simplicity to fundamental economic notions, we have to adopt a schematic and analytic method of geometry which we have elsewhere called the protolinguistic rather than the metalinguistic approach. What this consists of will become clear as we read further.

How To Build Up a Normative Notion for Economics

Modern economists admit, there cannot be a general rise of 'values' although there can be a general rise of price. They also admit, on the other hand, that the proper notion of value is the touchstone of sound economic theory. By examining the definition of value in any textbook of economics we can roughly determine the philosophical, metaphysical or theoretical basis of the particular school. These will be found to be as varied and subtle as with schools of theology and religion. God and gold, in the language of economics have often been referred to as complementary terms referring to life-values here or hereafter. How gold enters the economic world, circulates as ornamental or money-value and finds place in vaults of Wall Street, Lombard Street or in Moscow, lending itself to be a standard of value-reference for complex and mysterious reasons, as in the case of the concept of God in theology, has already been studied. Enough has been said to indicate in a sketchy preliminary fashion how there can be four distinct compartments in which gold as a value can operate. The adoption of the Gold Standard in England before 1931 and the climbing down from it and the idea of 'created credit' and capital is a long story in the history of the evolution of economic value which we cannot here enter into. Capital-credit-value, at the present moment, is what makes it possible for 'new money' to be put into circulation by groups of bankers who wish or agree to do so, of which the ethical implications and justice have been questioned by us already. In the world of opulence the circulation and value phases of gold give us the pattern of relation-relata complex involved in the idea or notion of value. Complementary to this, the world of economics of the days of the physiocrats which we have analysed in the *Tableau Economique* of Quesnay, gives us a simplified picture of a normative economic scheme. Gold circulation and Quesnay's *Tableau* together give us some initial indications of how we can build on them a normative notion of value.

'Immature' Countries Have to Make up Their Minds

Economic policies of governments must show net value

production for making the country wealthy. The Physiocrats gave primacy to agriculture in this matter. The gold-rush-economic-world gave capital the primacy. Abstract credit is the culminating factor at which the so-called advanced countries have arrived. Abstract credit itself has become, at present, a major world economic issue with many-sided and delicate implications. An impending crisis that will affect the whole credit structure of the West is to be expected within reasonably short time limits. Agricultural countries like India have now to make up their minds one way or the other, whether they want to imitate the West into the wrong side of the economic fabric represented by capital and its evils, or if they want to build up a stable world of economic abundance in favour of those in rags rather than those with bags. These two economic worlds, however, cannot live together, just as crabbed age and youth cannot live together. The relation between the two worlds of abundance and opulence is such that there is a philosophical principle of incertitude involved as between them so that any conscious programme conceived, which gives primacy to the one, at once compromises the other. Just as in the case of the Heisenberg ***Uncertainty Principle*** in modern physics, and the time honoured error of *jñāna-karma samuccaya* that Śaṅkara puts forward so ably in his writings on *Vedānta*, no state could have a programme which adopts both kinds of progress.

The Cross-Roads Indicated by Rousseau and Voltaire

We have already once tried to explain the sectors or the zones in the economic world which cannot be mixed promiscuously, but more than presenting an arbitrarily imagined and over-simplified picture, we have not been able to go into all implications.* We have had occasion to quote Rousseau in support of the immiscibility of the two worlds and programmes corresponding to each. The striking reference to this very fundamental economic law by such an intuitive and penetrating mind such as that of a Rousseau warrants repetition of quotation here:

---

* See page 143 below.

> Above all do not try to combine these two projects; they are too contradictory, and wanting to be related to both by a composite way of progression is to want to miss both.[13]

We know that between Rousseau and Voltaire the age called that of reason was ushered into being in the history of European thought. Between these two names, one erring on the side of the sentimental and the other on the side of a matter-of-fact attitude that often went beyond its own bounds of a normal and candid outlook, we had a revaluation and demolition of old values for new. Any one who has read *Candide* by Voltaire cannot fail to discover that it was an attack on the love of fortune hunting whose last picture marking the utmost limit of absurdity to which such a tendency could be pushed in human life, has been painted by him to hold it up to ridicule in the strongest possible terms.

Wealth is not Money nor Poverty Merely Pennylessness

Textbooks on economics generally take pains to make the student distinguish between what is wealth and its independence of money. Although the distinction is drawn, the rest of the discussion continues to give primacy to the money aspect of wealth. The standard of life measurable in terms of money value is not questioned and generally passes as valid. This is as misleading as when a young man says that he enjoyed his holiday by spending such and such an amount. The absurdity implied is a subtle one and hard to expose. Money and enjoyment do not belong to the same order of reality and one cannot be the measure of the other. In fact wealth and money could belong to two opposite and reciprocal worlds which have nothing to do with each other. Certain relations in science, we know, vary inversely and others vary directly. Although it might be true that direct proportion might hold good between money and the pleasure it yields, it is a poor yardstick for general over-all use. A simple cup of coffee costs ten times as much in one country than in another, while the cheer it brings remains the same. In a country where the economic progress has been money-based, giving opulence the primacy over aboundance, the polarity or ambivalence that is evidenced and reflected in the prices of foodstuffs, as compared with a country that gives primacy to abundance is to be traced to the existence of two distinct value worlds which are hard to compare by common standards of measurement. A subtler form of vectorial mathematics is here applicable and the usual statistical mechanistically conceived statements could give an altogether false picture of good or bad economic conditions. In any attempt that we might be making in fixing a norm for economic life, especially if it is to be applicable to the One-World that we have in view, we have to make due allowance for the possiblity of reciprocal and mutually exclusive worlds. Just as in Vector Analysis we have to think of the **tensors** and **versors** as different, there are subtle considerations in economics which we have to keep in mind if we are to avoid violating fundamental laws consciously or unconsciously. The clarification of a norm in economics alone could remedy such possible errors which prevail at present. The greenness of a colour cannot be measured in terms of redness, but the intensity of incandescence could be measured in terms of candle power. Monetary standards can measure only horizontal aspects of value while Value as such on which happiness depends eludes such measurements. What we mean by these terms, horizontal and vertical, is precisely what these articles are expected to make clear.

IV

Economics is Value-Wisdom

A comprehensive definition of economics is that it pertains to wisdom about human values. The tendency in modern economics is to confine the world of economics to the market-place transactions that refer to man's physical needs. The *Columbia Encyclopedia* defines it as "study of the supplying of man's physical needs and wants". The pragmatic attitude that is behind such a banal way of defining economics is unmistakable. Marshall and others have not delimited the scope of economics to such a drastically earthy extent.

Ruskin goes to the full scope of economics even beyond the utility values when he says:

> There is no wealth but life: Life including all its powers of love, of joy and of admiration. That country is the richest which nourishes the greatest number of noble and happy human beings.[14]

Between these two views of the scope of economics we have to arrive at a normative definition.

Economics is for Man

We have to admit in the first place that economics is for man and not man for economics, which latter might have no regulative or normative central principle at all whether in the world of existence, of knowledge or in that of axiological values. Economics has to cater to the inner or outer wants of man at all levels from bread to freedom. All constitutions of states start by a guarantee of these primary factors that touch human life. Man does not live by bread alone and losing one's soul would be more disastrous than profitting by the gain of the three worlds. Any science of economics worth the name must put man at the core both as the 'subject-matter' and 'object-matter' of all economic endeavour. Although economics does not directly promise human happiness in so many words, no economics that does not refer to human welfare or what amounts to the same — his happiness — could be interesting or significant.

Poverty and Unhappiness are not Directly Proportionate

The notion of sin is a basic assumption in theology. To modern economists scarcity corresponds to the notion of sin in theology. It is on this basic assumption they build up false theories of economic backwardness or immaturity without reference to any norm to evaluate the standard of life. It is the same as referring to a good Christian applying strange and outlandish norms. An opulent or an abundant economics must equally have the happy man as its yardstick, instead of a monetary standard which would be like measuring something uncertain with another more uncertain. Julian Marias writing on the Commonwealth, brings out this point of poverty and 'poverty' when he says:

> Economic poverty is not equivalent of vital poverty; . . . when poverty remained simple poverty, it inspired in me a deep respect, mingled with admiration, and it seemed to be not far from a state of well-being or if you prefer, happiness.[15]

The Empire State Building in New York requires hundreds of thousands of dollars to keep it warm for its inmates during more than half the year of cold which has to be subtracted from the standards of life of the Indian who lives at a temperature that maintains body temperature approximately year in and year out and through each day and night. How to measure the welfare involved by a monetary standard of life is one of the questions that stare us in the face, which, like many other myths, prevail in the mind of the average modern man who claims to know such matters. Inner and outer man have to match with inner and outer good or goods to spell happiness, through wisdom. Such is the scope of economics understood from a One-World and global human basis.

The Relation-Relata Complex of An Economic Norm

The fruit of the forbidden tree stands for the context of all that is considered evil in Christianity. Although stated in the language of fable or myth the story of Adam and Eve gives the start for Biblical spiritual speculations. What does economics amount to in its simplest of terms, is the question that must be squarely answered before any scientific economics could result. Man finds himself placed in an economic situation which calls for some good qualities on his part, whether of head or of heart to deal with, in a way conducive to the Good of all and the General Good. Virtue and wisdom go hand in hand and are to be treated as dialectical counterparts. Individual and collective happiness have to be thought of together and life here and hereafter in all its grades referring to the present or the future, cannot be omitted from the full scope of economics properly understood.

As we have seen, the emergence of Value through correct economic wisdom and corresponding behaviour, on the part of man, is what economics is studied for. In a statement such as, 'there can be general rise of prices but there cannot be a general rise of values' which is a textbook dictum already accepted, it is easy to derive that the almost mystical or metaphysical notion of Value, which has further been referred to as the touchstone of all economic theory, has or ought to have a central place in economics conceived as a science. In the notion of **net product** of Quesnay and of **surplus value** with its subdivisions of **absolute** and **relative values** in the writings of Karl Marx, we attain to a degree of subtlety which is on a par with philosophical and theological speculations in the name of economic theory. It would be, therefore, quite in place to examine that situation in simplest and abstract terms which is the basis of what is known as the emergence of economic Value to Man.

The Use of Proto and Meta-Linguistics in Economics

Man as the central core or nucleus of the situation equally concerned with the plus and minus sides, the subjective and the objective sides, of the relation-relata-complex involved is the measure of good or bad economics. A good economist is one who both saves himself and saves others from errors in respect of human values. With the neutral and abstracted idea of a man representing all men involved we have to place him in his proper economically concieved relation-relata-complex. There is the good within him like a streak of gold in his heart and there are other goods which enter into and exit from their relation-relata complex holding interest or significance for him at a given moment or place. There is primary or preliminary or negative wealth as well as commodities or goods with use value or price value or exchange value all of which have to be thought of together in the process of flux of economic life that repeats itself year after year, decade after decade or century after century in human life. There will be periods of economic depression or rise fairly general like the seasons, or like night and day, and there will also be local changes like climate or weather that is temporary. Man has to be fitted and studied in his economic environment which vary according to time and space. The alternating cycles that are normally expected and actually registered in economic life have also to be fitted into a living normative picture of the economic life of man. All these factors have to be imagined as clinging together as if hanging by the same peg, if the normative notion desirable for regulating economic thought should be effective.

It is difficult for the mind of man to grasp all the factors that thus come to a single focus of attention, and it is therefore that we have said in an earlier section that proto-linguistics has to come to the rescue here. Charting, mapping, graphs, schematic representations with one or more factors that vary reciprocally, concurrently or in direct or inverse proportion, with a polarity, dichotomy or ambivalence as when we are asked to think of aspects of happenings that are interdependent in economic life such as demand and supply, collection and distribution, interest and discount etc. require a monadic abstract model or pattern in visualizable terms. In fact the cobweb charts now employed in equilibrium analysis has paved the way to the use of proto-linguistics as against descriptive statistical or formal or verbal definitions etc. which pertain to the world of language which itself requires to be further examined, verified or confirmed from a more meta-linguistic standpoint such as that of mathematics or logical calculus.[16] An algebraically expressed formula in economic calculus would thus have a meta-linguistic character while a graph with the use of Cartesian correlates which is also mathematical but belongs to analytical geometry, is proto-linguistic rather than meta-linguistic. A unit economic situation in a descriptive pictorial language and the various phases of value that gold could have in relation to man have already been examined. How the same scheme could be used in other branches of precise thinking has also been explained in various articles of the present writer ranging from education, science and even theology and logic. Like vector analysis this is a new approach that is here recommended for clarity and certitude in the language of a normalized Science of sciences for the One-World of tomorrow.

The Four Limbs of an Economic Situation

Just as the sun and the sunlight belong together we have to think of economic problems subjectively and objectively at once. In a science like that of geology it might be sufficient to examine fossils or rocks microscopically or megascopically as specimens in a museum. Where human welfare and wealth are involved, we have to approach the subject more unitively, and totality of a unit economic situation has to be first visualized in living and real terms. In trying to be positive, economics cannot afford to be merely 'objective' in the sense that Compte meant. In fact Compte failed to bring sociology and economics within the scope of his positivism as he himself admitted. Just as the first fall of man in the *Bible* is the starting point for Christian speculation which concerns welfare of man in the life hereafter, economics has to have a simple starting point for normative thinking in what concerns good economy here on earth. Instead of relying on myth or fable for supplying this neuclear pattern of all economic thought in the name of positivism, we have to resort to another modern device which is becoming more and more accepted by modern economists themselves which is that of charts of equilibrium analysis. If it is conceded thus far, it would be easy to see that every simple or primary economic situation examined as a relation-relata-complex consists of four limbs comprised within two main axes of reference referring to the space factor and the time factor respectively. Nothing can take place without space and time being involved in it whether it is physical space or mental space that we are thinking of. Actual and perceptual or even conceptual space have here to be first fitted into a natural psycho-physical frame of reference to enable us to arrive at a norm in economics which, as we have seen, concerns the inner man and the outer man inasmuch as the inner and outer 'good' which enter into economic circulation, motion or transaction. Economics means movement as well as values that have inner or outer significance.

The charges of preferring scarcity as a primary assumption in economic theory which persists, like original sin, vitiating economics from the days of the gold rush to the present-day and the legitimate stigma attached to this branch of knowledge as a dismal science or of mammon worship would be justified more or less if we do not give to economics the total basis on which both, natural abundance and opulence artificially created through a special kind of scarcity economics, have equal place. Negative and positive wealth have to be treated together as one whole unitively understood.

In one sense economics could be simply visualized as an event that takes place as between two sides of a counter, dividing one from the many, whether persons or goods that might be involved. There are goods of qualitative value and goods of quantitative value that are exchangeable in space or in time. Individual transactions and transactions on a social or national scale involve one or many counters real or implied. Representatives of different classes derive the benefits of these transactions taking in a frame of time-space, quality-quantity factors. The man, the transaction and complex of values involved must all be capable of being thought of together before economic intelligence, sagacity or value-wisdom generally, could operate and could lend itself to study or intelligent scrutiny. The economic policy-maker must predict wrong or evil and remain on the right path leading to general good and the good of all involved. The political parties of any country in their rival election manifestos invariably devote a paragraph to their economic creeds which in the effect of dividing the people of any country against themselves, is as effective if not more effective than religious schisms. It is therefore of the utmost importance that a normative notion must be supplied for this science which otherwise would be no better than rival religious or sectarian groups that already spell unhappiness by their very existence.

The Emergence of Absolute Surplus Value with Marx

The notion of Value is the touchstone of sound economic theorization. From net product, rent, profit and interest to the culminating notion of **Absolute surplus value,** aspects of Value have been found much mentioned in the writings of economists from Quesnay to Karl Marx. The distinction between absolute and relative surplus values is a mystical or metaphysical one. The following extract from Marx's *Capital* will make the complications evident to the lay reader:

> A prolongation of the working day beyond the time during which the worker was producing no more than an equivalent of the value of his labour power, and the appropriation of this surplus value by capital — this is the production of absolute surplus value. It forms the general foundation of the capitalist system and the starting point of the production of relative surplus value. The latter pre-supposes that the working day is already divided into two portions, necessary labour and surplus labour, the period of necessary labour is shortened by means which enable the equivalent of the wage of labour to be produced in a shorter time. The production of absolute surplus value depends only upon the length of the working day: the production of relative surplus value revolutionizes out and out the technical process of labour and the way in which society is subdivided into groups.[17]

In the introduction by C. D. H. Cole of Oxford, a well-known authority in English Economics, he starts off by saying; 'Karl Marx's Capital is not an easy book to read'.[18] If this is a fact with fully trained economists, we can concede that, as far as the common sense reader is concerned, these and similar paragraphs must remain a closed book for ever as in the case of the most cryptic sayings of any book of the theology or esoterics.

Hegelian Absolutism Implicit in Marxist Economic Theory

We can see the affinities of the theory implicit here to that of Hegel which through Engels has afforded the philosophical foundation and supplied the frame of reference for Karl Marx. We have to remember that Hegelian Absolutism, when further elaborated, leads to the triple notions of **thesis, antithesis** and **synthesis** which interact and absorb each other or one another by a mechanism known to dialectical thought, that would take us back to pre-Socratic philosophers in the history of European thought. It would not be a far-fetched generalization to state that Marx's *Capital* contains mystical or esoteric secret doctrines which it is not easy to analyse and state in positively clear terms as required of any science.

The Fall of the Absolute

The difference between the Absolute and the Relative is itself a subtle philosophical one. When Einstein's theory of Relativity prides itself in being different from that of Newton or Euclid of classical times, the vogue in science at the present-day seems to be in favour of the non-absolutist way. Philosophers themselves have raised the slogan of the 'Decline and Fall of the Absolute!' The very first sentence of a book devoted to twentieth-century Analytical Philosophers which bears the above slogan as the title of its first chapter reads:

> It is a remarkable tribute to an enormously muddled but brilliant German professor of the nineteenth century that almost every important philosophical movement of the twentieth century begins with an attack on his views, I have in mind Hegal . . . . .[19]

To use the words 'Absolute' and 'Relative' expecting the usual reader to grasp its implications existentially, subsistentially or in the domain of Value is thus a difficulty at first sight unsurmountable. If we could make use of proto-linguistics the task at once becomes easier.

We know that as between a Bradley and a Bain in the logical tradition of England there is still a great unbridged methodological and epistemological gap. Bradley is a dialectician, but Bain still confines himself to the framework of the tradition of Aristotle which is that of the world of syllogism. These two worlds are far apart and at the same time they interpenetrate in a subtle way. The relativistic outlook of Bain is transformed into the absolutist way of thinking in Bradley. This absolutist way, in fact belongs to the pre-Socratic tradition of dialectical thinking, while the relativist way to the usual world of objective realities and formal relations. To give to both the absolute and the relative their legitimate places in a total scheme, is the task that we have to accomplish here without taking sides with either exclusively. This would imply a revaluation of methodology and epistemology, on a total unitive basis which we shall do with recourse to a later chapter.

Phenomenological Implications of an Absolutist Outlook

How the Cartesian tradition was broken through by the phenomenology of Hegel, further amplified by the English philosopher Hamilton and elaborated through various stages by Husserl in recent times, is a long and complicated story which we shall not enter into. We shall content ourselves by stating that this notion of Absolute Surplus Value has to be fitted into some sort of post-Hegelian philosophical context if it is to make any intelligible meaning at all.

Without stopping to examine whether phenomenology, in its latest form, was subscribed to, directly by Marx and Engles or not, in order to be able to fit this mystico-metaphysical theory of Absolute Surplus Value into its proper context, we are obliged here to build up a spatio-temporal relation-relata-complex so that we could arrive at a normative notion for the restated science of Value that we have said economics must conform to, in the world of tomorrow. The following quotation from Edmund Husserl, referring to a **world of facts and affairs** and a **world of a values,** a **world of goods,** a **practical world** which could inter-subjectively and phenomenologically co-exist penetrating each other trans-physically, in terms of intentional immanence and transcendence at once, and which could belong to any person thought of in the first, second or third persons singular or plural, masculine or feminine, representing the final stages or unconsciously affiliated, would serve for us as spring board to enter fully into our own further speculations leading to the finding of a scientific norm for economic thought.

In this way, consciously awake, I find myself at all

> times, and without my ever being able to change this, set in relation to a world which 'present' for me, and I myself am a member of it. Therefore this world is not there for me as a **mere world of facts and affairs, but,** with the same immediacy, as a **world of values,** a **world of goods,** a **practical world**. Without further effort on my part I find the things before me furnished not only with qualities that befit their positive nature, but with values — characters such as beautiful or ugly, agreeable, or disagreeable, pleasant or unpleasant, and so forth . . . . These values and practicalities, they too belong to the constitution of the **'actually present' objects as such** . . . . The same considerations of course just as well to the men and beasts in my surroundings as to **'mere things'**.[20]

Circulation of Value on a Phenomenological Basis

On such a phenomenological basis let us now visualize the Circulation of Value. If economic theory turns round the notion of Value and is related to good or goods in the abstract on one side and to the mind of man who practises good economics on the other, it is but natural to see that such a notion is made to belong to its proper background scientifically and philosophically. We have seen that Quesnay himself, who has been called the father of modern economic theory and to whom even Adam Smith wanted to dedicate his work on the *Wealth of Nations* had his favourite notion of Value which he preferred to call **net product** of agriculture, understood with reference to a unit country like France. The farmer produced true wealth as opposed to the sterile activities of the industrialists whose labours were lost in the sands of vain effort and cancelling out on price rises. Net **product** was a value that circulated in annual cycles changing hands from class to class of the three main stratifications of society, as it were, cutting vertically across these stratifications instead of merely circulating within each of them, like water in a bed of sand. This same idea of two kinds of value, one that was not true value and the other which mattered, was thus at the basis of the scheme of normal economic phenomena, even with the Physiocrats.

With Engels and Marx we see this same idea further fitted into the context of Hegelian idealism or absolutism in spite of the materialistic and historical perspective in which Marx and Engels wished to examine the notion of Absolute Surplus Value. We have purposely chosen this extreme position taken by Marx for discussion here so that between Quesnay and Marx, whom we have tried to examine, we could extract two fundamental and interrelated notions which refer to relative and absolute value.

Proto-linguistic Terminology

In proto-linguistic language the relation between these two sets of values could be represented by two lines that cut at right angles. This has been developed in the Cartesian language of co-ordinates. The same graphical schematization could be adopted in economics with great economy of mere verbosity. Ricardo's rent, value, interest, profit, capital and credit and pure credit creation by Wall Street, Lombard Street or Moscow would all fall on the plus side of the vertical axis. If we should think of the four limbs of economic life, as conventionally accepted by textbook writers, which are the **land**, the **labour** the **entreprenuer** and the **capital** we could make these four factors accord with the **negative-vertical**, the **negative-horizontal**, the **positive-horizontal** and **positive-vertical** aspects respectively of the unit economic situation whether applicable to small scale individual transactions or to economic phenomena viewed in a larger historical setting of Western conditions. Unexploited land should be understood as potential or negative wealth not thinkable in terms of coin or currency which refer to the horizontal aspects of wealth. Big business and commerce, called justly by Quesnay as the sterile stratum, would refer to horizontal competitive, collective and mutually distructive aspect of value. Inflation and soaring prices are produced when this aspect of economics is strained beyond certain limits. Vertical interaction between trust and credit, within healthy economic units, is what is most desirable in the interests of general economic happiness or welfare for all involved in that particular unit. World economics has to be imagined as harmonised and scientific expansion of the four-fold factors involved so that there would be proportionate growth and not lopsided monstrous accretions or bloatings of one limb at the expense of the others. The preservation of the identity, purity and integrity of the peasant population is all important, as the negative base of the vertical is the real source of all true welath as we shall presently explain.

Vertical and Horizontal Values and Their Circulation

When Quesnay opines that commerce and industry are unproductive of net gain for any unit norm in economics he is merely referring to the **horizontal value**. When on the other land Karl Marx refers to Absolute Surplus Value, he refers to the emergence of a subtle qualitative abstration in the world of Value which makes its effect felt in total historical or social setting of any considerably large area, treated as an economic unit. This is the **vertical value**. This is like cream that comes to the top of a can of milk or like honey that is stored by bees as extra when all the wants of the individuals of the bee-hive, whether drone, worker or queen, have been satisfied which is the share of the credit making financier. Wealth has the habit of getting polarised as credit in centres of high finance while the polar counterpart of the same wealth could exist in its negative potential form in far flung corners of the globe. Sheep that graze on the meadows of Australia, is the real wealth of which the credit available in banks is only a poor reflection. Money does not multiply but when sheep multiplies its reflction in the form of abstract credit could bear interest, to make credit ascend or descend vertically to serve human wants. Thus there is a return of rent paid to the landlord and to the farmer as Quesnay in his *Tableau Economique* has made abundantly clear.

Thus there is too, inevitably, a circulation of wealth in which it changes over from goods to cash of various grades and orders known to economic textbooks as commodity, consumer goods, produce etc. It is hard to imagine all the phases, virtual or actual, positive or potentially negative, as referring to time or space, as price value or use value. The course of value transformation or metamorphosis is a mystery which none except the most gifted of intuitive persons can clearly visualize. In broad outline however it is possible to generalize and state that the course of value describes a kind of figure-of-eight in its change over or alternation between the four aspects of value that we have postulated.

One has to see the circulation of wealth in Quesnay's *Tableau* first and then one has to fit this circulation into the four limbed phenomenological world of values that we have outlined, (supported by a quotation from Husserl above). Finally, one has to visualize the emergence of Absolute Surplus Value as a result of action that is brought to bear on the total economic situation in the form of brute labour coming from the workman's muscles and that subtler vertical counterpart of the same labour-principle, conceived in the abstract as a social, qualitative, historically necessary, element which is the use value as opposed to the price value of a product.

The coat that a tailor makes to fit a particular man has a limited and personal or **qualitative use-value** while ten yards of linen which might cost the same as the coat made by the tailor, has a general **quantitative price-value.** The use value is thus a vertical factor while the price value of ten yards of linen which is exchangeable with the coat (as Marx points out through these favourite examples) is a horizontal factor. Many other examples are possible and it would be hard for the reader to extract the difference between these two sets of values, which it is most important to distinguish, without a proto-linguistic frame of reference. Every notion of value has implied in it four distinct aspects, which have always to be kept in mind together before any conscious economic thinking or planning could take place whether on a small or a big scale on short term or long term.

The course that gold, as a visible economic factor, takes to enter into human affairs and effecting its exit, after functioning as different values, vertical, horizontal, positive or negative, have been examined by us in the chapter 10. We have also tried in an initial fashion to indicate in the form of a table like that of the forbidden fruit the same four aspects of a primitive or simple unit economic situation in it. In that chapter we have accomplished but little more than to come in sight of the bare outlines of a normative notion in economics, as a science of values, in human life here. These initial fundamental outline factors of the normative notion, as far as we have got to draw from the same, further definitions, clarifications and schematic representations, in respect of this elusive subject, are to be where such false doctrine and consequent charlatanism could otherwise prevail.

Outline Features of an Economic Norm

> The first step is to place man in his proper economic environment conceived in terms of Value.

As the sun and the world lit by the sunlight belong together, we have to imagine a phenomenological world of values of which the core is man himself. Man is the measure of all things, and more so when in economics, we are directly concerned about seeing man and making him happy. One and all, **general good** and the **good of all**, have to be fitted as reciprocal aspects of the same dialectically conceived verity. When all are happy the individual is happy, and when individual happiness is not guaranteed the collective programmes of happiness or welfare would defeat their own purposes.

The Pure and Practical Aspects of Value Have to be Distinguished

There is a **time-axis** and a **space-axis** with either of which as reference, we could think of an axiological world. Planned economy cannot give primacy both to the world of opulence and to abundance consciously at the same breath. Two rival gods cannot be propitiated by the same prayer. There is an innate reciprocity and inverse variation between these two ambivalent aspects of economic life.

We have used the terminology of analytical geometry to refer to these aspects proto-linguistically, as the **vertical** and the **horizontal** aspects of Value. A series of Value worlds could lie along these axes. One could think of something like a unit or **monad** in economics which could be graded quantitatively along the two axes with the positive and negative polarities that belong to one or the other of these. We have already referred to these four aspects in passing. In the next section we shall examine them in greater detail and try to define them more precisely, insofar as such definitions could be indulged in without a fuller treatment in a regular treatise, which the subject fully deserves. Leaving such a task for someone better qualified and to the future, we shall here content ourselves, in finally indicating the circulation of value in the economic world so that the normative notion that we are attempting to usher into view, may have that living element, without which economics would lack any reference to living movements as such and give us only a static picture instead of a dynamic one. Good economics must spell progress and a life more abundant. The goal of economics must be to free man from want or suffering both inner and outer. Here its programme might have common boundaries with that of spirituality though not with any static and closed religion as such. **True economics, when it works, takes man from a lower world of Values to a higher one, in a vertically conceived scale of Value-worlds.**

There are the lower worlds of negative wealth which have also to be given their legitimate place in the polarised worlds of values, so that we could plan both an abundancist and an opulencist economics however, compromising with the mutually exclusive value worlds. The innate contradiction between the two can be transcended by a unitive approach, which would make economics the preserve of the expert of experts. The relation-relata-complex of value factors in which economics has to live and move, when properly understood, has to avoid major errors and consequent disasters. Sometimes opposite effects can accrue from pressures applied wrongly, in the delicate set-up of economic life. One has, in fact, to be greater than a *Yogī* to be a fully sure economist. Planned economy is generally full of pit-falls. If the country still survives it is not unlike the patient living in spite of wrong remedies applied by the doctor. Ascending and descending economic policies can be applied only by way of adjusting the internal conditions of a country with its external relations, so that a favourable balance could be struck, and progressive pressure maintained with an eye to different kinds of human values.

If after the reading of this fourth section, the reader would concede that there are two distinct economic worlds of human value, one of abundance and the other of opulence, and that there are between them two axes of reference where positive and negative value factors reside, and also concede that in broad terms there is an alternating circulation measurable in decade or century units, of a kind which has to be kept healthy in good economics for any economic unit, the rambling discussion that we have been obliged to adopt hitherto would have served its initial purpose. Above all, it is for a law of Economics to recognise that the innate ambivalence makes it impossible for an abundancist economics to be consciously planned side-by-side with an Economics of opulence.

V

We propose in this last section, to try and arrive at indicating, though in a preliminary fashion only, the principles, laws and definite notions that must underlie economics if it is to be recognized as a science. We shall adopt a decimal system of numbers for the systematic taxonomy of the items, examined in a graded fashion.

1. Economics is a branch of axiology. It refers to human values both inner and outer.

1°1. Economics is a science of value-wisdom as it refers to life here as opposed to life hereafter where we are more properly in the domain of religion.

1°2. A Utopia or a heaven which refers to ideal conditions of life here or hereafter are envisaged respectively by rival enthusiasts who propose to better the lot of human being here or hereafter.

1°3. The danger of tenaciously adhering to favourite items of such a programme of values, is common to both these branches. Superstitious creeds and dogmatic or doctrinal orthodoxy could vitiate both fields, except when looked upon with a living human aloofness and dispassion without selfish axes to grind. Both these fields offer equal opportunity for charlatans.

1°41. Good economics, as it applies to a given unit, could yield either opulence or abundance, but not both except by very rare coincidence.

1°42. Like a mirror-image and its original, is the difference between these two economic worlds. They form complex value systems both at the pole of opulence as well as that of abundance.

1°43. Prices can be artificially raised or lowered by economic planning, but the One Value that spells human happiness is to be understood as a state of balance, equilibrium, stability or harmony between the forces of satisfaction and wants that operate within a unit economic situation.

1°44. In the absence of a normative unit notion of value the idea of raising the standard of life can have no meaning. Raising the standard might be at the expense of abundance and in favour of opulence which must spell economic insecurity, instability or lopsided progress which is only progress in appearance.

1°45. **Price value** depends on exchangeability in the market and **use value** is the intrinsic significance for single individuals. The former may be called horizontal while the latter is vertical.

1°46. There are values that yield short term benefits to an individual or group which are horizontal, and those which give long term benefits may be broadly distinguished initially as vertical.

1°47. Inner and outer values in life meet from opposite poles in the self which is the Absolute Value that each human represents to itself.

2. A happy human being is the normative goal of

economic endeavour. Collective happiness is only the resultant of individual happiness.

2°1. The individual is only happy when he makes another happy or works for general happiness of mankind.

2°2. Unilateral economic transactions bringing benefit to one party while making another a looser, violates the most fundamental of all economic laws, viz., that all economics is for both parties in any transaction.

2°21. Aggrandisement, selfishness, domination, explanation and injustice are various attributes signifying the absurdity involved in one-sided or dualistically conceived economics. Charlatanism, cheating and robbery are also applicable in such dealings in actual or figurative language.

2°3. Absolute Value has no limbs; it refers to a state of felicity when all concerned are, and each concerned is, happy at once and for ever. Wealth has four limbs: production-consumption and trust-credit. The former pair represents the plus and minus sides of the horizontal and the latter the negative and positive aspects of the vertical.

2°4. Normal, perfect and economically healthy circulation of wealth is when all the above four aspects alternate as successive phases of the economic cycle of activity.

2°5. Sterile circulation tends to be wholly horizontal while productive circulation passes through vertical levels. Surplus value is an abstraction which gains its meaning with reference to an absolutist or verticalised notion of wealth.

3. Pure values are those that have unity in both ends and means. When means and ends are divorced, wealth becomes pillage or booty.

3°1. Wealth is best when it is self-sufficient. The resulting value is human happiness.

3°2. Capital is credit ready to support economic undertakings.

3°3. Trust is what ensures endurance and security to wealth.

3°4. Price, money, currency, exchange-value and token-value are aspects of wealth as it moves or circulates horizontally.

3.°41. Bank rates have their plus and minus aspects tending to come to balance or equilibrium as between interest and discount.

3.°42. Short term and long term economic transactions compensate or contradict each other by virtue of the principle of double gain or double loss.

4. Dialectics of the **one and the many** is involved in all economics. This is most evident in insurance, which involves no visible goods in the transactions. Advertising is for the broadening of the basis of the **one and the many** dialectics implicit. The business counter is the point where the limbs of business, involving one-and-the-many relations of long term or short term duration, have their locus both abstract and concrete. Time compensates for space and quality for quantity etc. at this locus.

4°1. A normative notion in economics is like a monad or a Monad of all monads conceivable or possible as units in economic life. We have to distinguish between monads in which horizontal aspects dominate over the vertical, and the positive over the negative, in each of the axes of reference. These monads might be supposed to exist in vectorial space in terms of tensor theory, giving room to absolute or relative monads or the Monad of all monads. For the sake of simplicity we have to conceive them as belonging to a flat surface consisting of two correlates, time or interval being the absolute element involved. The elaboration of this kind of economic monadology based on the four limbs of economic activity is mostly the work of future experts who accept the basis of the above.

4°2. In the *Wealth of Nations* of Adam Smith and in the *Tableau Economique* of Quesnay, some unit country is kept in mind which is mostly arbitrary. The Quesnay unit is more natural and normal than the 'nation' vaguely considered by Adam Smith which would more really apply to the mercantilist units in economic life of such places as London, The Hague or Rotterdam and regions round it only. The so-called economically underdeveloped units have wealth only for exploitation by the so-called developed nations according to such notions. To the extent this notion of wealth is not normalized it is not right to think in terms of it.

4°3. The number of happy individuals that a state can produce is the real measure of its economic well-being.

4°4. Happiness has to be judged with its natural human counterparts. No mother could be considered wealthy if the child is poor, no king without subjects, no master without servant, no husband without wife etc. Unilaterally conceived riches, wealth, money or happiness as an over-all value, has no sense. It is absurd.

4°5. If food that is grown in a country is not available to the mouths that feed on it, in a normal and natural way, an economic absurdity of the lack of living correlation of value takes place. Human intelligence often causes more trouble by mechanistic arrangements of production and distribution for money-profit, making the human lot worse than before. A fish-wife in a coral island cannot get the coconut that grows near her hut, because of its money and exchange value which makes it beyond her economic reach. Horizontal forces cut across the peace and self-sufficiency that would have naturally prevailed when vertical forces are left alone. The *laissez-faire* policy has herein its justification.

4°6. The outcome of horizontal economic endeavour is competition and that of vertical, cooperation.

4°7. When two farmers resort to litigation, both lose what each should have gained vertically by agriculture. A double loss or gain is implied which is dialectical in its implications. The children of both might starve instead both having abundance.

4°8. A State Reserve Bank employee gets a higher standard of living conditions when in service; but his children become homeless on the day he retires and there are scenes of weeping on that day. Long term security is not always implied in a higher standard of life.

4.9. Fear of constant insecurity of being fired or laid off at short notice often stares in the face of people who enjoy very high standard of life. This is poverty entering by the backdoor when the life of getting-and-spending gets a horizontal accentuation. Such a life is full of tension and exacting on the nerves.

4°91. Working women in cold countries are often thrown out of city tenements for not being able to pay winter heating expenses in advance by a certain date in autumn. Long term insecurity is a keen form of poverty, hidden under high standards of day-to-day individual living.

5. The one and the many dialectics when it acts in conjunction with the principle of economic intervals of short-term or long-term changes of value, gives us the normative notion of what constitutes the core of economic life.

5°1. To decide controversial questions, like the one that has been engaging rival schools of expert economists in London recently, on whether the European Common Market would improve the economics of each country involved or not, they have to be first viewed in the perspective of the vertico-horizontal complex involved. Broad-based the perspective of the one and the many relations would spell gain, but individual nations might lose much during transition.

5^{0}2. Advertising is a supreme example of how by broadening the basis of the **one and the many** and by intensifying by repetition the value aspect of some good or goods, monopolistic economic domains are built up. Here no goods need be involved, only ideas.

5.^{0}21. For advertising, having advertising itself as its item of business and news agency for its own sake, shows how economics can thrive on airy nothing.

5^{0}22. Film advertising thrives on the features of a film star which itself is flimsy.

5^{0}3. Banking and insurance thrive on mere book-keeping and that with other people's money. It is strange to hear, in spite of this that religious mendicants who take after the example of a Christ or a Buddha preaching the Kingdom of God or *Dharma*, for all humanity, without any return gain, are considered even in India by modern plan-economists, as economic liabilities than assets. There is a strange irony here.

5^{0}4. Some holy cities of the East and some civilized ones of the West, thrive on exaggerations of sacredness or of sin as their main article in trade. Prostitution as well as holiness could both be flourishing industries of a questionable character.

5^{0}5. Mere lewdness or obscenity could sometimes take the place of an article of trade. It breeds sterility or immoral prosperity without true economic goods.

5^{0}6. A man of good repute anywhere is an economic asset. A woman is more so.

5^{0}7. The correct way of getting and spending is represented by the model economic man of parsimony, right abstinence and wholehearted love of general welfare and the welfare of all, with only added gain or life, more abundant to himself in every way.

5^{0}8. Gandhi and Tolstoy and all leading saints of all climes and times have had great economic forces implied in them linking one with the many, broad-basedly for enduring time spans.

5^{0}9. Economics is as much for man as man for economics. Economic ends and means have their meeting point in him.

6. Credit and Trust accrue round persons or corporations with the value called **Good will** which is a great economic good. Goods are only secondary in importance. Production and distribution take place when credit meets Trust.

6^{0}1. Prodigals and fortune-hunters belong to the credit side while misers and hoarders belong to the trust side.

6^{0}2. Trust could be lost as with the sterling now, and credit could be dishonestly created as attempted through the ECM. World opinion can effect the combined structure and make it burst like a bubble.

6^{0}3. A carefree life in natural abundance is worth more than the life of a multimillionaire ready to commit suicide from his sky-skraper window.

6^{0}4. Grains and eatables hidden under bamboo beds make more real wealth than empty refrigerators containing sometimes only half a bottle of Coco-Cola.

6^{0}5. Winter in the West represents an accumulated weight of poverty unknown in climes that make the land filled with mud huts and people in rags. A good climate is for all, and is not to be measured in money value.

6^{0}6. Market fluctuations are either due to spatial or temporal scarcity of wanted goods. Both these factors could exist together with their four limbs so that inflation becomes an economic mystery. Conscious remedies often make the patient die earlier due to 'experts'.

$6^{0}7$. The Lloyd's Bank represents merely the reflected glory of the sheep that graze in the pastures of Australia. The labour is on the part of the grazing sheep.

$6^{0}8$. Abstract labour as well as surplus value are metaphysical abstractions used by writers on economic theory. Mathematically, there is vertical and horizontal labour. These produce positive or negative values of price or of use.

$6^{0}9$. A woman conceiving and giving birth involves negative vertical labour. A man at digging is in travail of a positive kind in the horizontal. When treated as recreation they become interchangeable and cancel out naturally in the joy of living.

7. Work becomes no work when it becomes natural and enjoyable.

$7^{0}01$. The iron law of subsistence-wage level marks the horizontal line of separation between the world of opulence and that of abundance. Economically advanced countries tend to be poor abundancistically and underdeveloped countries tend to be poor in opulence that can only express itself by its streamlined bursting balloon glory of emptiness.

$7^{0}1$. Ascending of wealth into the domain of symbolic credit and its descent to meet necessities and to exist again stored in the form of potential trust, have to be visualized imaginatively before a programme of peace and prosperity could be spelt, by finance ministers of any economic unit of a country or community.

$7^{0}2$. Roads and communications could by themselves be good as well as evil at the same time. Bandits as well as benefactors could enter protected areas by these means. Why should there be fortifications if easy communications are all for good.

7^{0}3. Taxation tariff walls and trust monopolies imply barriers of dubious value in world economics. Indirect taxation shares in profit unjustly, resulting in a state compromising its own prosperity or unit within another unit countering interests of each other.

7^{0}4. World Bank might be a name for an illegitimate monopoly of credit.

7^{0}5. Contraband traffic, cartels and created-credit are signs of the times indicating a world economic crisis.

7.^{0}51. The ascending pyramid of credit draws people upward into sterile domains of more and more getting and spending.

7^{0}6. Unemployment and leisure refer to the same state of affairs. One is hardly recognizable from the other. When unitively treated both are good. Dualistically treated, both become separate problems, one accentuating the evil of the other.

7^{0}7. The honesty of limited liability is questionable.

7^{0}8. A simple breach of trust can be implied in coming off the gold standard when that was not understood in the beginning.

7^{0}9. Hard currency, key currency and other terms which are given consideration often affect settlements of internal debts unfairly by bringing in artificial considerations or concessions that bring advantage to some and disadvantage to others.

8. Economic theories like that of population control end in dogmatisms that refuse to die when proved to be superstitions.

8^{0}1. Celibacy is held up as a virtue or sign of holiness like 'immaculate conception' within certain types of religious belief. The same aversion to procreation persists as family planning as refracted through the orthodoxy of some protestant sects whose priests are allowed to marry. Even scientists do not escape this influence and talk with a quasi religious fervour when they speak of normal sex in men or women and the need for its control.

8°2. Every decent textbook of economics devotes at least a paragraph to say that Malthusian ideas which originated with priests has long remained disproved scientifically, but the idea persists and continues to haunt the minds of people who want to save nations. The fact that other intelligent nations like China and Russia pay mothers for adding to population shows how opinion is based on mere false prudery or sense of guilt in sex or in sin merely. When Hitler employed this method of population control to exterminate races that he hated personally, as known through Eichman evidence, why should it be over-suspicious to think that foreigners could use this against their enemies actual or potential?

8°3. Birds migrate, plants distribute their seeds far and wide to survive but man is at his wit's end about living space for his progeny when half the surface of the green earth is still vacant. Experts would make the common man believe that there is no standing space in the earth. Hundreds of thousand acres are said, at the same time, to be available in the same newspapers to be given to the poor to cultivate, even in states like Kerala which is supposed to suffer from overpopulation, by expert opinion. To think of killing future progeny to solve this problem that does not really exist can only be called suicidal madness.

8°4. There is no good so precious as a young and growing human being, male or female. Let anyone challenge this statement.

8°5. When there is too much fish it is used as manure

but when too many humans are born they say no use could be found for them. No wonder, sensitive persons have called economics a dismal science.

8°6. Tariff walls, curtains, barriers, impediments by permits needed, licenses and papers of all kinds, make of the world a prison house instead of being a place for common man to live and seek his normal happiness as a human being, freely. The world is tending to resemble a big concentration camp. All wrong impediments must go. Slavery is not yet abolished. It persists in other forms, more keenly.

8°7. Bread and freedom must be guaranteed for happiness both general and individual. The *Bible* for a sinner must only be at least as important as a loaf of bread now. The former refers to a vertical need which must be met in horizontal terms of everyday life. Bread without freedom and freedom without bread defeat the purpose of both and either. Economics has to be approached dialectically, not with unilateral aim.

8°8. Pure factors like credit and trust must translate themselves into actual benefits in everyday life by the contract of **all for one and one for all**. The quantitative slogan of the greatest good of the greatest number would then be seen to be meaningless. Everybody should be considered his human brother's keeper.

8°9. A sum of money could be spent in two different ways for the benefit of others, by fractional benefit to many and full benefit for a few. The calculation should be based on life-unit's needs rather than mechanistically as illustrated in the parable of the talents in the *Bible*. Funds of public bodies often spent neither for individuals nor for humanity at large tend to become absurd waste. The Kingdom of God could be economically interpreted as, in the regions here, instead of relativism prevailing in respect of benefits in life, is replaced absolute sharing in full, against the generosity which introduces barriers of both time and space.

10^0^1. The highest form of cooperation is unlimited liability between the one and the many, understood dialectically. This will yield double gain where double loss prevails.

10^0^3. Money-centred scarcity economics cannot escape the nickname of mammon worship that has been applied to it. The dismal science becomes lighted up with hope when human being's good is kept in mind. Topsy-turvey economics, by placing wrong accent on human values, is to be avoided. The goal of economics determines its character, as a tree is known by its fruit.

10^0^4. **From each according to his ability, to each according to his need** is a dialectical verity to be applied to economic theory more and more. Mechanistic and statistical approaches cannot accomodate this verity.

10^0^5. The quadrants involved in economic life tend to make the science full of possibilities, probabilities and incertitudes. The science of economics must be restated dialectically, normatively and absolutely with the fourfold aspects of value cohering together in living terms.

10^0^6. The hunger of one man, woman or child at the remotest corner of the world must concern all men at all time and all human resources applied to it, at any time and place. Such is the desideratum of One-World Economics.

10^0^7. Putting economic barriers against fellow men is a crime against humanity.

10^0^8. Class distinctions spell sterility of Wealth and its stagnation within stratifications in human society which must be kept mixed and homogenius for economic health. Caste or race notions create complicated economic boxes one within another.

10[0]9. The honey in a bee-hive represents the surplus value coming from an agreement between one bee and the whole hive.

11. Man and Humanity must be treated as dialectical counterparts if One-World Economics is to be a science, referring to general good and the good of all at one and the same time.

Appendix

The items given in this article are to be treated as broad indications for showing the lines along which any future revision of Economics on a 'One-World' basis is to be envisaged in a complete treatise which is largely the work for the future student. We give below (see page 145) some schematic representations with reference to items above wherever very specific. General reference to the whole way of looking at economic theory is implied throughout.

Notes

1. p. 163, Lee's Translation, Penguin.
2. p. 1, *Principles of Economics*, 8th edn.
3. p. 38, *Ad Valorem*.
4. p. 25, Prof. K.K. Dewett, *Modern Economic Theory*, Punjab University.
5. p. 13, *Ibid*.
6. p. 12, *Elements of Economics*.
7. *Time*, Sept. 15, 1961.
8. *Ibid*., February 17, 1961.
9. p. 426, *Elements of Economics*, Thompson.
10. p. 122, *The Listener*, July 27, 1961.
11. p. 372, *Anti Duhring*, Engels.
12. p. 360, *Ibid*.
13. p. 384, Translated from the *Contrat Social*, Editors, Garnier, Paris.
14. cf. *Ad Valorem* of Ruskin.
15. *Deccan Herald*, 1st Oct. 1961, Bangalore.
16. This difference has been fully explained in a monograph submitted to the Union Academic International, Brussels, by the present writer in the year 1960.
17. p. 555, *Capital* by Karl Marx, Vol. II, Everyman's Library, London.
18. p. xi, *Ibid*., Vol. I.
10. p. 1, *The Age of Analysis*, Mentor, New York, 1956.
20. p. 107, *Ibid*.

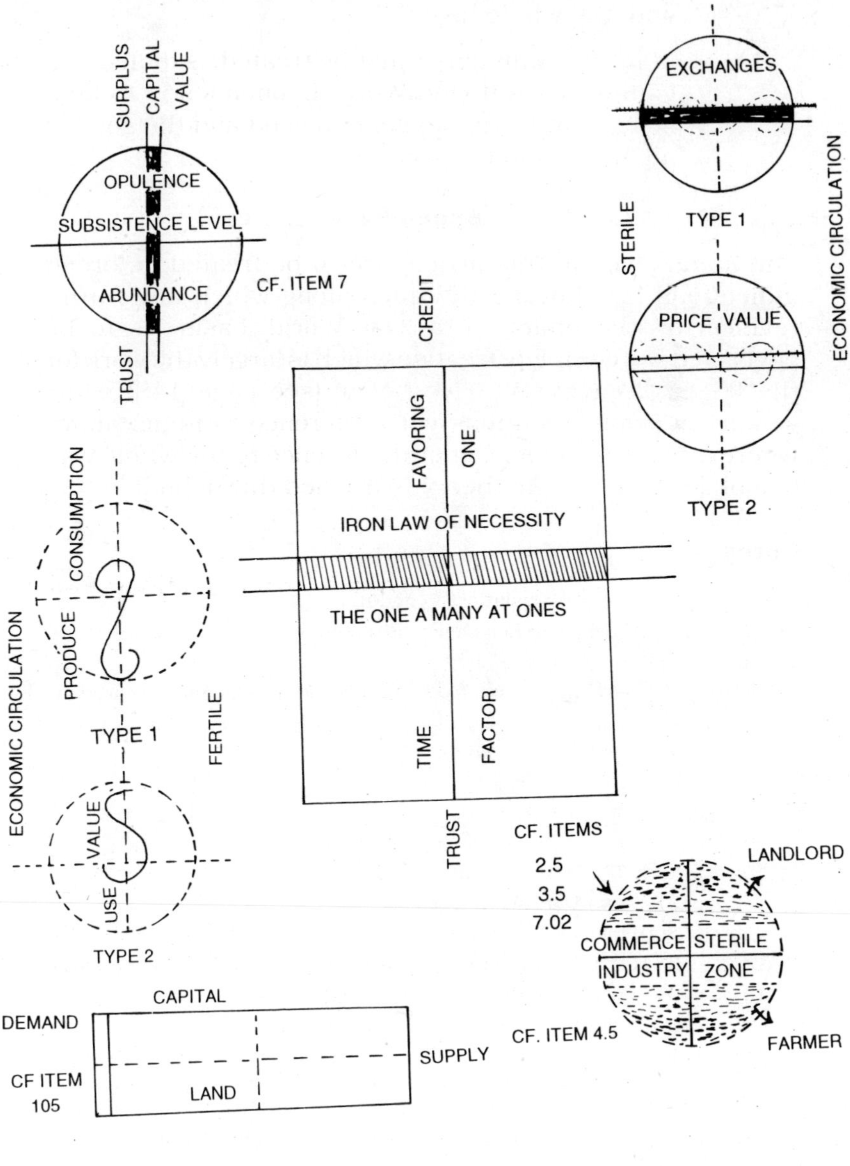
SURPLUS
CAPITAL
VALUE
OPULENCE
SUBSISTENCE LEVEL
ABUNDANCE
TRUST
CF. ITEM 7
EXCHANGES
TYPE 1
STERILE
PRICE VALUE
TYPE 2
ECONOMIC CIRCULATION
CREDIT
FAVORING
ONE
IRON LAW OF NECESSITY
THE ONE A MANY AT ONES
TIME
FACTOR
TRUST
CONSUMPTION
PRODUCE
ECONOMIC CIRCULATION
TYPE 1
FERTILE
VALUE
USE
TYPE 2
CF. ITEMS
2.5
3.5
7.02
LANDLORD
COMMERCE
STERILE
INDUSTRY
ZONE
CF. ITEM 4.5
FARMER
CAPITAL
DEMAND
CF ITEM
105
LAND
SUPPLY

12

Proto-Linguistics Applied to Economics

A VERTICO-HORIZONTAL scheme of correlation based on the correlates of Descartes has been tacitly kept in mind or overtly referred to in many articles by the present writer on varied subjects. In economic thought, which is perhaps one which is most intricate, this same proto-linguistic or geometrical scheme could be advantageously employed.

The following extracts taken from Ruskin's *Ad Valorem* lend themselves admirably to reveal the fact that even the best writers besides Quesnay, Adam Smith, Engels and others on this elusive subject, have kept in their minds some tacit scheme of correlation without knowledge of which most of what they wrote would remain closed to the common reader. After resorting to Greek Mythology and the Bible to aid him to express himself, Ruskin wrote in a language that could vie with the cryptic language of the *Upaniṣads*, as follows:

> This being the nature of capital, it follows that there are two kinds of true production, always going in an Active State; one of seed and one of food; or production

> for the Ground, and for the Mouth; both of which are by covetous persons thought to be production only for the granary; whereas the function of the granary is but intermediate and conservative, fulfilled in distribution; else it ends in nothing but mildew and nourishment for rats and worms. And since production for the Ground is only useful with future hope of harvest, all **essential** production is for the Mouth; and is finally measured by the mouth, as I said above, consumption is the crown of production; and the wealth of a nation is only to be estimated by what it consumes.[1]
>
> So that, finally, I believe that nearly all labour may be shortly divided into positive and negative labour; positive that which produces life, negative, that which produces death; the most directly negative labour being murder and the most directly positive, the bearing and rearing of children: so that the precise degree in which murder is hateful on the negative side of **idleness**, in that exact degree child-rearing is admirable, on the positive side of **idleness**.[2]
>
> In all the ranges of human thought, I know none so melancholy as the speculations of political economists on the population question.[3]
>
> The general law, then, respecting just or economical exchange, is simply this: There must be advantage on both sides . . . .[4]

Such paragraphs could be multiplied. Textbook economics admits already the four-cornered game of economic activity with the land, labour, entrepreneur and capital, keeping the four corners of the field. The famous *Tableau Economique* of Quesnay also presupposes a scheme. The subtle difference between the **price** value of a thing and its **use** value is brought out by vague examples as that between some yards of cloth and a coat by Marx and others. One such example does not, however, make it a generally valid difference to be understood scientifically.

Now, the four-cornered game of economic activity accepted by textbook writers could be viewed in two alternative ways: One in which brute factors like actual toiling and slave driving are implied as the horizontal aspects (*fig.* 12.1a) and the land and capital theoretically considered as pure (vertical) aspects (*fig.* 12.1b.). The pure or the practical aspects could be given primacy by the economist depending on whether he is of earth earthy or accepts, like Ruskin's human values conducive to life more abundant, instead of Mammon-worship. The difference is radical.

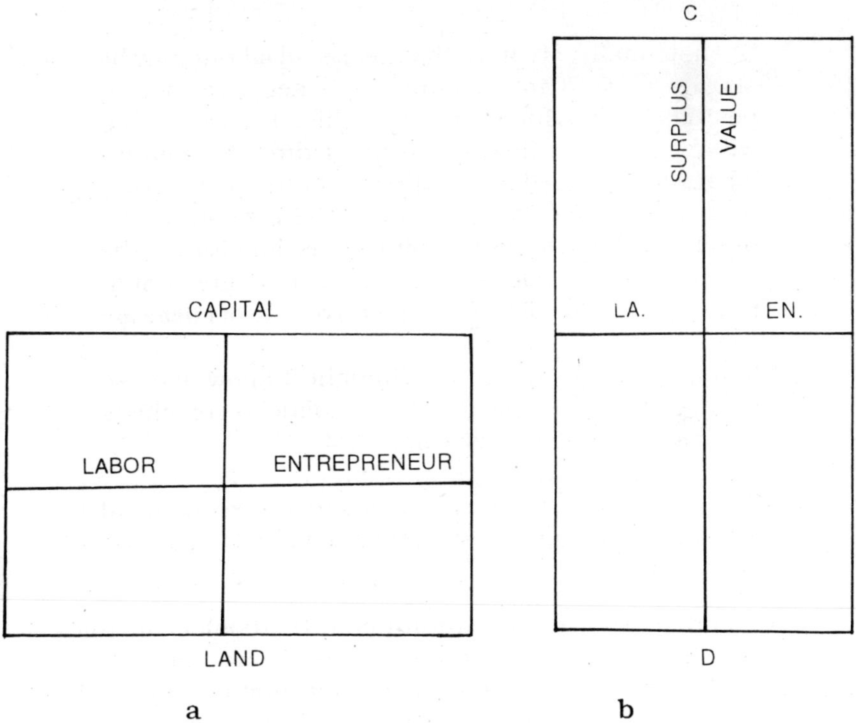

fig. 12.1

A simplified *Tableau Economique* as Quesnay might have proto-linguistically represented it, would be as given below (see *fig.* 12.2).

Now if we try to clarify the subtle implications of the paragraphs we have taken from Ruskin with the help of the same proto-linguistic approach, we would get the following schematic representation for the item marked 266 (*fig.* 12.3) and item marked 256 (*fig.* 12.4).

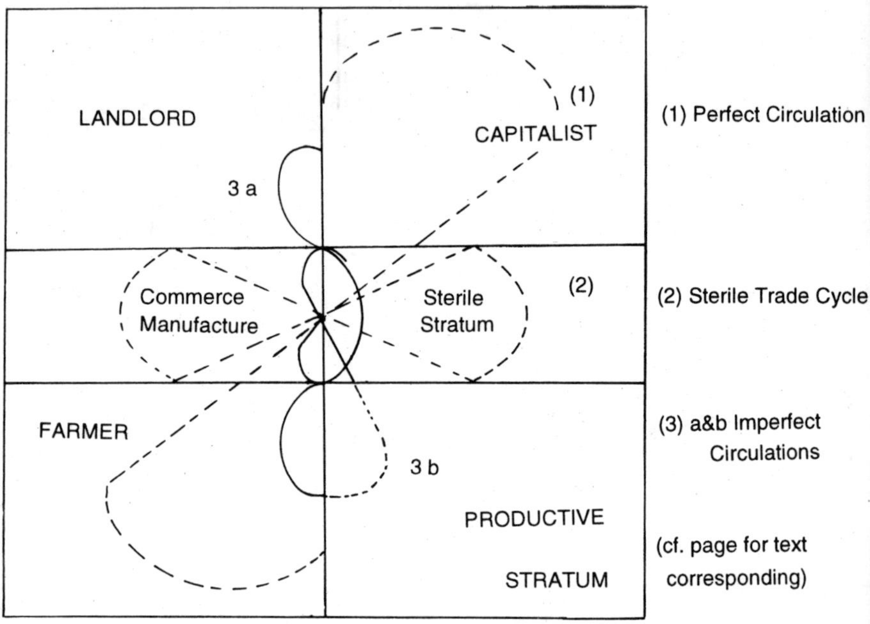

fig. 12.2

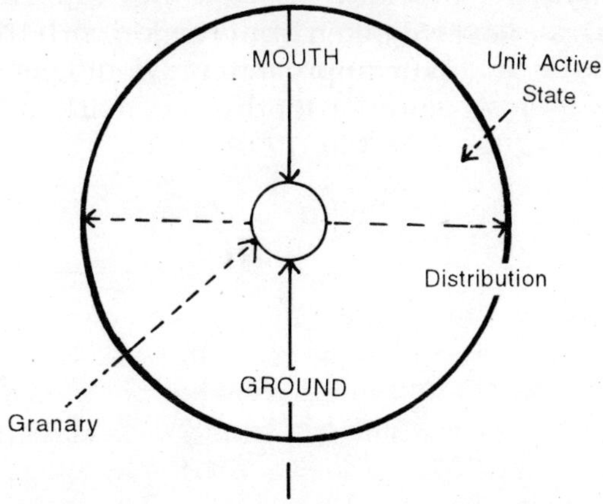

fig. 12.3

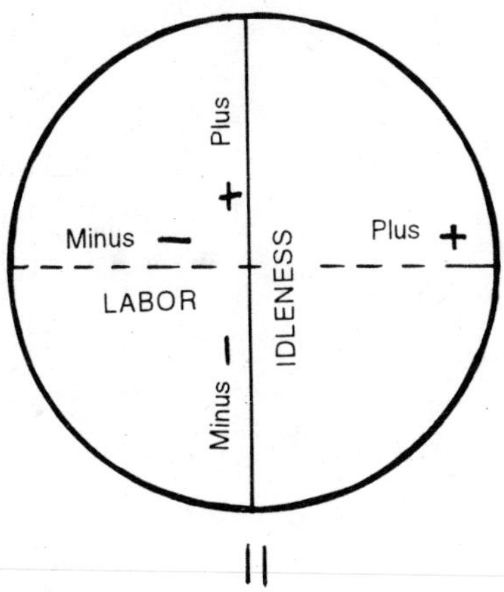

fig. 12.4

Notes

1. *Unto This Last*, Item No. 266, see *fig.* 12.3.
2. *Ibid.*, Item No. 256, see *fig.* 12.4.
3. *Ibid.*, Item No. 279.
4. *Ibid.*, Item No. 241.

Part III
One-World Education

13

Introduction

A GENTLEMAN is different from a boor. Education in the ordinary sense could be said to be what makes a gentleman out of a boor. The word itself comes from the Latin **ex** and **ducere** (to draw from, or out), and the more modern of educational theories today have insisted on this aspect of education. Classical notions of education are diametrically opposed to such modern ones, which thus believe in drawing out what is already present in the child, rather than in putting book-learning into him by hard lessons to learn involving the tears and drudgery of classrooms. This change in perspective was ushered into existence by a bold man called Jean-Jacques Rousseau, who is sometimes referred to in encyclopaedias of education as the Father of Modern Educational Theory.

In spite of such recognition given to him, with his picture appearing on the frontispiece of Monroe's *Encyclopaedia of Education*, Rousseau's theories are still a closed book to many moderns. His *Emile* might be the Bible of educationists, but it contains too many enigmas which have puzzled and continue to puzzle even such intelligent modern minds as H.G. Wells, who calls Rousseau a hypochondriac who believed in shedding his sentimental tears into the *Lac Leman* of Geneva. Rousseau remains an enigma to modern educational authorities today, and his name hardly figures in the training courses of teachers at all. The modern teacher knows Montessorie, Froebel and Pestolozzi. He understands the project-method of John Dewey, and how the school and society have to be related organically according to the standards of what is called the project-active school based on a pragmatic socialized outlook. The study of nature is also understood by him to be important — not in itself, but because of its benefits to society. The Herbartian educational theory flavouring of post-Kantian speculation is too theoretical and bookish to appeal to the minds of modern experimental educators. Even Herbert Spencer as a naturalistic educator and the ideas of John Locke are considered as being outside the scope of education as understood in a pragmatic setting. One learns by doing, and play and work in the modern school room have to go hand in hand, instead of being divorced from each other. It is here that Montessorie, Pestolozzi and Froebel are still respected in the modern educational world. Otherwise, the humanities are seen to recede into the background in any syllabus of modern schools generally.

One-sided Approach

Instead of programmes built around book-knowledge as the humanities are bound to be, one hears of programmes based on interests and possible useful activities commonly referred to under the designation 'project-method'. How does it work is a more important question than in what philosophical light does one understand it. That is the problem involved. Thus, the whole centre of gravity of modern education has drastically changed its position; there is little Latin and less Greek, while grammer and syntax have been thrown to the winds. Science has displaced humanities, thus putting outside the pale of the field of normal education of a young man or woman of our generation all of those subjects in which human values are directly involved. Aesthetics, ethics, economics and education are subjects that are studied without any normative reference presupposed by them. Mill's utilitarianism could thus go hand in hand with this kind of approach in which science and technocracy have a lopsided chance to enter the minds of young scholars or pupils, whether at college or high school.

The Tragic Paradox

These processes, it is true, are conducive to the education of a citizen of a welfare state, or of one that has got to develop vast territories in order to build bridges or long tunnels or otherwise exploit the resources of a big country to the best advantage of the beneficiaries directly concerned. Thus, educational progress in its outward march goes from one technocratic victory to another, producing heroes interested in exploring other planets than our own, and forgetting values nearer home residing within the Self of man himself. A bomb gives power to a nation so that it could dominate and dictate to a neighbour, even if it does not do so openly. Armies are maintained and the stockpiling of armaments goes on, instead of the carrying out of good intentions expressed at international conferences piously intending the golden day of world disarmament. Tensions mount up in the meanwhile, and cold wars, like subterranian fires, kill life by various forms of injustices that are not allowed to erupt into the open. Conflicting ideologies create situations far worse than in the days of the slavery that was supposed to have been abolished long ago. All this results from a tragic paradox hiding at the core of education itself.

This paradox can be stated in terms of the two standards revealed by the story of H.G. Wells, of the great school-master who fell dead while he was lecturing at the Ondel School on the occasion of ceremonies there over which Wells himself happended to be presiding. The conflict was clearly between the two mutually exclusive positions represented by the slogans, "Love thy neighbour as thyself", and "Britannia rule the waves". No educator except perhaps Rousseau ever faced this paradox squarely. He said that it is impossible to educate a citizen and a man at the same time. State educational systems are seen to shut their eyes to this obvious verity, and pretend ostrich-wise that it did not exist. Neither Montessorie nor Pestolozzi nor Froebel is prepared to face this paradox with its tragic implications. Herein lies the basic drawback of modern education. One has to love Pakistan on the one hand, and watch millions of refugees suffer and starve on the other. This is what it amounts to. There is a helplessness here which should only need to be proved once, yet still the educational policy-makers look on helplessly and suggest watered-down paliatives falling far short of curing the disease.

The hand of God is revealed to no man, and there is no panacea for all ills. We can only travel from error to error, and those who say there is an absolute answer to such questions are derided in these days of scepticism, relativism, and the approach of trial-and-error. Final answers are suspected of being dogmatic as in the Middle Ages. "Down with the Absolute" is the modern slogan. "Let us invade the domain of knowledge piecemeal, and never try to storm the citadel wholesale". Such notions indicate the prevailing trend of modernism.

It is no wonder then that Rousseau stands condemned as a sentimentalist and that his ideas sound strange to modern ears. He speaks, for example, of a form of negative education which holds that a child should be allowed to be a child before being a grown-up. Such a doctrine of negative education cannot be fitted easily into what gives meaning to education as could be understood at all in the West today. This is the reason that modern educators, as mentioned already, have nothing to say about the book *Emile*. The paradox in education was faced by Rousseau, but the same paradox killed the great schoolmaster of Ondel by pulling his loyalties in opposite directions.

What we have to say, therefore, from the standpoint of One-World Education consists of recommending a fresh study of Rousseau to see how he is able to resolve the paradox and develop a theory of education in which the tragic implications of it are no more allowed to work havoc. Any theory of education must be capable of reconciling the two rival or conflicting positions of educating a citizen and a man at the same time. Such is the educational problem that confronts us in this book, for stating which we have just finished clearing the ground preliminarily.

Four Stages of Education

Education is a process to be conceived of in terms of a lifetime. There is the education of childhood, the education of the adolescent and the adult, the education of the man of affairs whether as a citizen or as a householder, and there is also finally the education that applies to a pensioner or a man who is thinking in terms of passing on from this life to the next. The child must not be deprived of play, the adolescent should not be deprived of the legitimate enjoyments of life proper to his age, including the pleasures of romance and love. The man of more mature years, when tried and weighed down by his responsibilities and worries, must be allowed some retirement and rest. And fourthly and finally, the man whose next event in life would consist in facing his own death has to find a more serious solution. Kālidāsa in his *Raghuvaṁśa* refers to just these stages which he visualizes under ideal conditions when he describes the citizens of King Dilipa's time as learning lessons in infancy, seeking pleasures in youth, practising austerities in advanced years, and finally learning to leave the body beautifully by the practice of *Yoga*.

These four divisions readily suggest to us four different types of education which we could distinguish as: (1) Negative Education of Rousseau; (2) Naturalistic Education of Herbert Spencer; (3) Pragmatic or Socially Responsible Education of John Dewey for a man at middle age combined with some contemplation proper to his age; and (4) a programme of full-fledged Idealistic Education which covers spiritual disciplines such as *Yoga*. Of the four broad divisions thus conceived, Negative Education would take us to the age of 14 or 15, varying only slightly in respect of a boy or a girl. Adolescence could cover the ages of 15 to 20, comprising the period of Naturalistic Education. From 20 to 45 could be called the period of practical social adjustment proper to Pragmatic Education. And finally, a fully contemplative discipline would apply from the age of 45 until death. Keeping these broad features in mind, it is thus possible to think in terms of four such stages of education in which we would expect variations both in respect of the activities proper to men and women, as also in respect of the content of both theory and practice involved in each of the stages of the process.

Education as a Bipolar Process

Here we have also to remember that education is a bipolar process. It always involves a relationship between the teacher and the taught, who are sometimes referred to as the **educator** and the **educand**, respectively. The personality of the educator is considered all-important to the process, which has sometimes been compared to an osmotic interchange of essences between a highly evolved personality called the Guru and the less evolved educand who is called the disciple. In certain countries, under certain prevailing theories of education, the personality of the educator is not given as much importance as in other traditions, philosophies or schools of thought. Adjusting the pupil to the needs of fitting into a society correctly does not involve the teacher's personality as directly as when Rousseau and Emile consider themselves as inseparables. In advanced years, when a man is engaged in problems of life beyond death, the guidance of a spiritual teacher or Guru comes into the picture again more imperatively. In Naturalistic Education, the open book of nature itself could be treated as the education, as one of the counterparts of a dialectical process. The workshop or the project in Pragmatic Education need not necessarily involve respect for a personal teacher, because hydrogen and oxygen can be shown to combine to make water irrespective of whether the student loves or respects the teacher or not.

Thus, the bipolar process called education has to be studied in all its phases and aspects as it progresses through the broad stages that we have indicated, and each phase has its own type of bipolar process to be imagined as proper to it. The education of a woman has to differ drastically from that of a man, because of the difference of the functions they have to fulfil in their lives. It is always the personality of the pupil that has to be given primacy in the forming of any educational theory. Furthermore, the interaction between teacher and taught has to be secured and maintained as a constant and uniform one so that the process could develop or unravel harmoniously throughout life, and more especially during the stages that we have tried to distinguish above as the Negative and the Idealistic, marking the first and the last of the four broad divisions.

Conclusion

Such are some of the guidelines which are suggested here for us to formulate a One-World Education. We know of no other textbook which satisfies these basic requirements than Rousseau's *Emile*. Other precious indications can be found in works such as those of Kālidāsa. Education and economics and ethics are all presented in a blended form in various parts of his works, whether poetic, lyric, epic or heroic. To glean educational theory from them would require detailed research into them which we cannot undertake here, inasmuch as these remarks are merely meant to be broad guiding considerations for the time being.

14

World Education Manifesto

HUMAN problems are many. Most of them concern individuals. There are also total problems facing humanity as a whole. Nowadays it is an accepted dictum that "wars begin in the minds of men". It is also well realized now that modern war is a menace to humanity. To avoid this great danger, or at least to meet it with intelligent certitude, the answer lies in a whole-hearted and thoroughgoing love of fellow men and a reliance on Absolutist Wisdom. When we take it for granted that the atom bomb is not in keeping with the dignity or destiny of mankind, education conceived in terms of a whole life-time and as applying to the whole of humanity at once, is the only factor with which to counter this ever-staring disaster which threatens the race.

The educator has the pupil or the child as his only tool or rather counterpart with which he is to accomplish this great task of saving humanity and securing its peace and happiness. With this tender and formative factor, sometimes for convenience called the **educand**, the person of mature age or understanding, called the **educator**, has to enter into a fruitful relationship in the continued process called **education**.

The two persons involved are dialectical counterparts of an educational situation. The individual personality of the educand has to be influenced by an education that is compatible with his age, sex, stage or type. The innate tendencies in the educand have to be adjusted progressively through the process so as to unfold his potentialities as fully as possible, so that throughout the process and in later life, he can play the happy role of a member of the human family, and thus contribute to the general happiness of mankind.

Whether this goal is stated as peace on earth and goodwill to men, or in more religious terminology as the whole-hearted love of God and one's own neighbour, or in terms of social order, the well-being in a work-a-day sense, whether conceived as a political ideal for the world of tomorrow for world citizenship, or even as the will to power of the idealist, the universal and human basis of education that should prepare him to lead a better life, with which we are concerned in this Manifesto, must remain the same.

The Bipolar Relation

If the intervention of the educator in the natural unfolding of the personality of the **educand** is to be successful, it is necessary to establish scientifically correct educational relations between the two persons involved. Here the understanding of the **personal factor** and the laws that underlie the bipolar relation are matters of primal importance.

The educator in his own person represents the second pole by virtue of which the various subjects, the relational, emotional or environmental factors that might confront the educand in the process, have to be eliminated or selected, graded or regulated and presented to him without any violation of the bipolar character of the process. This condition has to go on unhindered and harmoniously for many years before education can have any tangible effect. The educator has to adjust himself to every kind of educational contingency that might arise, in which he might have to play many a role, initiate many orbits of interest or activity, improvise many an experimental or educative situation, and stimulate intellectual interests in the pupil in many desirable and natural directions.

The Personal Factor and World Happiness

In other words, the two persons have to be treated as belonging together to a dialectical situation in which both the counterparts are of equal importance. The science of education has therefore to be conceived not only in living or organic lines, but also in dialectically conceived terms. The prevailing mechanistic approach, although called scientific because of the use of brass instruments, measurements and even experiments, has ended in a sterile accumulation of impersonal quantitative data and statistics which leave the personality totally outside the discussion. Educators even avoid references to the **personal factor**, and if they do so at all, perhaps include a last paragraph on the subject apologetically. Thus important human values, not to speak of higher ones, are glaringly omitted from any programme of education.

The present Manifesto is an attempt to present the case for an education which would help to enhance the value of the person along scientific, open and dynamic lines without closed or static dogmatisms. Localized traditions or closed cults are here discredited. A classless and casteless humanity without frontiers or barriers made by traditional ideas, however superior in themselves, is kept in mind here. Further, the **personal factor** here involved in this living bipolar process of educational adjustment is to be a central or absolute concept or entity envisaged for developing systematically and methodically, the theme and thesis of this Manifesto.

This Manifesto is further conceived as a universal or World Manifesto because the high hope that the peace and happiness of mankind should be the primary concern of any programme of education worth the name, whether individual or collective.

I

Division 1 : General

The Need for a New Manifesto

When organizations such as the UNESCO are in the field it

is legitimate to ask the question, why there should be need for a manifesto of this kind. The reasons are:

Firstly: That the programmes of the UNESCO are based on the recognition of the present set-up of soverign states, each with its own closed pattern of cultural or citizenship values, not properly conceived on any human or one-world basis. In respecting the wishes of member nations and not encroaching on their sovereingnty, the UNESCO has to be very careful not to draw any loyalty to itself in any absolute sense. At best it can gather statistics, act as a clearing-house for information, promote literacy all-over, under what is called a programme of "Fundamental Education", which term, vague as it is, has been recently described in a UNESCO publication[1] as in effect merely "the educational arm of social and economic development".

Community projects and the training of leaders in rural areas figure prominently in the programmes of this body. It is not easy to see how the humming bee-hive-like secretariat with its **pilot projects**, the gathering of educational data, and the compilation of international educational statistics from dry governmental reports coming in from the numerous member states, large or small, can effectively include within its scope in a practical or tangible sense, personal or human values which would make at least one human a better man. It is true that some cultural publications are attempted and the fostering of international understanding made at the level of a college debating society or a getting together party is also sometimes included in UNESCO programmes. It is not hard to discover that the millions of dollars spent by the organization are lost in the sands of such works as surveys which hardly interest anybody, or in works mostly consisting of stenography, typing, translating, collection, collation or clearing of information on a world-wide scale, or sometimes on items of travelling or on conferences in far-flung parts of the globe.

The International Bureau of Education which had been doing the same kind of work since the days of the League of Nations has now been largely absorbed into the UNESCO, but the same work goes on in Paris now on a slightly more glorified or outwardly streamlined form. How the individual **educand** in a personal sense could ever be reached or influenced by all this peripheral paraphernalia which leaves him outside its close scrutiny, and how it can help in the making of a better man or even a better citizen in a human or world sense, remains a puzzle.

Secondly: The possibility that the UNESCO which takes for granted rival citizenships, endangers besides compromising, the role of that body as an effective world organization. The United Nations Organization itself, of which the UNESCO is but a limb, can only hoist flags of individual sovereign states under or alongside its own flag. Although such spectacular and symbolic acts might have a very indirect educative value, the status of the UNO remains at a very impotent, dull and relativistic level. How much more inferior is the status of the UNESCO, which can do little more than arrange exhibitions or shows or imposing assemblies at which rival power groups and their satellites get a good chance to sling mud at each other on its well-equipped and publicized platforms! There is further, the constant danger in the surcharged atmosphere of these assemblies, which have no tangible common goal to draw together a united loyalty, of cold wars being fanned at any moment into hot flames, when war-minded men are made to sit side by side at the same desk or table.

Reason for Failure: Education is often defined as meant for citizenship. If two rival citizenships are imagined without any middle ground between them, war clouds can find in this situation ever favourable conditions to rise and spread at a minute's notice.

The way out of this difficulty is a secret of the dialectician. Mere logical reason can never attain to the root of the problem, much less solve it. The really wise men of the world who, at any given time can scarcely be found, might hold this secret, but such could never hope to get a hearing at these loud assemblies, which are conceived, as it were, from the peripheral rather than from the central point of view.

The problem of education for peace has to be approached from an altogether opposing angle than the one from which so far it has been approached by these world bodies now in the field of world education. Even with an amended constitution, such bodies can never be expected to cope with the task of preparing humanity for peace, because of their origin and their intrinsic nature.

The Contradiction at the Core of the Problem itself

The *raison d'être* of this Manifesto and its ample justification will become evident when we recognize that there is a subtler philosophical contradiction lurking at the very core of the problem of education. Little attention has been paid to this even by leaders of educational thought. Training colleges go on teaching the theory and practice of education decade after decade, paying no attention to this, which effectively compromises all programmes of state education. The future of education itself must remain sombre until the time when this secret of a philosophical or contemplative order becomes sufficiently understood.

Why this verity has so far remained unrecognized in education is because involved in it is the paradoxical conflict of basic principles of human nature. Rousseau was laughed at for his paradoxes. Yet, although he was much misunderstood and maligned, he still enjoys the recognized position of the father of modern educational thought. Rousseau himself is a puzzle to moderns who have forgotton the idiom in which he wrote. In his classical treatise *Emile*, which is devoted to education, he puts his finger right on this very contradiction and states it as strikingly as possible when he writes:

> Forced to combat Nature or social institutions, one has to make a choice between making a man or a citizen; for one cannot make the one and the other at the same time. (*Book I*)

A citizen or patriot is obliged to protect the frontier of any political unit he may belong to. He has to kill or die, an imperative necessity which even a contemplative such as Socrates could not escape from. In modern days necessity of this kind becomes more binding than ever. Only under very special conditions may a conscientious objector be just tolerated. The generality of men are just citizens for war time, and are mostly treated in the educational world to be so, if not already so. The hereditary and religious attachments that an ordinary person might have also make him in many cases willing to die for "the ashes of his fathers and the temples of his gods", as stated in an old ballad. Nelson, that model hero for English school-boys, applied the telescope to his blind eye when he was told that an English ship was sinking. His motto: "England expects every man will do his duty" pertains to the same closed context.

In one of his books devoted to education, H.G. Wells describes the conflict which troubled very much and perhaps indirectly caused the sudden death of a martyr to the cause of education, Sanderson of Oundle. In a whole volume, *The Great Schoolmaster*, Wells describes the last speech made by this senstive and conscientious educator who wished to be true to English tradition and cultivate patriotism in his pupils by making them sing *Rule Britannia*. He had to cultivate also in the Sunday school hours and at those periods for religious lessons, that other attitude implied in the biblical words, "Love thy neighbour as thyself". The actual story as it happended, records how while on a school anniversary day, all was happy and gay and Wells himself was presiding, when the poor schoolmaster actually collapsed while the contradictory phrases above-mentioned were hardly out of his mouth. He was making a very spirited speech on the subject of this very contradiction, and had hardly said 'Amen' to "Love thy neighbour as thyself" when he collapsed, and thus became for ever a martyr to the cause of true human education.

A later philosopher than Rousseau, one who perhaps had a slightly better reception than Rousseau by the Western world, reiterated the same implict contradiction lurking at the core of our ideas, of a philosophical nature, pertaining to the growth and development of the personality or consciousness of man. Bergson wrote:

> since the time of Aristotle, and which has vitiated the greater part of the philosophy of Nature, is to see in vegetative life, in instinctive life, and in the life that is based on reason, three successive degrees of the same tendency that developed itself, while they are three divergent directions of one and the same activity which took by itself many divergent directions in the process of growing up.[2]

The Indian philosopher Sankara also refers to this inner philosophical contradiction which touches the human spirit when treating of the impossibility of attaining salvation by combining knowledge (*jñāna*) and works (*karma*). In his commentary on the *Gītā* he wrote :

> The conclusion, therefore, of the *Bhagavad Gita* is that salvation is attained by knowledge alone and not by knowledge conjoined by works.[3]

Modern Educational Endeavour

UNESCO AGAIN

If we refer again to the UNESCO it is just to point out that even when we take a closer look at the work of that body, we find there is no serious educational theory implied in it. The same publication already quoted admits more glaringly the empty and peripherally dissipated content of its own work when we read from the preface the following:

> Readers of *Educational Abstracts* are familiar with the term 'fundamental education' used by the Unesco to designate educational activities which aim to help people to take an active part in the social and economic development of their communities. The term is now widely used in many countries though the forms of educational activity which it describes and the subject-matter of its 'teaching' vary considerably with differences in the local needs and conditions. Again the term itself is not an exclusive

> one and some countries have adopted different terminology — such as 'social education', 'mass education', and 'community education' to describe similar activities. 'Fundamental Education' has been recently described as the *educational arm of social and economic development.*

When we notice that the word 'teaching' in the above quotation is put by the writer himself (or herself) in quotes and take into account the grave implication of the last part of the quotation which we have italicized, it is quite safe to say that by the admission of its own sponsors, the UNESCO has no educational content or message worth the name, and that it does not actually deliver the goods which it is under contract, as it were, to deliver to the people of the world.

The same applies to many great educational establishments, such as some of the important universities, especially of America whose legal validity and honesty have recently been questioned and challenged by young men who have become alive to the sad defeat of true education in them.

THE NEW EDUCATION MOVEMENT

If we turn to other educational endeavours of our times we have the New Education Movement or Fellowship of Europe, which has spread to the New World also. The epicentre of this movement is Geneva, that famous international city where the spirit of Jean Jacques Rousseau, the unique citizen of Geneva, may be said to be still presiding. We have said already that Rousseau is still recognized as the father of modern educational thought, for which his inclusion as such in the *Cyclopaedia of Education* of Monroe is sufficient evidence. Rousseau himself may be said to be the inspirer of the New Education Movement which started in the same city. It would therefore be but natural for us to hearken back to Rousseau in our effort here to place ourselves correctly in relation to the educational trends of our time so as to be able to relate this Manifesto to its own natural background or starting point.

Mistrust in the Father of Modern Education

Although the mortal remains of Rousseau were removed to the Pantheon in Paris one hundred years after his miserable and lonely death as a hunted and persecuted person, his name is still lingering in the charming lakeside city of Geneva. His much misunderstood or ill-understood theories, act still as an anathema to the orthodox, not only of religion, but even of politics and education. Rousseau is still a dear yet puzzling enigma to Europeans generally. Yet Europe cannot do without him either. They neither accept him nor reject him totally. As an original thinker and a contemplative of high stature, his name stands out more prominently than any other single name in the history of modern thought. Together with his contemporary and spiritual or intellectual counterpart, Voltaire, what is called modernism may be said to have been ushered into being and given its dialectically revalued character, as a few of the modern intelligentsia can still recognize.

Rousseau has remained a puzzle even to those who should have been naturally disposed to give him recognition. Even Frenchmen of high academic status have misjudged him, not to mention persons like H.G. Wells, who, in his *Outline of History* lightly brushes him aside as a sentimentalist of no importance. It is interesting to note that the general editor in a footnote has taken care to pull up Wells on this point. Even Henri Legrand of the University of Paris, who presents the Larousse edition of *Emile* in his prefatory note on this work of Rousseau, admits his confusion when he says, "One finds oneself confusedly troubled with what one meets with, by all that is old-fashioned, the naive and the baroque" in the book. He adds further, "*Emile* is far from us . . . . this is true, for it contains the greater part of the illusions and paradoxes of Rousseau". (p. 6)

Developments in Europe after Rousseau

Rousseau's influence on education brought others who could follow only in a general way the sense of the trail he marked out for them. The deeper dialectical secrets of

Rousseau, though still interesting to them, eluded their grasp. Pestalozzi, Froebel, Loyola, Montessori and Decroly are some of the names that have come down to our times after Rousseau.

They approached education from the active experimental angle, in which a programme of education began to be conceived on the basis of **interest** rather than in terms of **bookish subject-matter**. Education was concerned with **drawing out** what was in the child rather than in **driving in**. The child begins hereafter to be given more importance than the teacher. The heuristic method of Herbart insists that the teacher should not tell the answers to questions in the classroom in advance, but somehow try to **elicit** them patiently from the child, and that the old knowledge in the child has to have the new grafted on by the **principle of apperception**. The child had to be left free for play and activities. Occupations interesting and natural to the child had to be provided for. Rousseau, though not his followers, even provided for a **negative stage** in education, when the pupil was not expected to learn anything at all, but just **be a child first before becoming an adult**. The child with Rousseau was to be brought up in isolation and loneliness under the guidance of a single governor without being interfered with by any outside extraneous or social influences. He spoke of three main kinds of education, that which belonged to Nature which could well be left alone; that which belonged to things, with which the educator could not do much even if he wanted to, and the education that man could give where the full role of the **personal factor** as a bipolar relation was recognized by him. When Rousseau went so far as to recognize the **personal factor** in this dialectically scientific manner, he became a puzzle to his followers, and they began to leave him alone. Private education thus had to part company with public education.

Impersonal Public Standards in Education

Education on a general scale is the responsibility of governments and the position from which governments may be expected to look upon this problem must necessarily be a standardised, impersonal and public one. This is the reason why in spite of the profound impression that Rousseau made in the world of educational thought, he was coldly left behind after some years. Governments were more interested in making the cannon fodder called the true patriot or the citizen, and whatever else it wanted to make of the educand was only of secondary importance to it.

The phenomenon that we have been watching in recent times, of the rapid popularity that Montessori gained in the educational world is to be explained by the fact that here for the first time the tiny tots who were the educands had something conceived along modern lines for their education. **Paedocentricity, activity, freedom** from interference, non-bookishness, **experimental material** based on the **natural interests** of the child, rather than subjects compulsorily to be taught, letting the child be a child first before becoming an adult — these were features which came from the new orientation given to education of which Rousseau himself was the initiator.

As a result, the **Montessori Method** was recommended and promoted by one modern state after another, although, as merely consisting of **sense training**, the Montessori Method may be said to have stumbled into this popularity by mere dint of Montessori's original attempts merely to correct defective children whose senses functioned inadequately. The scientific aspects of her method later became adapted so as to include the infant who was more normally human in endowments. Still, some of the roundabout artificialities of the method which have come from its abnormal origin could be discovered as lingering on in the Montessori Method as it is put into practice at the present-day, even in its revised form.

The Declaration of Geneva

Rousseau's home city again comes into the story of world education in the famous Declaration of Geneva promulgated by the now forgotten League of Nations. This was meant to guarantee the freedom and protection of the child in the world of free human rights. It was a kind of Magna Carta born in the minds of some educators who were also leaders of thought in that interesting European city which enjoyed the admiration and respect of President Wilson of the U.S.A. who was instrumental in choosing this Rousseau City as the home of the League of Nations. There to the present-day the Eastern or Western pilgrims can visit the Ile Rousseau at the heart of the city near the Quay Wilson, dominated by the more than life size bronze statue of Rousseau surrounded by tall poplars and accessible by a causeway. The Citizen of Geneva, as he is called on the pedestal-inscription, lives on by reputation and continues to puzzle, and thus add a new dimension to the atmosphere of this city situated at the very heart of Europe. The Declaration of Geneva is but an expression of the all-embracing spirit of Rousseau who may be said to be the latest of modern dialectical philosophers not yet fully understood in the West, but whom the East is likely one day to rediscover and possibly respect even as a world-teacher.

Rousseau, more than a mere Modern Thinker or Educator

Rousseau was a contemplative and dialectical philosopher who could view education for the first time from the standpoint of the science of dialectics which is still a vague term to most modern intellectuals. He had more than paedocentricity, activity or freedom to contribute to education. By being a contemplative he is not to be looked upon as belonging to the Age of Reason on a par with his contemporary Voltaire who often mocked him in his writings. Rousseau must be included among the contemplative perennial philosophers who transcend their own epoch and the geographical region where their influence was first felt. While Prof. Legrand whom we have already quoted as introducing *Emile*, strangely mistrusts Rousseau when he says, "*Emile* is far removed from us, because it contains some of the errors and manias common to people of his age", he is seen soon almost to contradict himself when he continues, "In appraising in its wholeness the spirit that animates the book, we are able to see hazily something that is profound which agrees singularly with our modern soul." From such contradictions and from the very fact that the modern educator is unable to shake off the profound impression that Rousseau has succeeded in making on him, however much he might seem to disown him or be ashamed of him, on specific items of educational doctrine, there is no doubt that the dialectically revalued notions of Rousseau are the soundest available ones in the Western world for the erection of the superstructure which we envisage in this Manifesto for World Education.

The Dialectical Idiom of Rousseau

The idiom of dialectics has become forgotten in world literature. Paradox is of the very stuff of this dialectical way, because it is in paradox or in dilemma that human conflicts and problems make themselves evident in everyday life. Life has the everstaring question of "To be or not to be". What is mistaken as old-fashioned or naive in Rousseau by the best of trained thinkers, really belongs to the natural and inevitable style of the timeless contemplative way of higher wisdom. This is referred to as *yoga* in the *Bhagavad Gītā*, (IV. 2) which Kṛṣṇa as the teacher in this contemplative textbook of dialectics, himself deplores as a precious heritage tending to be lost again and again in the world.[4]

The J.J. Rousseau Institute

Following on the footsteps of Rousseau, it was right that some leading educationalists of Europe established at the beginning of this century a Rousseau Institute of Education at Geneva. This is also alternatively named "The Institute of Educational Sciences". This Institute, although it was the mother of the International Bureau of Education which, in its turn, has culminated in UNESCO, with which it is organically linked at present, as we have already noticed, is now receding into the background in favour of those peripherally conceived items of educational endeavour that can no more be said to have any tangible value in the context of World Education, as pointed out above. Educational endeavour has therefore to be given a fresh start and impetus, and this is what this Manifesto represents. The sterile sands of mass education have all but absorbed the nourishing waters of educational effort, and it is time that educators the world over rallied to retrieve the cause. The hour for a Manifesto of this kind is therefore with us now.

Fresh Breezes from the East

Western civilization has all but forgotten its contemplative idiom. From the days of the discovery of the telescope, technical advances through the conquests of science have overpowered the normal imagination of the Western mind. What it might have contributed to human happiness in the form mainly of human comforts, has been taken away by its other hand by its trail of smoke and gas. Obsessed by pride or confusion, the common man has no clear training in the appreciation of normal or natural human values in everyday life, not to speak of moral, spiritual or contemplative life. All goodness or kindness has been ruled out by him as sentimental and uncritical dogmatism on blind faith. Rousseau became outmoded because as a proud European he was still capable of shedding tears into his favourite Lac Leman without any apparent reason whatsoever. He loved the lake and that was all. He became laughed at and was bypassed by the rest of his own people who took pride in their status as men of reason and not 'sentimental sissies'. That extra dose of humanity which they found in the Citizen of Geneva was too much for them to understand. There is however, a small group, even in the West, who are able to recognize in Rousseau a first-rate contemplative philosopher and World Citizen, in spite of his personal, so-called shortcomings which have become cheap subjects of derision directed against him by the common ill-educated man or woman. Rousseau's neglect of his own children was enough to turn their minds against him without taking into account the pelting and persecution that his own people made him suffer.

We shall not be considered far from the truth if we should generalize about the small group we have referred to, and say that they represent people of an Eastern outlook living in a Western clime. The cold winds known as the 'Beeze' in Geneva can freeze or numb all tender emotions from man in that harsh climate. The tender and sensitive plant that was Rousseau's spirit, could not thrive in a harsh climate. Eastern breezes may still raise and revive his noble soul, and rediscover him for the cause of an educational programme which knows no distinction of East or West, North or South. A pilgrimage to the Ile Rousseau surrounded by its greenish lake and its white and black swans ever swimming round his statue, would not be a bad idea to undertake by Eastern lovers of contemplation when they visit Europe. Let them sit and meditate for a while under the tall poplars for a change!

Rousseau's Absolutist Concept of Nature

What Rousseau is never tired of calling Nature should not be confounded, as has often been done, with the word 'nature' as used in such expressions as "the return to nature" or "a nature-poet". Outside nature is one thing, but Nature with a capital letter, conceived synthetically as an Absolute inner principle, which gives us notions of right and wrong, and which is the basis of conscience, or an axis of reference in the educational, moral and spiritual progression of man towards his high goal, belongs to quite another order.

According to Rousseau, who refers all education, except social adjustments in a practical utilitarian sense, to this innate and imperative urge called Nature, it is more than just habit cultivated during a lifetime. Nature should fall in line with Nature if it is to be good, and Nature itself should be thought of as transcending the limitations of life here and now, reaching into the past or future and giving a direction and purpose to life in a sense teleological as well as ontological. Natural inclinations like the verticality of a plant which would regain itself even when tilted and placed at a more horizontal angle from its original natural position, is the favourite example that Rousseau cites to show there is an innate sense of goodness, rightness or justice rooted timelessly within the human spirit. The positive content of the term Nature as intended by him is brought out into relief when in a certain section of *Emile* he elaborates spiritual life under what is called Natural Religion, in his "Profession of Faith of the Savoy Vicar".

Rousseau and Social Education

It is true that the question of social adjustment in education finds little favour in the educational programme envisaged by Rousseau. This is not an omission nor a prejudice. As with the philosophers of India, the world of men, sometimes referred to as the 'madding crowd' by poets, is a factor to be avoided rather than included in any sane programme of education based on contemplative principles. Desire (*kāma*) and anger (*krodha*) arise from the rivalries of men, and these evils which are referred to as belonging to the triune portals of hell in the *Gītā*, when taken together with miserliness (*lobha*)[5] stem out of the penchant for activity (*rajas*) especially competitive activity which, in the struggle for existence, the world of man necessarily implies. Love of social life (*loka vāsanā*) is a thing to be avoided by the spiritual aspirant, even according to the teachings of Saṅkarācārya in his *Vivekacūdāmani*. While philosophers like Dewey have stressed utilitarian and pragmatic social adjustment by education, Rousseau has remained more truly a contemplative idealist, loyal to his ideas of goodness and Nature which represented to him high absolutist values in life, and which were very precious for man. He was interested in gaining the soul, even at the loss of the whole world.

Rousseau's Negative Education

Rousseau is bold enough in this direction to lay down the law that should regulate the earliest years of the educand. He says it has to be 'negative' in character. The implications of this doctrine of negative education is none other than what is known as the *nivṛtti marga* or the **via negativa** that has been known to *Vedānta* in India and to pre-Socratic philosophers in the West. Outgoing action, whose tendencies are characterized as *rājasik* is an evil which, however, has to be respected only insofar as it is inevitable or necessary.

"Sufficient unto the day is the evil thereof", is the dictum that holds good here, and the *Gītā* doctrine of *niṣkāma karma* or dispassionate action, which has confused even Indian thinkers, is nothing more than an intelligent and intuitive dialectical way of not getting trapped by horizontal interests in life which spell activity, attachment, and consequent tension.

Negative education consists in bringing up the child protected from the evils of society, like a young plant that is fenced-in and protected from passers-by. The child is to be brought up in solitude as in the forest schools of India of ancient times. He has to be guided by a single teacher who would regulate, interpret, select or prepare favourable educational conditions where nature would have full chance to assert herself in the child, till it attained to full manhood or womanhood. Rousseau's Nature would correspond to the **categorical imperative** of Kant and to the creative **élan vital** of Bergson.

The whole process is maintained in the direction of Natural Goodness by a teacher who represents in himself the same principle. In Rousseau we see that for the first time education is considered as a bipolar process between a preceptor and a disciple, as with the *Guru* and *śiṣya* understood in ancient Indian education. Nature with Rousseau is thus nothing other than what is good in human nature. What we have done in this Manifesto is just to give a more correct name to this very Human Nature, giving it its proper status according to a science of the Absolute, as a notion common to the educator and the educand at once, in the process of education. This common basis of educational relations we have named for scientific correctness as the **Personal Factor in Education**.[6]

The Echo of Time-Honoured Indian Concepts

Rousseau writes: "For being well conducted, the infant should follow but one single guide".[7] Again, he emphasizes the strict bipolarity to be secured between teacher and taught in education, in referring to his educational relations with the pupil Emile in the following words:

> Emile is an orphan. It is not important that he should have his mother or father. Entrusted with their duties I succeed to their rights . . . . and I would even wish that the pupil and the governor should regard themselves such inseparables that the passing of their days should be with them always with a common object.[8]

The ancient Indian idea of the relations between a *Guru* and *śiṣya* are here echoed unmistakably.

In the education which we have touched upon as **negative** as with Rousseau, the pupil is to be protected from the glare and pomp that society offers. Not only the infant but even the adolescent has to be so protected, as we read in Book V of *Emile*. This noble passage is as follows:

> Would you like, therefore, to initiate and nourish in the heart of a young man the first movements of a nascent sensibility and turn his character towards a beneficial life and to bounty? Then do not allow to germinate in him pride, vanity, envy, by the misguiding picture of the happiness of men; do not expose at first sight before his eyes the pomp of courts and the feasts of palaces, the attraction of spectacles; do not make him promenade in social circles and in brilliant assemblies; do not show him the exterior of high life in society before he is in a state capable of appreciating it in itself. To show him the world before he understands humans, that would be not forming him, it would be to corrupt him, that would not be to instruct him, but to misguide him.

It is not hard to notice how close a family resemblance this passage bears to what the ancient Indian educator conceived as the life of the *Brahmacārin* (the initiate in the way of *Brahman* or the Absolute) in a *Gurukula*, a forest school where teacher and pupils lived together.

SOLITARINESS

The cheap fling at Rousseau is that he conceived of an education in anti-social terms. This is because he lauded solitude for man, as conducive to happiness. In *Emile*, Book IV, he wrote: "A being who is truly happy is a being who is solitary. God alone enjoys a happiness that is Absolute". When the *Bhagavad Gītā*, VI.10 reads: "The *yogī* remaining in a lonely spot by himself should constantly engage in *yoga* secretly, with his relational mind subdued and free from expectant waiting and greed", the contemplative pattern of life common to East and West alike is unmistakably reflected.

From the day when he submitted an essay on the corruption implied in the Arts and Sciences to the University of Dijon in 1750, Rousseau never tired of attacking the evils of Western civilization as we understand them in their vastly amplified aspects at the present-day. Rousseau was a champion of those human values which are deep-seated in the human heart.

The mystical note in Rousseau attains to sublimity when he puts the following words in the mouth of the Savoy Vicar:

> For elevating myself as far as I could to this state of happiness, of strength and of freedom, I exercise myself at sublime contemplation. I meditate on the order of the universe, not for explaining it by vain systems, but for admiring it endlessly, for adoring that wise Author who makes His presence felt therein. . . . . O God that is kind and good in my confidence in Thee the supreme wish of my heart is that Thy will should be done. *In joining my will with it, I do what Thou doest.* I submit to Thy bounty, I believe that I partake in advance of that supreme felicity which is its prize.

The correct contemplatively mystical pattern with a gentle touch of ecstasy and the *advaitic* (non-dualistic) note revealed in the part italicised by us in the above quotation, is sufficient to reveal the personality of Rousseau as a *yogī* or a Guru or even a solitary recluse or *muni* as we understand them in the context of Indian spirituality. He could not have been less of a true Christian or a true brāhmin because of these traits in his personality. While Rousseau's statue sits neglected in the little island we have pictured, regarded askance by the proud moderns, he might one day be garlanded or offered incense, flowers, water and fruit by some Indian devotee if one day such a one should come to recognize his status as a *jagad guru* or World Teacher. Rousseau would surely have felt more at home among the mystics and saints of India rather than in the cold climate of Europe, except perhaps in the early spring, when the Nature he loved would adore him in response. Rousseau's personality and message has to be rediscovered at least in the cause of World Education.

Rousseau's catholicity of outlook even in religion is reflected in the following quotation:[9]

> I regard all the particular religions as so many salutary institutions which prescribe in each country a uniform way of honouring God by a public form of worship, all of which could have their reasons for being so in the climate, in the government and in the genius of the people, or in some other cause of a local order which would render one preferable to the other according to the time and place. I believe all of them to be good when they are able to serve God by them in a convenient manner. The essential worship is that of the heart. God has no regret about any homage paid to Him when it is sincere, under whatever form it may be offered to Him.

The *Gītā* (IV.11) which says that "all humanity treads the very path that is Mine" reiterates this same verity, as also the motto of the Guru Narayana, "One Religion and One God".

Rousseau and Gurukula Education

Quotations could be multiplied to show that Indian doctrines of education such as *Gurukula vāsa* (living away from society under a single Guru), *guru-bhakti* (maintaining a strict bipolar relation with the teacher), *brahmacarya* (walking in the absolutist light of Nature or Goodness) and other related concepts such as *dhyāna* (meditation), *yoga* (contemplation), when understood shorn of any local colouration or exaggeration that might stick to them, follow on the best lines of thought opened out to the modern world by Rousseau, who describes himself simply as *un ami de la Verite*, a Friend of Truth.

Importance of Correct Notions about Educand

In his own preface to the first edition of *Emile*, published at the Hauge in 1762, Rousseau says: "One does not understand the child . . . . Commence, therefore, by studying better your pupil, for very assuredly you do not understand him". Here he rightly touches on the central problem of all education. Again, in *Emile*, Book V, he insists: "Let us understand first of all what she (Sophie) consists of and we shall then be able to judge better where she lives". Here it is implied that the objective environment of Sophie has to be understood together with understanding her. The dialectical or contemplative way has to treat these conunterparts together when they belong to the same factor or situation.

In his section on religious education he repeats: "Begin therefore by studying human nature and what is most inevitably present in it which constitutes what is best in humanity". Here he refers to the knowledge of the generic or collective personality of humanity taken as a whole. When he comes again in Book IV to the discussion of notions of human justice he says: "Here now, is the study which is important for us; but to do so properly one has to begin by understanding the human heart".

These are various possible perspectives or views of the Personal Factor in education. They have all to be included in a synthetic picture of the personality in which the educator and the educand, the eductional counterparts of a given situation could be discussed at one and the same time, by the help of a central concept of the factor which is common to all phases, aspects, types or environmental patterns involved in education, as a complete life process both collectively and individually understood.

In this first part of the Manifesto we shall put the mark of punctuation where a synthetic picture emerges. The more analytical aspects of the personality will be discussed in Part II, where the starting point will be indicated by treating problems such as distinguishing sex differences or the specific attributes of a Peter or a Paul.

Division 2 : The Personal Factor: A Synthetic Perspective

The Personal Factor as a Distinct and Central Concept

In religion we speak of the 'soul' which is what is subjected to a progress called 'spiritual'. Soul is the central concept here, without which theological sermons would be difficult. Education needs a similar concept which should be more positively or scientifically conceived. The terms **libido, persona, psyche, sub-liminal self**, conscious or subconscious ego, are terms already available which have their own particular connotations coloured by their usage or origin in abnormal or analytical psychology or the psychology of psychic phenomena. **Individuality** can apply to humans and animals indifferently. Education has to do with **specifically human** qualities. *Homo sapiens* is distinguished by an elaborate brain and can attain to the heights of a superman if desired, through contemplation, or to the state of a World Citizen by social and political adjustment. The notion of the personal factor has to give room for all these possibilities and qualities of the self of Man. The term **personal factor** is what we propose here.

(a) There are **two distinct sides or aspects** to the **personal factor**. Knowledge is what education connotes primarily. There is the synthetic knowledge of the subjective self that we can know when we contemplate it in silence or in seclusion to cut down or minimise external impressions that reach us. This inner aspect of the **personal factor** is what can sense its own presense as a light within, which in reality is not strictly localized within us in any actually objective sense.

(b) The **second aspect** of the **personal factor** is what philosophy distinguishes as the non-self. This is what is to be known as distinguished from what knows in the subjective self. Both these are synthetic concepts and are thus to be treated within the range of this first part of the Manifesto before we come to the anlytical aspects of the **personal factor** in the latter half.

Personal Factor a Reality, though Approach is by Way of an Abstraction

Although the **personal factor** is admittedly a mental abstraction, it has its status in Reality as something that both exists and subsists. It exists in the sense that its presence is necessarily felt, and it subsists in the sense that even when its presence is not felt by the sense, it enters our consciousness as a formal idea or entity which we are bound to take into account in any intelligent understanding of the personality involved in education. In spite of being an abstraction, it is thus capable ofbeing understood realistically. Actual life-problems do not therefore lie outside the scope of the personality as we conceive it here.

The Intuitive Approach

The tendencies that constitute the **personal factor** could be studied on a chart or with the help of a schematic representation for the purposes of understanding them unitively and globally as held together by an absolute life or consciousness principle. Rousseau puts this same verity in his own interesting way when he is speaking of God's own type of intelligence as follows: "All truths are for it but one idea, as all places one spot, a single point, and all time one single mements".[10]

The idea of the **eternal present** or the **dialectical moment** is implied here in dealing with the subject of the personality of man; for it has to include in its treatment both psychic and physical factors at once from a neutral standpoint. Bertrand Russel would call such an approach that of Neutral Monism and Descartes' definition of intuition would also include this philosophical approach. All philosophers employ intuition of one kind or another. The correct dialectical way in metaphysics has been employed by Bergson in recent years. Neo-Platonic dialectics, Hegelian and Marxian dialectics and Pre-Socratic dialectics of Zeno and Parmenides are possible aspects of the same intuitive absolutist approach, which is still to be clearly codified and stated methodically and systematically. The *Bhagavad Gītā* is one of the world's greatest textbooks in dialectics. Plato in his Socratic dialogues refers to dialectics as a hymn. Our Manifesto has to approach the **personal factor** from the same contemplative angle, and this should not be considered its drawback, but rather its special advantage. Matter and mind can be treated unitively only by such an approach which need not necessarily be considered therefore unrealistic or impracticable.

Concentric, Central or Peripheral Grades of Reality

Consciousness is a spark at the core of life. This very statement implies central and peripheral aspects of consciousness which may be called by different names according to their grade of materiality or mentality. The methodology of contemplation calls for the concepts of such concentric grades in the **personal factor**. Contemplative epistemology would justify this and give it full validity. Organic life, instinctive behaviour or intelligent conduct in the open world are various grades of personal life, with reference to which the **personal factor** has to be conceived as a unitary concept or **norm** of thought in the science of education.

A Schematic Representation of the Personal Factor in Order

Just as a map need not be considered a fetish, the use of a

schematic representation of the tendencies in the **personal factor**, so that the human intelligence, which is apt to be too analytical or synthetical, could grasp the ensemble or the pattern of correlation of tendencies, should be considered quite normal in our study of the **personal factor**.

It is often objected that life, being very complex, does not admit of treatment in a simplified manner. It is to be admitted that the totality of life taken in actual detail is complex, but what concerns us in the complex totality need not necessarily be complicated. The simplification of life-tendencies in the individual for the purpose of perceptual treatment to help our ideas about them is therefore legitimate, permissible and helpful to the educator. Insofar as it can serve the cause of World Education, such a method will have its place in the present Manifesto, because much of what we have to say would otherwise remain vague or discursive.

The Personal Factor, an Organism in the Process of Creative Evolution

Let us now think of the **personal factor** in terms of a simple living organism. We know that growth and division are the two main expressions of a living organism. We borrow from Henri Bergson's *Creative Evolution* to help us to visualize clearly what this organism at the basis of the **personal factor** represents:

> The veritable and profound causes of division were what life carries within itself; for life is a tendency and the essence of a tendency is to develop in the form of a branching shoot of corn creating by the very fact of its growth, the divergent divisions among which it will divide its own vital urge. This is what we are able to observe with regard to our own selves in respect of that special tendency we call our character. Each one of us by taking a retrospective glance at his own past history will be able to state that his personality as a child, although an indivisible whole, united within itself in a melted form the persons which could have been there, because of their nascent

> state; this indefiniteness so full of possibilities is in itself one of the greatest charms of childhood. But the personalities which thus interpenetrated become incompatible on growing up, and as each one of us lives but one life, we are forced necessarily to make a choice. We are in reality choosing ceaselessly, and we do abandon many things . . . . The route that we trace in time is scattered over with all that we began to be and all that we could have become. But Nature, which has at her disposal an incalculable number of lives, is not subjected to such sacrifice. She conserves the diverse tendencies which have diverged on growth. She creates with them those distinct series of species which do evolve independently.[11]

In this quotation one can disitinguish the dialectical approach adopted by Bergson, the latest inheritor of the tradition from Socratic and Neo-Platonic times. Here living realism goes hand in hand with philosophical abstractions of a highly intuitive order. The *Vedānta* of India knows of the five concentric zones or sheaths called *kōśas* that contain the Self. The one consisting of food value (the *anna-maya kōśa*) is the most peripheral. Books like the *Pañcadaśī* of Vidyāraṇya refer to these aspects of the Self (*ātman*) in a manner reminiscent of Bergson's approach. In Plotinus, *Vedānta* and Western dialectics may be said to find a meeting place.

The Method of Correlation by Two Axes Cutting at Right Angels

It was Descartes who invented a scheme of correlation consisting of two lines intersecting at right angles. This convenient method has been generally adopted in mathematical graphs as also by psychologists like Beatrice Hinkle in drawing the distinction between extroversion and introversion, which imply the objectivity and subjectivity respectivity, of life tendencies.

In treating the most elementary of life expressions in connection with the **personal factor** it will help us to centre our discussions round the explanation given by such correlated schematic representations, without getting lost in eleborations that have no end. The first of these sketches is given here (*fig*. 14.1), and represents graphically without any poetic or literary effusions that might misguide our imagination, all that is significant for us in the present Manifesto.

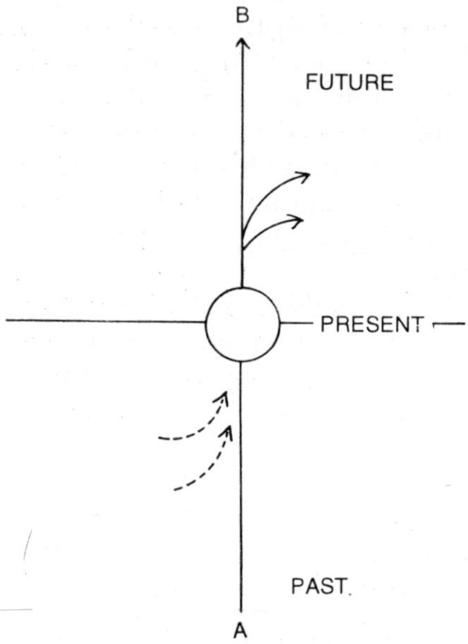

fig. 14.1

Explanation of Figure 14.1 : The vertical axis *AB* represents the life duration of the individual organism. The horizontal or lateral axis marks the present with its multiplicity of interests that vary concentrically in their attraction to the individual. *O* is the centre of life where the past and present meet in the dialectical 'moment' or 'eternal present'. The dotted arrows between *A* and *O* represent virtual tendencies which converge to meet and melt into the matrix of the organism; and the linear arrows above between *O* and *B* show the divergent tendencies as they choose between alternatives in life progression, or 'creative evolution' as Bergson would put it.

The Personal Factor as a Unit in Psychic Life

The pattern of the **personal factor** at the zone of nervous functioning is brought out graphically and in living terms in the following abridgement of a passage from *The Principles of Philosophy*[12] of M.E.H. Starling of the University of London:

> How the physiological processes in the nervous fibres on their arrival at the brain could excite a conscious sensation, we are not able to decide or discuss . . . . No sensation is the immediate or the unique product of the stimulation at the peripheral end of the nervous fibre, but the sensation that is most simple includes a judgement, which is to say that they produce neural activities of a complex order resulting from innumerable currents of the past and the present which are poured into the central nervous system . . . . The first reactions of a baby are those by which it procures its nourishment . . . . *An elementary unit in psychic life as in neural life* should be a complete reaction. It is from the reaction and not from the sensation that a constructive psychology is to be built.

A careful reading of the above paragraph will reveal that Starling here is reconstructing synthetically what constitutes a complete reaction directed towards an object of interest, and how it has its circulation between the central and peripheral nervous system so as to make us imagine a unit in consciousness. We can find here the same scheme of centralization and alternation of phases in relation to the same two axes that we have adopted for a correlated picture of life tendencies. Living duration may be seen to enter into the picture and not merely events in space.

The Zone of Physical Functioning Typified by the Heart-Beat

Let us now take the functioning of the heart as typifying physiological functioning in general. Terms such as sex diastole or systole are sometimes used in psychopathology which will justify our claim here that the heart-beat could be taken to represent in its positive or negative, actual or virtual, qualitative or quantitative phases, other larger rhythmic cycles which take place within the limits of the body in the form of nervous or other circulations like the one described by Starling above. The same two axes of correlation could be used here as in the case of the progression of an organism in duration.

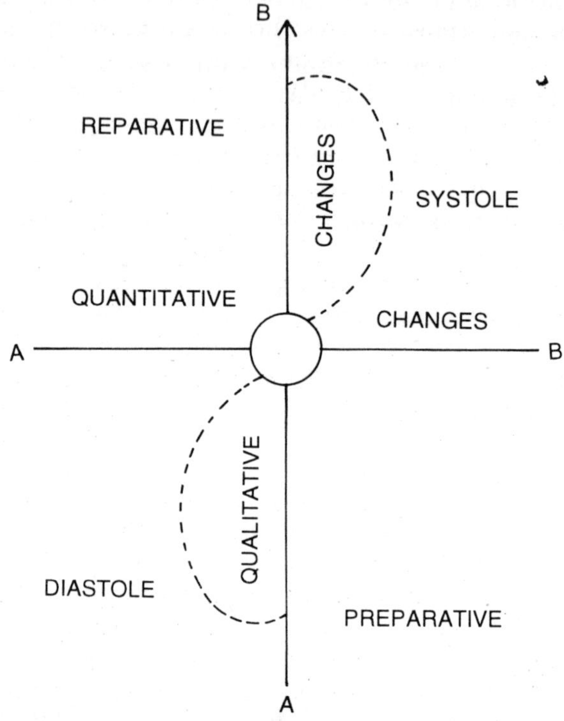

fig. 14.2

Explanation of Figure 14.2 : The two axes crossing at right angles represent qualitative or quantitative aspects respectively of the functioning of the heart. There is the same rhythmic alternation of phases which are marked clearly enough in the figure itself.

Reconstruction of the Personality in Education

For fear of getting lost in elaborations which should more legitimately find place in a thesis rather than in a simple Manifesto of the present kind, we shall confine the rest of our discussion of the **personal factor** to the explanation of two more diagrams in which the various items or component parts are brought together. For more detailed justifications, evidence, documentation and examples, the reader of this Manifesto is referred to our book already mentioned *The Personal Factor in the Educative Process.*[13] Bergson, Rousseau, James, McDougall, Ribot, Rivers, Dumas, Payot, Watson, Claparede and others are the authorities largely relied on in reconstructing, recreating and revaluing notions connected with the personality in education.

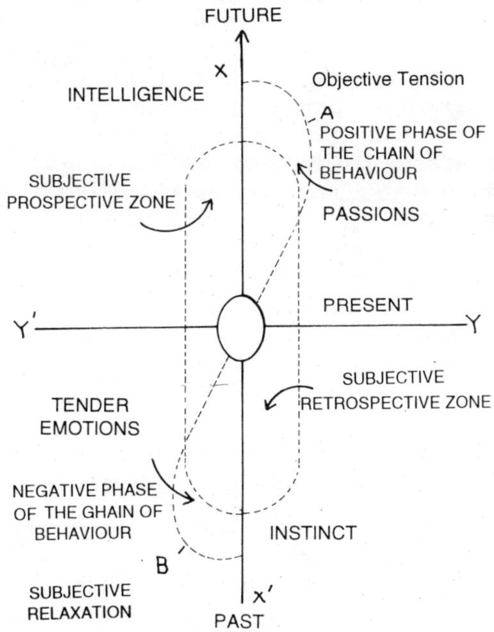

fig. 14.3

Explanation of Figure 14.3 : In this figure *X'OX* would represent subjective consciousness, and the axis *Y'OY*, although also subjective in the sense that it is also to be understood as being within the consciousness of the individual, yet pertains to a stimulus-response order of reflexes or automatisms of the personal consciousness when related to the simple present. The terms 'subjective' and 'objective' are to be understood synthetically here. Those elements of consciousness which are related to the past and are thus the background aspect of the personality are indicated here by that part of the vertical axis *OX'* and the corresponding portion of the vertical axis *OX* will stand for consciousness which has to do with the exercise of the will. Point *O* represents the centre of consciousness in the eternal present or dialectical moment. A distance measured from the *Y'Y* axis at whatever point it may be, by its length will indicate that psychic state of tension or virtual relaxation in which some object of desire influences positively or enters negatively into the personal consciousness of the individual.

The four compartments comprised within the two axes would stand, on the positive side to the top, for waking consciousness; that on the top left the field in which virtualities (which have still an objective status as in very realistic dreams) have to be placed; the lower left quarter being the domain where potent virtualities with no name or form exist as related to instinctive dispositions, vague memories or other psychic states connected with tender emotions. The quadrant on the lower right would represent the vaguest of backgrounds of the consciousness in which there is only an amorphous matrix which consists merely of a general sense of well-being or of ill-being. The sense of solidity, liquidity, taste or sound, are able to revive here shapeless memories of the past world or worlds which constituted the experience of the self in the most synthetic or general of senses. These memories are called *vāsanās* (vague instinctive dispositions), related to the five elements with which, in principle at least, consciousness ever enters in contact. The *prius nobis* of Aristotle and the *turīya* or fourth state of the four-limbed self mentioned in the *Māṇḍūkya Upaniṣad*, may be said to belong to the past which gets lost in the Eternity of the Unknown and the Unknowable at the point *X'*.

The curve *OAOBO* shown in dotted lines would represent a **complete chain of natural behaviour**. If we take the example of grazing cattle, it would be possible to disinguish the psychic factors involved at each point in this curve to active and passive phases of bovine life which here has the form of a figure of eight. One half of it falls into the waking and the other half into the other three subconscious states that we have just distinguished. Dream virtualities are really inversed in time as a series of events in duration so that at the Point *O* opposing tendencies meet ambivalently and neutrally. The neutral *O* in consciousness is the Absolute in its purest sense, spoken of in the last section of the *Māṇḍūkya Upaniṣad*, where the ego sense is cancelled by its own opposite, and where all contraries and contradictions meet as if in the Truth of truths or the Light of lights. Reality and illusion, existence and subsistence, and all other pairs or counterparts melt into unity in this core which is small or big at once. Life functions or activities that we prize as superior or despise as degrading are cancelled out in a neutral attitude in a perfect man who is able to live and have his being in what is represented by this centre of life-pulsation. This light is the seed of all and the most potent factor in the personality of man.

The next peripheral zone marked in the plan of the personality here is the seat of affectivity in general, which consists mainly of emotions and passions. Passions are positive in character by objectivity and by their prospective orientation. Emotions, on the contrary, are retrospective and are forms of regret. A reminiscent mood is a form of regret and all memories may be said to be regrets that hurt the personality and cause psychopathological states. Emotions and passions taken together when the polarity between them is barely evident, gives us that zone which may be called the **zone of affections** of the personality, where sublimations, repressions and conflicts known to psychoanalytical schools and the various factors of psychopathology have their movement or being. A perfected *yogī* is one who feels the joy of balanced or harmonized affectivity or sensibility, who is satisfied in the self by the Self, as the *Gītā* would put it.

A thoroughgoing discussion of these matters properly elaborated would take the legitimate space of volumes. We shall therefore stop by referring finally to movements in thought or in pure consciousness. We can easily see that these movements still conform to the same pattern of the **personal factor** into which we have fitted most other aspects.

The Structure of Thought-Processes

John Dewey writes:

> There is thus a double movement in all reflections: a movement from a given, partial and confused situation that is suggested which is complete and comprehensive (or inclusive) and returning from the suggested whole — which as it is suggested is a **sense**, an idea —a return movement to particular facts in such a way as to relate the ones with the others and to relate them to additional facts on which the suggestion had attracted attention. In a general way, the first of these movements is **inductive** and the second **deductive**. A complete act of thought comprises these two movements; that is to say, an effective interaction of

particular facts observed (or which one remembers) and the suggested general sense.[14]

The above paragraph, whatever its detailed implications may be in the light of Dewey's philosophy, at least brings to light the double movement that we can distinguish even in the poor domain of personal life which consists of what we have called 'movements in thought'.

Analytico-Synthetic Scrutiny

If such movements in thought are capable of analysis by such respected pragmatic philosophers of modern times as Dewey, the analysis of consciousness by an Eastern Guru such as the Guru Narayana, when it enters into the same subtle preserves where contemplative philosophers love to dwell, should not be brushed aside by the proud modern as just speculation that is too sentimental or theoretical to command our attention at the present-day. The most nuclear picture of the personality of man at its innermost essence or core could again be studied by reference to the two axes of correlation that we have adopted here. Such an analysis could correspond to a dissection in biology, only here the subtlest of aspects of inner life are brought under an analytico-synthetic scrutiny.

The Component Elements of the Core of Consciousness

Let us take two simple sentences for the purpose of analysing the component elements of consciousness in the most nuclear form as it is felt within each person. First let us take the sentence 'This is a pot', which is a statement of an overt fact or mental event cognized at a certain instant in life.

Here the word 'this' would represent the vague background of suggestive material which consists of universals. It has no specificity. The inductive functions of thought have their origin in this. In the concept represented by the word 'pot' an object in the outer world is located in time and space in a specific manner with a certain name or form that may help to cognize it. The linking word 'is' is the act of thinking whose movement is the central neutral point that we have already noted.

If, secondly, we take another sentence such as "This is knowledge" we get to the subjective core of consciousness in which all references to the outer world of sensations is absent. At the base of the vertical axis we should put the connotation of the generic universal concept implicit in 'this' which can refer to every kind of particular knowledge. The word 'knowledge' itself would have a specific (not generic) content which includes comprehensively all possible knowledge of a pure order that man is capable of cognizing, whether through intuition or positive intelligence. When this has a specific human content it would represent a supremely or uniquely high value like the *summum bonum* of Plato. Specific knowledge of an absolute order, as opposed to generic knowledge, is here implied. The vague foundations of this same knowledge is a Wisdom-awareness which is the basis of all reality. There is a movement between this foundation-aspect of Wisdom-awareness and specific knowledge. This we can know by contemplation in its most willfully active phases.

The **personal factor** in its innermost aspects may be schematically represented in the same manner as we have represented its more peripheral aspects, in the manner shown in *fig.* 14.4.

Without trying to explain more elaborately the implications of this sketch, we shall content ourselves in concluding this first part of the Manifesto by quoting from the *One Hundred Verses of Self-Instruction* of the Guru Narayana:

> The powers of wisdom are many; all of them under two divisions,
>
> The 'same' and the 'other', could conclusively be brought; Merging into that form which makes for "other-same-ness"
>
> To clarity of vision one should awake.

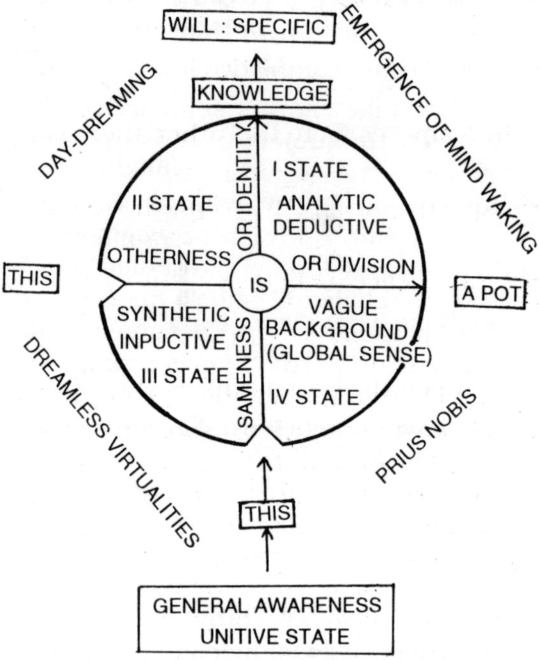

fig. : 14.4

To subdue even somewhat the obduracy of the 'other'
Is hard indeed without wisdom's limitless power;
By such do gain mastery over it and unto her who is Wisdom,
The anti-sensuous One, close access attain.

What appraises manifold variety, the 'other' that is;
And the 'same' is what unitively shines;
Thus understanding the state aforesaid, into that state
That yields sameness, melt and mix and erect sit.

Following up further the said powers — a second division:
One of these is an attribute of the 'same', while the other

Qualifies the never-to-detachment-attaining harshness
Of the 'other': thus making two kinds of these again.

On to the 'same' as on to the 'other' there constantly alight
Their respective specific powers; though not proportionate
By spin-emergence as between these two in all,
All predications whatsoever come to be.

In 'this is a pot' the initial 'this' is the harsh
While 'pot' is what makes its specific attribute;
For the mind with its myriad magic of Great Indra to come to be,
Understand, 'this' to be the nucleus.

In 'this is knowledge' the initial 'this' is 'same'
While its attribute is cognitive consciousness.
For the mind and all else to vanish
And the good path to gain, 'this' should one contemplate.

(Verses 36-42)

Here we see that Eastern Wisdom of a contemplative order can meet modern thought neutrally and on a par, in what pertains to this central notion or norm in education.

It is a strange coincidence that while the last paragraphs of the above were being typed, the headlines in the dailies announced: (July 22, 1957): "East-West Philosophers Find Basis for Discussion: Warsaw Conference Ends: Nearly fifty eminent philosophers from twenty East and West countries tonight wound up a four-day conference here at Warsaw amid statements that had 'established a dialogue'."

This Manifesto on World Education is also meant to make East and West, North and South, meet in the One name of Human Happiness dear to all mankind.

II

In part I of this Manifesto we were able to arrive at a global and synthetic perspective of the **personal factor** in education. Our aim was to reconstruct an integrated though schematic picture of this in the light of a time-honoured intuitive approach, known to philosophers, Eastern or Western, of antiquity or of recent years.

In this Part, we are retaining this reconstructed image as the basis of what we have to say concerning the varieties and modalities of the **personal factor** when more analytically viewed. We have to distinguish here not merely the basic aspects of the personality **implicit** in the **personal factor**, as we have called this central notion, but also those **explicit** traits of the **personal factor** which exist in a more overt sense. In other words, those characteristics of the **personal factor** by which we should be able to appraise the difference between a Peter and a Paul, instead of merely referring in generic terms to any Rāma or Kṛṣṇa, must stand out in relief from the comparatively stable (though not altogether static) psyche of Part I.

Education should be understood in terms of changing man for the better. Such a change must manifest in behaviour, whether in the individual or in the general pattern we call civilization.

Unity of Ends and Means

The education of gentleman as known in the West has here to be thought of in the same breath as the perfected model of spiritual life as conceived in the great religions of the world. Insofar as these models have given us patterns of a good life worth perpetuating, they should be conserved. In evolving the gentleman or the perfect man of the future, we might have to put into the melting-pot many of those petrified moulds which the conservative orthodoxies of various departments of human life have thrown up to the surface through the changes or upheavals of history. Living and dialectically revalued notions of piety, sportsmanship, chivalry, social responsibility, statesmanship or even citizenship have to enter into the makeup of the educated gentleman of tomorrow. Contemplation, which knows no historical limitation, has also to be given its full place in such a normative model as we have to keep in mind. The man of tomorrow must be one hundred per cent human and thus represent the highest human value in himself.

To accomplish this end, the **innate** and **overt** aspects of the personality have to be adjusted and balanced. A scientifically understood **norm** has to apply to the **image** and the **mould** it fits into, at once. In other words, the subjective and the objective have to be justly and truly comprehended. Disequilibrium, maladjustment and lack of harmony or beauty have to be avoided. As a head-dress must match the man or woman concerned, so the behaviour-pattern available for the educated person has to agree with what he represents in himself, as the effect of his education up to that moment. Thus **ends** and **means** have to meet unitively in the process, and more especially in the final stages of **positive adjustment** in education. The ends and means have to meet, at least in Infinity or Eternity, so that some behaviouristic cap or other has to be chosen, whether one likes it or not. Such is the implication of Absolute Necessity which in a practical sense culminates with Death and in a theoretical sense with Eternal Life. The Crisis of Man, whether actual or spiritual, has to be met with the benefit of the best wisdom available to man and in keeping with the dignity of the race.

When Shakespeare says that a man's dress "declareth the man" in him, or when proverbs tell us of the verity that birds of a feather flock together, or again when the *Bhagavad Gītā* states "What a man's faith is **that he even is**" (XVII. 3) or even when a modern psychologist is able to recognize with Th. Ribot: "The man of great passion is confiscated wholly by his passion, **he is his passion**"[15], we are touching one of the laws of fundamental personal dialectics. It is also said that, "as a man thinketh, he becometh".

In the human world of actions and opportunities which is spread before each individual, there are many items that, through necessity, taste or refinement, he would select to adopt as his own. **Man is ever equating himself to things or thoughts**.

The hat that a woman would wear, the food that a boy might select when seated at a feast spread before him, the pattern of behaviour to which he would naturally conform, not to mention the occupations corresponding to his aptitudes, have all to be understood as regulated by the laws of personal dialectics implied in each case. These laws could be used diagnostically besides being rules to be followed. The Sabbath could be for man and *vice versa* according to the necessity or contingency involved in the situation. Education **must** meet the individual and the individual **must** fit into the available pattern in the world of activities and opportunities.

Division 1 : Content of Education

From Simple Sensations to High Human Values

If a simple **sensation** reaching the organism may be said to mark the **alpha** of the educative process, the **omega** of the series may be said to be marked by the appreciation of **high human values**. In this Manifesto this is to be conceived as a positive and progressive adjustment of personal tendencies reaching out to the highest of human values within his reach. Even in the final stage of perfection sensations are not totally abolished, but tend to recede into the background to occupy a secondary position. The personality does not live in a vacuum, but in a graded scale of behaviour patterns. It fits into a field of creative life expression with a starting point and having a culminating target to reach. Activity and affectivity require catering to, in this process, without violating laws of human dialectics which concern his **existence**, his more formal or intelligent **subsistence**, and the **values** that might attract or repel him at each intermediate stage. The process is not mechanistic but **living, creative and organic**.

If we should consider a simple sensation we find that the **stimulus** that starts it through **centralization** from the periphery, attains to the **core of consciousness**. Instead of resulting in a simple unit response, as wrongly supposed by some mechanistically minded physiologists, simple stimuli invariably produce whole, complex, or integrated responses, resulting in **ideas**, through a characteristic **central delay** after the **irradiation** of the primary impulse. The ideas attain to a higher or lower status in consciousness, according to the **facilitations**, inverse or onward, going towards the higher or lower centres, already there in the form of **habitual dispositions** connected with instincts and memories.

If we rely on Rousseau's educational psychology here, rather than on being misled by stimulus-response psychology (dominated by its brass instruments and gadgets which what is called experimental education has brought into vogue in the West, and which may be called a form of scientific superstition peculiar to the age), we can easily see that personal life, with which education is concerned, hardly consists of unit sensations, the total of which makes up life. On the other hand, the simplest sense-stimulus gets translated and **verticalized** into an idea, integrated and raised to the status of an interest or a life-value. Sensations and perceptions have to be understood unitively. As Rousseau points out: "Simple ideas are nothing but sensations that have been compared. There are judgments involved in the simplest of sensations."[16] That an idea is also an idea of value we shall see on page 217.

Vertical and Horizontal Worlds of Values

If modern philosophy admits of the notion of Monadology of a Liebnitz in which the Monad of monads corresponds to God, and if the cosmology of Descartes admits of a universe in which etherial fluids move round a vortex, it should not sound strange in these days of space-time continuum, and of the drastic revision of our theory of knowledge, methodology and value notions, that we should, for the sake of brevity, begin here to refer, as it were, abruptly, to vertical and horizontal worlds of values.

In the *Contrat Social* Rousseau himself uses this contrasting set of values in his discussion, as follows:

> As I meditated on the nature of man, it seemed that I discovered therein two distinct principles; one of them rose to the study of eternal verities, towards love, justice and true morality, to those regions of the world that the sage loves to contemplate; the other lowered, rendered it slave of the senses, and of passions, which are its instruments, and was **thus opposed** to all that was suggested by the first principle.

Once the sensation gets integrated into a **value-idea**, by the very interest that it implies thereby, it can exert a vertical pull upwards, hypostatically, or become a lowering weight that can, by a **descending dialectical process**, bring the consciousness in relation to simple existents that are of interest in the sustenance or joy of life. Taste, smell, touch, sight and hearing can unitively work hand in hand with natural elements or **entelechies** as Aristotle would call them conceived as value factors (and not as mere objects), to make a whole string of values, from simple existent ones to the high ideological ones of the Platonic World of the Intelligibles. A contemplative psychology, epistemology and methodology are implied here which we cannot discuss at length in this Manifesto. We shall, however, have occasion to discuss the epistemological and other implications of this contemplative intuitive approach to the **personal factor** in some of the sections that follow.

The Basic Conflict and Unitive Treatment of Life Values

It is true that one cannot serve two masters, and that Caesar's domain is different from that of God. As Rousseau would put it strikingly, as it pertains to education, one "cannot make a citizen and a man at once". This contradiction at the core of the personal tendencies themselves has to be fully recognized in any science of education that deserves the name. In the scheme that we have adopted, the conflict is represented by the correlates crossing at right angles. Every aspect of personal life, within body limits or outside, is subject to the conflict. It is the task of contemplation, however, to resolve this conflict unitively, to transcend or overcome the confusion it might bring in the process of education, by developing a sound methodology, epistemology and a scheme of values proper to it. Within its humble limits, this Manifesto gives broad indications in this matter, of great importance. For the time being let us name this the **law of conflicting interests in education**. This is the second law. The first law was already implicit in Part I of the Manifesto, being the **law of unity, equality or identical total value**.

The Law of Polarity or Ambivalence

The third law and the second of the important fundamental notions that we have to formulate correctly in personal psycho-dynamics, may be called the **law of polarity or ambivalence**. In the domain of biology it was Bleuler who first defined this term. Other-terms such as dichotomy, polarity, synergism, antinomian principles, all expressing this reciprocal, interdependence, or relationship of a complementary or compensatory character, have been understood or used in physiology, theology, philosophy or cosmology. This **element of paradox or tragic conflict** in life, attains to the very core of our being. Hamlet's 'to be or not to be' is ever echoed in our hearts at every step we take, whether intellectual or physical. Piety and work are opposed, as also grace and sin. Groups of muscles balance one another; functioning itself delicately hangs in the balance as with the heart, which is energized by two distinct sets of nerves, one **positive** and the other **negative**. The **neutral core** of consciousness is the wheel's hub where conflicting spokes meet, as the *Upaniṣads* (and the *Tao Teh Khing*) would put this verity.

We should be content for the present to derive two secondary laws based on this principle of polarity. These could be stated as follows: III (a) The **law of compensation of interests** and III (b) The **law of equilibrium**. Their nature will be clear from the contexts as we continue.

Education Consists of a Series of Equations to Interests

There have been many definitions of education; that it is "a drawing out" or "a driving in of truth", that it is "a preparation to face the battle of life", that it is "the development of head and heart" or "of the whole man", that its aim is "social adjustment for utility" or "for leisure", that it is "for citizenship" etc. Each of them may be partially valid, but the best of them is one which treats ends and means unitively, and refers to the process in terms of harmony, equilibrium, balance, beauty or proportion in life tendencies. There is a cancelling out of counterparts, a constant search for agreement, accord or unitive peace with oneself or with the outer world involved in the best notion of education. Boyhood interests are equated with play, youth interests in seeking companionship, old age interests in thoughts good, bad or indifferent. One sphere of interest succeeds another, but the balancing of counterparts holds good always, and man tends by his natural gift of reason to rise in the scale of values, while the equilibrium of forces, acting horizontally, is ever maintained constant. A scientifically conceived education has thus the **law of equilibrium** implied in its end and its means.

The Content of Positive Education

We have noted that Rousseau considered the earliest phase of education as **negative**. Does this mean that later stages of education are **positive**, and if so, what is the precise content of such a programme?

When the child grows towards becoming a young man his **interests are directed to things** with which he wants to be related intelligently or actively. Common everyday science by which he relates himself to the physical world gives him interesting experiences by which he is able to dispel step by step, wrong or apparent notions with corrected or true ones. When his vision thus penetrates into the veil of appearance, his education may be said to be getting positively adjusted. One simple interest gives place to another, till one day he discovers that there are interesting events happening to himself. He then **compares himself with others**. This becomes the **second stage of the positive process** of education. He wishes to be self-sufficient and earn an honest livelihood and get finally a companion in life. Simple, natural, positive adjustment of tendencies go on up to this point without any tragic factors creeping into life. Later in life, education demands higher idealistic adjustment in which tragic conflicts incidental to life are conquered by a more positive yet unitive solution.

Thus, after the first stage of education, the whole of the remainder of the educative process has a positive content. Normal positive education is thus a harmonious ascent or vertical adjustment to life values. All tragic values, involving conflict, lie in the horizontal series of interests, from which the educand is to be saved as much as possible. To help the pupil in this way to adjust his urges progressively and harmoniously, turning him away from the harsh and tragic aspects of life, is the task of the educator.

The Onlooker the Best Educator, Even in Positive Education

Although we have just said that tragedy is to be avoided, this is not to be done wilfully by any interference or escapist doctrine. A born tragic hero must have a tragic situation to face to prove his worth. To hinder his self-fulfilment would be dangerous. Each type has its proper vocation in life, and this principle which the *Gītā* calls *svadharma*, "one's proper calling", requires to be respected absolutely. The inner man must be matched one hundred per cent with the outer circumstance which, though apparently involving two wrongs, sometimes when put together, works for one right. The **discipline by natural consequences** that both Rousseau and Spencer adopt in their educational theories, respect this principle of non-intervention or interference by the educator.

This is but a corollary of the principle of equalization and of the neutralization of opposing tendencies in the pupil throughout the process. The **plus** and the **minus** aspects of the sets of tendencies involved in any given interest of the educand must by themselves be allowed to attain to an equilibrium by his working out his salvation himself, through his own proper vocation. Forcing in any way would only distort the tendencies. Freedom, however, should not include freedom to go wrong and get maladjusted. The educator should expect from each **according to his ability** and give to each **according to his need**. He has to maintain a neutrality based on a **law of compensatory reciprocity** here, which is of the essence of the bipolar relation which, as we have said, is implied in education.

It is in this sense that the educator has been compared to an intelligent gardener who tends and watches, or to a good shepherd who leads his flock to fresh waters and green pastures. Socrates, who was concerned with the highest role of education, as the teacher of wisdom, still compared himself only to a midwife. Tolstoy has compared the subtle bipolar relation involved to the process of osmosis between liquids separated by a living tissue. The reciprocity may be illustrated by referring to two magnets packed together so that one would help the other to retain its own power without getting spent itself. A dialectical law of reciprocity is here implied. The *Guru* (spiritual teacher) and the *Śiṣya* (pupil in wisdom) were known to be related in this bipolar way in ancient Indian education. This is instinctively understood even by Indian peasant women to the present-day.

Educability of the Educand Need not be Doubted

Many modern thinkers have doubted even the educability of the educand. Among such, Th. Ribot put his finger at the very centre of the question when he stated briefly, "true character does not change". Voltaire who is the representative of the Age of Reason, put it more pointedly when he said, "Would you insist absolutely on changing the character of a man? Then purge him everyday with diluents till you have him dead". Guyau, Spinoza, Gall, Schopenhauer, Taine and Spencer are among the other thinkers who thought, education could not do much to change the nature of a man.[17]

This objection would at once lose its whole force when we adopt the standpoint attributed to Muhammed that if the mountain would not come to him, he would go to the mountain. Dialectically approached, according to a theory that is also dialectically correct, and with dialectical relations or conditions properly secured for the osmotic process to go on, education has still possibilities of full success in its highest aim. Some people like Voltaire have the perversity to obtain doubly wrong conclusions even when doubly right ones are possible. Reason can be wrongly used like an inverted telescope. Even extremely wrong opinions sometimes help us to see the truth of the opposite. Dialectics can resolve a double disaster into a blessing both ways.

The Dialectical Approach to Work-a-day Programmes in Education

At this stage it might be objected that this dialectical approach being such an airy subtlety, it cannot enter into school teaching in any tangible form. Gleaned from personal experience in teaching in various types of institutions from primary to university grades in different parts of the world, the following general indications may be set forth here as guiding principles for the educational practitioner:

(a) **Recognition of the background aspects of the personality of the child** which is the retrospective seat of the instincts, memories and global emotional dispositions connected with repose and relaxation, is a much neglected matter in actual educational practice as obtaining in the large public schools of today. The **background aspect** comes into evidence in the classroom when we find that certain children take more time for expression than others; but when they do begin to express themselves, they do better than those whose response was earlier and quicker. There is a kind of sub-conscious receptacle, where **impressions lie stored and delayed** before they become organized and **ready for expression**. The capacity of this receptacle varies with different children, and the teacher, who ignores this difference would be dealing wrongly with the child who might be forced to keep pace with less richly endowed pupils in this respect. Thus damage might be done which it would be hard to heal later on. The richer the negative aspect, the higher is the promise for the future.

(b) **Differing levels** of personal reaction to the same set of interests or situations, .is another matter which a mechanistically minded approach to education would tend to ignore with disastrous results in education. Defective children may show precociousness which should not be encouraged. Normal healthy reactions should be encouraged even when the attainment from the scholastic point of view might be at an inferior level for the time being.

(c) There is similarly a **personal rhythm** of progression belonging to the personality of each child which it would be disastrous not to recognize as the tendency happens to be in mass impersonal education. Slow and steady alternation can be superior to a quick rhythmic alternation, which might be due to a sick soul.

(d) There is even a **diurnal alternation** of emotive and intellectual, prospective and retrospective, positive or negative phases involved in everyday education which should be remembered both in framing the time-table and in balancing the curriculam. Analytical, intellectual exercise must occupy morning hours, and such subjects as history and light literary studies taken during the reminiscent, reposeful mood of the evening hours.

(e) **Complete reactions** are to be preferred to partial ones. This is another rule that mass education is likely to neglect. A **natural chain of behaviour** involves various phases which we have tried to trace in Part I of this Manifesto. The figure-of-eight that it traces involves a natural sequence which follows a certain living order peculiar to the **personal factor**. A cyclist going uphill can admire a sunset without compromising one activity by the other. Although "one thing at a time" is proverbially a "good rule", a properly compensated and balanced programme of daily activities helps to make education a pleasure to the teacher and to the taught. Here again a dialectical approach, equating work and play, helps in everyday eduacation.

(f) There is another long range of helpful possibilities in that innate urge in the child, to see himself as a person reflected in all he comes in contact with. **Personification** which is a general instinctive urge in child-life, has been found to be helpful already in teaching dry subjects like grammer where, for example, noun and pronoun are pictured as persons who take the place of each other. Personification is, however, a much more serious and deep-seated urge in the educand and an effective handle in education.

(g) The possibilities of **mutual personal adoption** or admiration between the teacher and the taught, when correctly accomplished as a condition in education, are well-known in the educational world. Mutual admiration can go to the extent of absolute hero-worship and then the handle that the right educator gets to shape the character of the pupil is very great. A good teacher often succeeds in making such a lasting mark on the spirit of the pupil, that it can change his character. Even if a small percentage of a mass of students should thus get changed, education should be considered a worthwhile undertaking in the interests of humanity.

(h) The personality of the teacher could help the pupil in **overcoming inhibitory crises**. The progressive adjustment that we call education has critical stages, some of which the pupil might find too difficult to cross unaided morally if not physically. The situations are many and varied, whether in the class-room, the sports-field, or in the larger world outside the school walls. Correct bipolar relations with a sympathetic teacher whom the pupil admires, likes, or better adopts willingly as his model, can work the wonder of enabling the hesitant, inhibited pupil to get past the spiritual or intellectual hurdles of various grades of inhibitions in life. Under this heading, hundreds of possibilities of effective education are open to the teacher, who, like the pupil, must be born for the specific job involved in the education that concerns both of them equally as partners inseparable for life. Thus we arrive at the basic notion and role of a Guru as tacitly understood in Indian pedagogics from the most ancient times.

Division 2 : The Personal Factor: Analytical Perspective

Having, in Part I of this Manifesto, dealt with the **personal factor** involved in the educative process synthetically (though not statically, as some writers with Cartesian duality in their minds have done) and having disposed of general matters of educational or pedagogic import connected with the everyday practice of education, as it exists at the present-day, it now remains for us to take a bird's-eye-view of the analytical and more positive aspects of education as a process of progressive adjustment to overt and larger situations of life, considered individually as well as collectively at once.

This latter aspect could legitimately be called the psycho-dynamical aspect of the **personal factor**, although the description of the earlier aspect would not be strictly psycho-statics, as usually distinguished in treatises on the subject of the "Human Personality and Its Analysis".[18] In considering one part or aspect of the personality as static we should be allowing or admitting unconsciously a duality of treatment of the unitive personality, prejudiced by the body-mind differences which still vitiate and compromise our understanding of the subject.

Our claim in this Manifesto is that this unitive concept of the **person** involved in education has not so far been given its complete, correct or legitimate place, in the centre of educational discussions. State educational programmes, not to mention programmes conceived by such bodies as the UNO or the UNESCO, to whom we should naturally turn for evolving a science of education, have so far either wilfully neglected it or unconsciously by-passed it, in their haste to produce on a mass scale those citizens who would defend the frontiers or ideological barriers within which they love to live. Thus we see that between the slogans of

"Education for Democracy" or "Education for a Classless Society" in the mouths of the gaints who dominate opinion or policy in such matters, there has come to be no common human ground where proper educational theory could have a chance to flourish. This Manifesto is not concerned with revising all aspects of educational theory, but only in presenting the **personal factor** involved even in public or positive aspects of education, as a central integrated notion, round which all theorization, which tends to be over-departmentalized and disintegrated without it, could be built. The notion of the **personal factor** would supply the peg from which all theoretical elaborations could hang, and could at least be a basis for future discussion, if not as a completed or perfected notion as conceived here at present.

Psycho-Statics and Psycho-Dynamics Treated Unitively

A dialectical treatment of a science is radically different from the same treated rationally, mechanistically, unilaterally or dualistically. There is subtle difference here, which being missed, would end our discussion in futility and frustration. If we should give **actuality** importance in the name of 'objectivity' then by that very token, we fall into the error of neglecting **perceptual** factors; and again, the slightest extra emphasis on the spiritual or ideological, would land us into a similar dualistic position which would compromise the correct understanding of the **personal factor**. The *Advaita* (non-dualist) philosophy in India aims at avoiding this duality by a neutral, unitive approach in the name of the Absolute. Modern philosophers like Bertrand Russell, although they do not go the whole way with *Advaita*, have been inclined to put their case on similar unitive lines. As an example, Bertrand Russell has named his position as that of Neutral Monism.

In these days of brass-instrument-psychological-study, based on an almost empirical stimulus-response psychology, the matter-mind duality still vitiates our educational thought, to its great detriment. The physiology of the dissection table suffers still from a similar prejudice from the dead grip of which Dr. Alexis Carrel and others have tried to save it.[19] But orthodoxies die hard, whether in religion or in science, and this Manifesto takes its stand on a bold unitive approach to the problem of personality by which a dead or static educator would be ruled out in favour of a living and sympathetic guide. Likewise the child would not be considered merely a stimulus-response bundle, or worse still, a piece of behaviouristic mechanism with no mind within it, as J.B. Watson would put it. Even a **bare theory of play** has not been found possible to be formulated properly on this mechanistic basis which seems still in full vogue in the educational world.

In this present age of reason and of the proud triumph of science, it is no wonder that the educability of the educand has been called into question. If the almightiness of education as a force to change the individual character with which a man might be born is to be discredited, that does not justify the extremely opposite position which empirical thinkers take with such insistent perversity. A unitive, neutral, yet 'positive' approach to personal adjustment in education is therefore what this Manifesto stands for.

A Common Methodology and Epistemology for All Sciences

After Protagoras' dictum in the fifth century BC that "Man is the measure of all values" which was reiterated in the Delphic inscription, "Know Thyself", we went forward twenty-two centuries to Alexander Pope who wrote, "The proper study of mankind is man". Even earlier than Pope, in the latter half of the sixteenth century, there was a young man who from his seventeenth year nourished the ambition of correlating all knowledge unitively. We refer to Francis Bacon whose *Novum Organum* was laughed at by his colleague, the eminent lawyer Sir Edward Coke who, when presented with it, wittily wrote on its cover:

> It deserveth not to be read in schools
>
> But to be freighted in the ship of fools.

Since the time of Bacon very few have dared to step into this ambitious project, for fear of being called names. Eastern thought, however, has tacitly and openly nourished this ambition, and the great dicta (*mahā-vākyas*) of the *Vedānta*, such as "I am the Absolute", "Thou art That", "All is the Absolute" and "I and the Absolute are One", which boldly enshrine the same position as that of Protagoras and the Delphic Oracle, only in different persons first, second or third, as applied to the central person involved in all of them, still keep alive in the mouth of the common man and the pandit of the contemplative soil of India this high aspiration of the spirit.

Transplanted from the natural Indian soil, such dicta might sound strange, especially in the West which is proud of its own background and which has had its own different history, where memories of the Inquisition linger on. It is but natural, therefore, that any global unitive approach to the Self or the Personality in man is dubbed as dogmatic and suspected in the West. This is because of the lack of a common methodology and epistemology implying a scale of truely human values behind an integrated notion of the Self in man.

REVOLT FROM PRAGMATISM

Prof. John U. Nef. of the University of Chicago who broadcast a speech explaining the Committee on Social Thought which he took great initiative in starting recently under the aegis of that academic body, expressed the growing attitude of dissatisfaction in regard to this question of neglecting the study, as he put it, of "Man as a Whole". In this Manifesto we are not therefore alone when we say that this neglect of the study of man in this manner is a serious lacuna which it is high time the educational world filled up quickly, without feeling uncomfortable or touchy about it any more. In Prof. Nef's broadcast speech we read the following bold declaration of faith in unequivocal terms: "I believe the pragmatists not only lost their own critical faculties but dimmed those of their students and colleagues. Critical faculties with qualitative distinctions and universal principles, are the basis of a creative cultural life."

Outlining the origin and background of the Committee on Social Thought in a handout of the Department, Prof. Nef, enumerating the problems of the creative life and of education which confront modern society, says firstly: "One is the loss of the common classical and Christian inheritance in the intellectual sense." While thus relying on something that belongs to the West he explains in his broadcast speech[20] "At this same time, some of us in the University of Chicago were trying to establish an independent enterprise in graduate study, which would cut across departmental lines, and would be devoted to those very problems which were either ignored altogether or left to the charlatans."

ATMOSPHERE OF HESITANCY

Whoever might be in the mind of the professor when he suspects the charlatans, and whatever may be the content, not necessarily exclusive in any sense, of the classical and Christian inheritance alluded to above, that he might have been thinking of, there at least seems to be some sort of hesitation here to be fully bold and open in respect of this new and interesting development in the educational world of today. We have reason to feel that this hesitancy is shared by the university authorities also, as we listen to Prof. Nef, when he continues in the same broadcast: "Despite the fact that the President of the University and the Dean of Social Sciences were members of the group, we still had trouble .... When the negotiations were under way for setting us up, the Dean rang me on the telephone: "I can never get us set up under the title, the Committee on Civilization", he explained in distress. "What title would you suggest?", I asked. "The Committee on Social Thought", he replied. "What does that mean?", I asked. "I don't know", he said, "but I think it might get us through the executive committee, because nowhere in the University is there any study of social thought". Here we find pragmatism with a vengeance! We have taken the trouble and the liberty of quoting here in detail because of the rare and realistic picture it gives of the hesitancy and suspicion that might be said to be representative of the modern world of education of which Chicago is a sufficiently important centre.

If East and West are ever to have a common meeting ground at all, it is time that we began to think in more bold and absolutist terms without any Kipling mentality about the impossibility of the meeting of East and West. Fortunately for us, philosophers are not altogether extinct in the West nor Guruhood in the East. If the best of each could be brought close together there is still possibility of a common ground in such undertaking emerging to view, as a hopeful sign of the times. Openness is not, however, the exclusive prerogative either of the East or the West.

How the "Principle of the Better" Enters Psycho-Dynamics

The **Principle of the better** that Leibnitz formulated, reconciling Cartesian and Aristotelian notions, is the same as that which we have already referred to as the Vertical Series of Interests in life (see pages 202, 203 above). When the idea is one that implies value, it becomes interesting to the living organism with its consciousness which seeks to live by a series of successive interests in life. The latest philosophers of the West still adhere to these notions and it has not gone out of date with philosophers or even with Leibnitz.

We have evidence for this in the report of the present incumbent to the Chair of Philosophy of the College de France — that unique foundation which has preserved the best learning that France inherited from classical times, and founded by royal patronage of Francis I as early as 1530. In its *Annuaire* for the year 1948. Prof. Louis Lavalle in summarising his course for the year, has the following: "But the idea could not be a mediating factor between spiritual entities (*les esprits*) except on condition of proposing to each of them an end which it could will, estimate and like. **It is in this sense that the idea is always an idea of value.**"

Although the correspondence may not be exact, the conclusions of Vedāntic or *Advaitic* thought in India, whose categories of Absolute Wisdom consist of the components of *asti* (is existing), *bhāti* (is conscious) and *priyam* (is desirable), can be seen to have the same or similar elements or categories of thought implied in them. The hope of finding a common basis for Eastern and Western thought is not, therefore, to be given up too easily.

Dichotomy Invades Even the Very Core of Consciousness

Let us revert here for a moment to an analysis of the component elements of consciousness as we did when we took a close and almost microscopic view of its dynamism in the last section of Part I of this Manifesto.

In the verses of Guru Narayana quoted there we got as far as distinguishing two conflicting sets of tendencies which were considered under the heads of 'sameness' and 'otherness' (*sama* and *anya*). It was pointed out there that detachment of contemplative self-sufficiency was not to be expected from the pursuit of horizontal interests which had to do with the 'harsh otherness' of the objectively directed tendencies.

Besides this primary conflict it has been indicated in Verse 40 there, that, within each of the two sets of vertical or horizontal values themselves, there is a dichotomy or polarity implied. The generic aspect of each of these sets of interest reveals dichotomous ambivalence in relation to the specific aspect of the same. The generic of the horizontal tendency consists of vague virtualities still belonging to the 'objective' order, while the generic aspect of the vertical is unitive and universal in its content. The specific aspect which comes to meet it does not belong to it, but approaches it, as it were, from an opposite pole of reality. As between the two axes and between each treated separately, dichotomy is operative. **Horizontal specificity spells bondage**, while **vertical generality tends to release the personality**.

We know we are treading on very speculative grounds here, and therefore let us fall back on some classical writers for support. Referring to the nature of the Word or Logos, Aristotle states: "The Word may be regarded under two aspects: (a) as multiplicity of particulars and (b) as a system of general laws on which the particular depends." Reason, Aristotle has to admit, is not part of the human soul, but distinct therefrom. *Nous* is introduced into the soul *ab extra* and Aristotle speaks of it as a divine element in man.[21] What is of special interest for us to note here is the *ab extra* or hypostatic status of Reason which stands for the specific aspect of knowledge, wisdom or awareness.

The Final Abolition of All Duality in Pure Consciousness

Although we have just said that dichotomy enters into the very core of consciousness we have to make it clear that this only applies to a psycho-dynamical picture. There is, theoretically at least, a centre in pure consciousness, where opposing tendencies are neutralized. Descartes, who was blamed for his dualistic treatment of matter and spirit, was still able to say, "In the fact of self-consciousness truth and existence are identical." The descending dialectics of Aristotle which postulated the *universalia ante re* and the ascending dialectics of Plato who arrived at *universalia ante rem* were reconciled by Scholastic philosophers, and Spinoza, who spoke of the higher intuitive way, refers to *scienta intuitiva*, a contemplative way, by which "the concrete individualities of imaginative experience are restored, but **at a higher level** where the individual things are no longer conceived fragmentarily and in isolation, but in their relationship to their dependence upon the infinite ground."

Without being tempted further into this domain of philosophical speculation, it is our object merely to say that whether known as *Logos* or *Nous* there is a point at which all differences vanish into **absolute oneness**, whether we follow Eastern or Western philosophy to the very limits of speculation possible.

The Dialectical Approach Superior to the Merely Rational

Reasoning based on formal logical methods leads to sterile speculations about the meaning of Truth or Existence. This meaning cannot live in an intellectual vacuum and flourish. The content of truth has to represent some human value falling within the range of normal human life. Unitive values in life emerge when opposites in consciousness are cancelled out or merged into the sameness of the vertical principle which we have tried to distinguish in previous sections and at the end of Part I of this Manifesto.

As pure time does not depend on night or day but can still be a living experience as Time, so there is a way of arriving at natural, normal, just, good, true or beautiful values in life through a dialectical approach to reality. **A programme in education may be credited to be well-founded to the extend that unitive values in life are met by unitive interests progressively or harmoniously as life unfolds through all its stages.**

This dialectical way in education may be said to correspond to the way of the *yogī* as known in Indian contemplative life. The *Bhagavad Gītā* which is a textbook of unitive human values, arrived at by the dialectical way, which it succeeds in defining with scientific precision, puts dialectical wisdom above wisdom plain and simple, the latter being devoid of a human import. Educational theory has therefore to be conceived in terms of producing a man who is filled with one hundred per cent humanity.

The Case for Integral Education or "Man as a Whole"

The education of "man as a whole" is an expression which we are beginning to hear frequently from educational reformers. Man-making, character-building, moral or spiritul education, meant perhaps more or less the same in older days. If character is fixed at birth by nervous patterns belonging to types, where is the hope for this expression to refer to anything practicable? Only by understanding the structure of the **personal factor** in all its aspects, subtle and gross, central and peripheral, in a unitive dialectical manner, given proper educational theory and an educator who can apply it correctly in relation with his pupil, can we hope to obtain full results, when all the conditions are properly secured. Herein lies the only hope for the future of education. This, in short, is what would finally justify a Manifesto such as this claims to be.

It must be pointed out here that the education which has come into vouge in modern life, largely based on a stimulus-response psychology under the leadership of the United States, errs glaringly in not providing for the education of man as a whole. John Dewey, the most eminent of American educationalists, admits himself this truth when he writes, "Particular S-R connections interpreted on the basis of isolated reflexes, are viewed as static **cross-sections** and the factor most important in education, namely, the **longitudinal**, the temporal span of growth and change, is neglected."[22]

It is interesting to note here, that by referring to the 'longitudinal' section as a factor most important in education, John Dewey, though, as we have seen, now being discredited as a mere pragmatist by his own disciples in Chicago, still gives us the hint that he is not only interested in the education of man as a whole, but also that his own scheme of the **personal factor** involved in education is not fundamentally different from what we have developed so far in this Manifesto.

The Four Zones or Grades of Personal Consciousness

Education as a bipolar process will be effective only to the extent that the deepest seats of consciousness are brought reciprocally into relationship as between educator and educand. It would not be out of place, therefore, to examine the other strata, layers, levels, zones or aspects of the personality involved in education which lie hidden, as it were, under the visible surface where stimuli and responses, in the overt sense, may be said to live and move. In adopting the scheme of correlation that we have chosen, we have really made due provision to refer to four aspects of consciousness, each of which refer to the four states of **waking, day-dreaming, sleeping** and **general awareness** which come within the common experience of all. These states need no proof (*fig.* 14.4). All conscious and subliminal aspects beyond the threshold of consciousness may be directly referred to and understood by them. As the greater part of an iceberg is under water, the self which is hidden below the stimulus-response aspect, is quantitatively as well as qualitatively by far the more important aspect of the personality. To give the three other aspects their place in education is what this Manifesto particularly insists upon.

We find a perfect psychological analysis of these four limbs of consciousness in the *Māṇḍūkya Upaniṣad* where, in a graded fashion, their inter-relationships are brought out. The whole of this short *Upaniṣad* is devoted to this analysis of the *Ātman* or Self which it first describes as *catuṣpāt* (four-limbed). The four states of waking, dreaming, sleeping and general awareness are referred to serially twice over in the text: first by way of their functions diagnostically, and secondly by their place in consciousness understood from within. In modern terminology we could label them as, (a) overt-objective of the waking state, (b) virtual-objective of the day-dreaming state, (c) the bright blissfulness of deep sleep and (d) the pure awareness of the deepest stratum of the consciousness which permeates all the others.

To attain to this last named seat of consciousness, and to relate it correctly with an educational situation in which the educator and the educand are involved as partners for life, so that the influence of the one on the other may be exchanged like a subtle osmosis, requires an expert understanding of the **personal factor** in its deepest aspects, as well as, in its most gross overt expressions. The **plus** and the **minus** involved have to be linked up properly, if education is not to be a haphazard "muddling through" or "licking into shape" as it has been alluded to complacently by some English writers.

The Rousseau-Emile Relation

Cheap and sensational spirituality of a pseudo-scientific order has reached the West from the East in recent years. In some well-informed circles this has given rise to some legitimate mistrust regarding such matters. The mention of the word Guru is enough to disturb the general atmosphere in certain contexts or cultural climes. When viewed without undue exaggeration on either side, however, we are able to find the same human nature working with the same understanding or insight everywhere. Humanity is one. This verity is again confirmed when we find that in the domain of educational theory and practice what has been tacitly accepted in the wisdom context of the East corresponds with the best flowering of thought in the West.

Here again, for us at least, concerned with this Manifesto it is a significant fact to note that the Rousseau-Emile relation, as so carefully and laboriously worked out by that much misunderstood sage of Geneva, corresponds to the *Guru-Śiṣya* relationship which has been considered through the ages in India as the main plank in the process of education.

Shorn of the Eastern tendency to be easily exalted in the name of spirituality and to fall into *a priori* generalizations on the one hand, and in the West, the opposite tendency of relying too much on the overt aspect of life only, the position as between educator and educand, as conceived by both the sides, reveals in all matters of scientific import, a complete agreement. Two magnets properly laid juxtaposed, and an osmosis arrangement properly set up, need a certain expert understanding, which is all that is implied in this relationship. If educational authorities could see this, the future of education in the world would be said to have some hope. Humanity could still reap benefit from education,conceived not haphazardly but according to precise and positive notions.

Four Stages, Four Kinds and Four Patterns of Behaviour Involved in Education

At this point we must pause a moment to explain the plan of the rest of this Manifesto, which might get lost in the by-paths and ramifications of the forest of educational theories, or in the vast mass of literature which has accumulated in what passes for educational practice, most of which this Manifesto boldly calls into question. Humanity as a whole

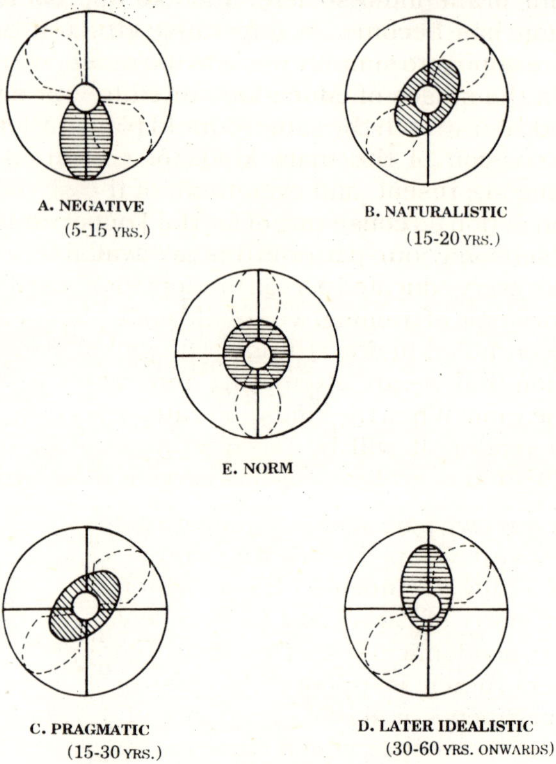

fig. 14.5 : FOUR STAGES OF LIFE

Explanation of Figure 14.5 : The central figure *E* represents the norm which may have different content with the sexes. In the scheme here, the male is mainly kept in mind. Figures A,B,C and D show striped core or zone which is oriented differently at the four stages of life (ages being shown in brackets). The dotted line shows the chains of behaviour (*see fig.* 14.3) natural with each phase. In A, the Negative Stage, when the relational sense and dependence is strong automatisms, habits, memory instincts and tender emotions should be availed of by the educator; in B, the Naturalistic Stage, there should be learning through play, excursions, experiences of a graded natural order and experiments to rouse curiosity; in C, the Pragmatic Stage, education is through directed socialized activity, leadership training and the ontological approach; and in D, the Later Idealistic Stage, higher positive adjustment should be achieved through relationship with the philosopher-guide.

being our prime interest here, a global approach to world education has become an imperative desideratum. If we therefore appear to simplify matters too much by referring to fours, in the stages of education suited to four ages in the educand, and stretch the same fourfold plan of reference into the discussion of the main kinds of educational theory prevailing at present, and even think of the actual world of men and action as consisting of fourfold opportunities in the form of set behaviour-patterns that are available, as if ready-made, for every educated person to adopt for himself according to his own type of training, we should not be blamed for being too pigeon-holed in our attitude. The global overall view of education that we are attempting here amply justifies this simplification. When the kinds and categories are clear to the general reader, it will be possible for him to see if this simplification is arbitrary or has been actually justified.

For our own part, in this Manifesto we have only followed the lines we developed nearly a quarter of a century ago in the form of a fully documented thesis which was submitted to the University of Paris[23] and thus received the hallmark of a modern academical seat of learning of good standing. Every statement therein is supported by cross-references, citations and experiments or actual experience of the teaching world (except in the section which comes at the end of the series touching the fourfold opportunity or behaviour patterns which is a fresh addition to the thought on this subject). This work has later being honoured by Dr. H. Wallon, Prof. of the College de France, Director of Higher Studies, in his *L'Evolution Psychologique del' Enfant* (Paris, 1941) by approving reference to it in his chapter in the "Person in Education" (p. 210). These circumstances must be sufficient guarantee for the present that this fourfold simplification is not made without respecting prevailing educational theories or in violation of correct formalities in presenting a new point of view on such a serious subject. The reader may refer especially to the chapters devoted to **type psychology** and the **negative**, **naturalistic**, **pragmatic** and **idealistic adjustments involved in education**. We have also the good company of Prof. R. Rusk of Dublin University who, in his work *The Philosophical Basis of Education* (London Univ. Press) follows roughly this fourfold classification of educational theory:

Negativism in Education, a Regulating Principle Throughout

Rousseau has been laughed at as a sentimental antisocial solitary or a lost soul. A careful examination of the educational programme of *Emile*, however, reveals that while he himself openly recommends negative education for the early stages only, there is provision made for the social adjustment of Emile as he grows to manhood. Rousseau lays the foundations of the modern vogue for experimental education and even for the **project method** when he makes Emile a carpenter's apprentice. But even when Emile lives a whole day at the farmhouse where the carpenter-Guru is allowed to displace the main Guru for a full unit period of a day at a time, the main Guru insists on being a fellow apprentice to learn carpentry with his pupil, so that the sustained influence and bipolarity of the *Guru-Śiṣya* relationship may not be broken. The three of them eat together at the farmhouse table, and discover maxims of dialectical social interdependence as represented in the beautiful antique etching, where Emile is taught, "Each one respects the labour of others so that his own labour may be respected." The main Guru looks on in the illustration[24] while the secondary teacher (the *upa-Guru*) watches approvingly as Emile becomes convinced of this verity by an experimental situation.

A certain unforced, non-interfered-with naturalness in the process that develops by virtue of educative situations that arrive by themselves, within the normal or natural course of the growth and adjustment of the pupil, is all that is meant by 'negation' by Rousseau here. Later, when it comes to religious education, the same negative attitude is seen to continue, as we have shown in the quotation given in Part I. In fact, Rousseau's negativism is the same as that so well-known in the Indian context of contemplative education as the *nivṛtti mārga* or *via negativa* as opposed to the *pravṛtti mārga* or *via positiva*. This is characteristic of all contemplative disciplines, whether of the East or of the West, and is recognised by mystics and philosophers, not to mention religious disciplines of monasteries where different doses of this negativism find place. The turbulant animal tendencies in the educand need controlling and holding in, even in the most pragmatically conceived programme of education. This control seems glaringly omitted in modern education, and hence the disastrously wrong results which are beginning to alarm state educational authorities already, by way of crime increase, in spite of providing amply for education in their budgets.

Naturalistic Education

Educational theories are many, but for the purposes of this Manifesto we are going to view all of them as belonging to one or other of the four main groups that we have referred to. The negative education of Rousseau has already been covered more or less to the extent that space here permits. Naturalistic education is not that of Rousseau though he has been mistaken for a man who stressed nature. Nature for him, as we have said in Part I, was not just nature as in the expression "back to nature", but nature with the capital letters standing for a spiritual principle of Absolutist Value. This we have tried to make clear already in order not to mix up Rousseasu's Naturalism with that of Herbert Spencer who may be said to be more correctly its representative. We shall tabulate here the distinction between them for ready reference:

Rousseau	*Spencer*
(i) Subjective Idealist	(i) Empirical Realist
(ii) Against Society	(ii) Education for Society
(iii) Puts Gooodness and other values foremost	(iii) Cultural education given a secondary status after utilitarian education, as education for leisure.
(iv) Attached to Pure ethical values	(iv) Attached to hedonistic ethics

In spite of these striking items of contrast, there are certain features of naturalistic adjustment as understood by Spencer which follow the same lines as those of Rousseau. Rousseau envisaged for his Emile a programme of adjustment to utilitarian social conditions. It was thus that he thought of making him an apprentice with a carpenter who was to be a second teacher under the master-influence of the first. The secret of Rousseau was that his idealism fitted within it, without conflict, and unitively, that correct dose of utilitarian programme natural to the age of the pupil. Therefore to label Rousseau as non-utilitarian or anti-social would be not to understand his unitive methodology, which held the secret of a vertical ascending series of values, without the principle of mutual exclusion or contradiction. As a small circle could lie within a larger one, without exclusion or duality between them, so the contemplative dialectical method allows of two positions being treated unitively, both of which could co-exist without mutual compromise.

Laws of nature were to be understood by the pupil through direct experience rather than from teaching. The experimental approach was, however, common to both these great educationists. The education of nature through things, as Rousseau would have put it, was what the naturalistic education of Spencer amounted to.

The maximum that we derive from educational institutions based on this Manifesto is that, where boys or girls between 13 and 17 are brought up, ample provision must be made for contacting nature and observing natural phenomena and for playing trades like carpentry or weaving, which would give a social sense of self-sufficiency and dignity by way of a horizontal orientation and balancing of personal tendencies. No direct affiliation to the harsh world of competition and profit should ever be implied in it.

Pragmatic Education

When we come to pragmatism, whose representative may be said to be John Dewey, we see that it is a natural consequence of the naturalism of Herbert Spencer and Rousseau who, as we have seen, makes allowances for the need for social adjustment. Within a larger scheme of idealism, they could be considered as pragmatists.

The **project method** of the active school is reflected in the carpentry apprenticeship that Rousseau himself recommends. More than in the case of Spencer, the utilitarian social adjustment envisaged by Dewey is without any rational idealism even of a Descartes or a Kant. These old-world philosophers mean nothing for Dewey, nor can he appreciate those negative elements which Rousseau finds important. A modified or revised form of stimulus-response psychology and a practical, realistic and even empirical approach to life is implied in Dewey.

We shall take but one or two quotations from Dewey to bring out the contrast. In defining character to be built in the pupil, he writes:

> In general, character signifies the power to act in society, organised capacity to function socially; this signifies . . . . social intelligence, power of execution, social interest and sense of social responsibility.[25]

Again, he makes the nature of pragmatic education more clear:

> The great thing to keep in mind then, regarding the introduction into the school of various forms of active occupations, is that through them the active spirit of the school is renewed. It has a chance to affiliate itself with life, to become the child's habitat where he learns through directed living, instead of being only a place to learn lessons having an abstract and remote reference to some possible living to be done in the future. It gets a chance to be a miniature community, an embryonic society.[26]

Rousseau would not have disapproved of these remarks except perhaps in the shutting out of the future of the pupil in favour of a very real present and a social adjustment that is too horizontalized in its content. Rousseau expressly selects carpentry alone for Emile, so that his pupil could ply this 'honest' human trade in the self-sufficient loneliness of his own home under the single teacher's supervision which is kept important as a condition applicable to the whole process of education. Social values, thus over-emphasized in education, tend to exclude some of the noblest aspirations of the human heart, and it is on such programme of education as envisaged by Dewey that mass education in American schools still thrives.

Pragmatic education has signally failed. To avoid its mistakes is the moral we learn here. While self-sufficiency in social orientation is an ideal worthy of perservation, full affiliation to economic, social or political value systems as they prevail in the harsh world of competition and strife must always be modified by a dose of negativism and idealism proper to the age, type or sex of the pupils in different types of institutions for pragmatic adjustment in education.

Later Idealism in Education

The last of the four phases of educational adjustment may be distinguished as **later idealism**. Higher values, implying personal tastes, love of art, moral, religious or spiritual sentiments, have to be cultivated here. Here also, various patterns are possible, and the writers who have faced this aspect of education where character and moral or spiritual education is involved, have been few. Ribot and Payot have approached it, giving primacy to 'Passion' or 'Will' respectively.

Even the few have approached the subject with differing ends in view. Some think of it in terms of a hobby, treating idealistic adjustment as of secondary importance and characterising it as **education for leisure**. Others speak of the end as **happiness**, a vague term which can include hedonism. Its content has yet to be made more clear and definite. The German idealists would think of education in terms of the **will to live** or the **will to power** or even reduce the **world as will** — as with Nietzsche, Hegel and Schopenhauer respectively. The pessimistic view of some would differ from the optimism of others, and to bring all under one caption would not be easy.

However, all involve a positive adjustment of the

tendencies towards a personal or human goal. Some may have the Superman in view. These, when understood in the unitive context of this Manifesto could still be treated as having a common trend which, we could say, belongs to that part of the adjustment of the tendencies of the **personal factor** which we have marked as the positive, prospective and intelligent.

IDEALISTIC DIAGNOSTICS

Some of the marks of an idealistically educated man might be critical acumen, analysis, precision, a clarity free from emotional or instinctive compromising traits which come from the negative side, expertness (called *dakṣatā* in the *Gītā*) in dealing with situations either intellectual, ideological or actual which would face the person at a given time, a keen sense of justice, an intelligent *savoir faire* and an equal sympathy for all mankind and even for all creation. Wisdom training in the use of the higher faculty of intuitive reasoning, called dialectics would be the crowning attainment of a programme of an idealistic education.

Such a love of Wisdom could be a master-passion or a final act of will, which could burn all lesser dross in the form of petty life-interests or instinctive or emotional dross, and lead to the total passion in which the passion becomes identified with the Person himself. The filling of the personality with the full human content of the **idea of humanity** or the ideal or perfect man, with all the specifically distinguishing virtues which constitute human nature, may be said to mark the highest limit of idealistic education.

Into the possible varieties which human life throws up in actuality we shall not look at present, lest we should see in it possibilities or varieties that vast hell cannot hold.

Starting with double suicide pacts of lovers, martyrdom, crime, gambling or cheating (as the *Bhagavad Gītā* would include in the list of persons revealing traits of Absolutism), all the Othellos and Desdamonas, Hernanis and Dona Sols, mystics lost in agony or ecstasy, those with ideas that are fixed for life, people of vengeance, hatred or devotion unto death, the Al Caponis or Bandit Chiefs, war-lords, bookies, racketeers, humorous actors like Charlie Chaplin, great comics, clowns, inventors as also the rake and the scholar (which is a natural combination), Da Vincis, the adventurer and explorer, a Pascal whose intelligence itself kills him prematurely, a Shelly or a Keats or a Burns or an Amiel whose sensibility overleaps its own limits, all come for consideration under positively or over-positively adjusted personal tendencies.

MASS RE-EDUCATION

There is more literature about the eccentrics rather than the normals, which latter class often lie buried in neglect by their very normality. Freaks attract more attention. True heredity is taken for granted. These other normal humans constitute a fund of positive tendencies available to humanity still for canalization and direction to great ends, if a programme of **mass re-education** in suitable colonies for young or old could be started.

What we have called the normal in this overstrung, overworked, sleepless, passionate or wilfull mass of denizens of the human world is given only to the natural, contemplative, unitive vision of the dialectical philospher to see. He can cancel out extremes in the **personal factor**, or accentuations of one set of tendencies at the expense of others. The synergic ambivalance or dichotomy involving antinomian principles in life expression (all these terms being familiar in different departments of philosophy, theology, neurology or psychology), when merged into **sameness** gives the norm in education.

Maladjustment in education is the most general danger to be avoided. In this task, state programmes, because of lack of a proper, complete or scientific theory of education, are, to say the least, not helpful at all at present. Juvenile delinquency and crime is alarmingly on the increase in the very countries which provide amply for education in their budgets. The remedy is misapplied. The plant is manured or watered wrongly by gardeners who do not understand their job. Young saplings lack protection, and chill breezes or desert winds play havoc with them. This Manifesto therefore pleads for the understanding of this problem of World Education on the revised terms indicated throughout, which is mainly a protest against what obtains in the name of education for humanity as a whole at present.

The four stages of education are schematically explained by *fig*. 14.5, the norm belonging to educational adjustment as a whole being given for comparison.

Sex Variations and Education

This Manifesto would be incomplete if it omitted to refer to the subject of sex in connection with education. Rousseau gives it separate treatment in his book *Sophie the Woman*.

To single out the traits distinguishing woman from man is a delicate matter because many men would have to be included among women, and *vice versa*. The generalizer would be blamed by both parties for the slightest partiality. Silence on the subject would be both chivalrous and wise. Such a double disapproval could at least thus be put off. But the dialectical approach need not fall into the error of partiality.

Let us start with the safe over-all statement that man and woman are equally endowed with perfect justice by Nature or God. The woman has the soul of the man she loves and the man likewise, however brave and masculine outwardly, can at times scarcely hide the woman within him. Good taste does not permit these truths to be stated blatantly, but cartoon strips do break into the conventional reserve in such matters, letting many a cat out of the bag. Jokes about married life occupy odd corners of newspapers, but the relation is never discussed seriously in public as a science. Except when armed with dialectics, this game becomes impossible to play. But dialectics here has the fullest scope for application in daily social life. Let us repeat the first law thus more completely: **Men and women enjoy equal gifts, but many men are to be treated as conforming to a woman's pattern of personality and many women as conforming to a man's pattern of personality.**

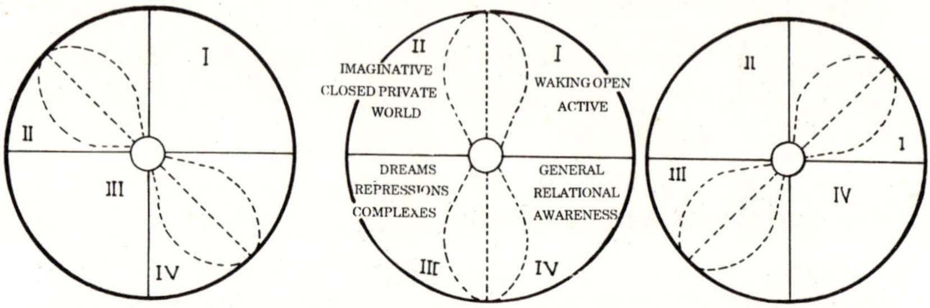

A: Girl 13-17

Maiden meditativeness and free fancy. Lack of interest in public events. Relational sensibility high. Suggestibility and easy educability.

B: Norm for both sexes

Applicable at all phases, not depending upon age.

C: Boy 13-14

Objective, active, cowboy pattern, relational sense crude. Suggestibility more an exception. Has to learn the hard way by experience or natural consequence.

fig. 14.6 : SEX VARIATIONS

Explanation of Figure 14.6 : Figures A and C give the broadest sex variations between the ages of 13 and 17. Many intermediate variations are, of course, likely to be in evidence as we actually meet boys or girls because they merge into the general context. Only the she-girl student and the he-boy student are represented here.

The second generalization which we would make is that if we take the boy and the girl at adolescence there are difference in their innate personalities which make themselves evident only to the observant educator. The girl would generally tend to conform to the **vertical negative** pattern or type and the boy to the **vertical positive**.

Taking the four phases together and confining our attention only to what interests the educator as an over-all normative picture that would hold true in all the four kinds of education, and making allowances for physical differences, the boy and the girl personalities may be said to have the same emotional or intellectual phases when qualitative or quantitative aspects are viewed globally.

Joan of Arc led an army, Hypatia taught philosophy and higher mathematics to the best Alexandrian philosophers of her time, Portia lacks no lawyer's acumen, and Elizabath was referred to as "imperial votaress", "in maiden meditation, fancy-free" by Shakespeare, and yet she could be a great ruler like Victoria. The adventures of a Hernani are balanced by those of Dona Sol. A Martha complements the gifts of a Mary. The **freak** here is hardly distinguishable from the **norm.** Taking our stand on the personality in its most synthetic sense, we are bound to say that, all in all, in terms of the content of consciousness or, educability, the sexes are to be treated as essentially the same, except that the adolescent girl is more educable that the boy.

Girls too in boarding schools are known to behave like tom-boys and worse than boys and play the role of bandits as well as men. As far as this Manifesto is concerned, it is neither interested in making a man, more a he-man or a woman more a she-woman. There are no sex differences to be encouraged in the Absolute neutrality of the Human Personality when it is correctly attached to vertical values which we conceive as the central norm for the whole of education.

Four Patterns of Behaviour with Corresponding Institutional Opportunities

If men and women have innate and outer personalities which alternate or change phases differently, if there are types which are statically fixed or dynamically flexible in endless variety, if all the varied kinds of educational opportunity or preparation for the different patterns of behaviour available for pupils are to be kept in mind, we would be obliged in education to think of an endless variety of intitutions to meet these varied requirements. If the meeting of all requirements correctly is an impossible task, as on the face of it, it really is, the same fourfold plan underlying the process could here be relied on again with advantage in simplifying the situation at least, so as to enable us to discuss the subject *grosso modo.*

We could think of a negative type of school where boys and girls, living separately, as in some of the new residential schools or retreats now attempted by some gifted educators in Switzerland. The modern Emile or Sophie could have personal co-educational attention bestowed on him or her by a Guru or Guru-couple, who would be a Rousseau or a Hypatia to them according to the laws and principles implied in the best type of education. The naturalistic school could conform to the model of some of the public schools in England, but avoiding their rough excesses, under an Arnold or a Sanderson of Oundle that Wells wrote about. The American type of high school with new features incorporated, would come near to what is desirable in the type of educational institution called pragmatic, if only the tension of horizontalism could be mitigated a little more out of respect for the vertical idealism that should finally prevail in education.

A World University of Higher Studies where the professors would be in free and daily intercourse with students, rising to the standards of the College de France or the Institute of Higher Studies of Princeton or the model of the newly started Committee of Social Thought of Chicago, would be desirable for later idealistic adjustment, when revised in the light of the indications given here. In evolving such models, the Indian soil, by its long tradition in contemplation, is a very favourable field.

Characterology and Type Psychology

Educational theory and practice are at present dominated by the important place given to brass instrument measurements.

From the time of the Alfred Binet tests of intelligence and the IQ which the modern pragmatic educator is so proud of, to the tests applied to the eidetic personality with ink-stains of Rorschach, the volume and variety of educational measurements have grown into large proportions. Psycho-biology with experiments and normative methods of enquiry that go worse than empiricism and on to Watsonian behaviourism which goes as far as denying any innate factor such as mind, are now in vogue. Gestalt-psychology brings its own contribution based on the configurations that influence learning, and what is called psychological profile is being mentioned. Psycho-analysis and evolutionary thinkers who advance the theory that "ontogeny is a repetition of phylogeny" put forward theories of the ambivalent subconscious mind, which would divide the personality into two halves or polarities at the basis of conflicts, complexes and repressions. **Extroversion** and **introversion** are spoken of, and the **cerebrotonic** and **viscerotonic** types have found a place in the general literature of modern writers, and there is a good deal of "little knowledge" in regard to many such pseudo-scientific concepts, in the mouths of ill-informed persons who rely on 'digests' for their education. Just to give a sample of the variety of theories about types in this field, we extract below the following from Dr. Claparede's *How to Diagnose the Aptitudes of School Children* (p. 233)

Binet	Subjectivists	Objectivists
Jung	Introverts	Extroverts
James	Ideologists	Positivists
Ostwald	Classicists	Romanticists
De Maday	Workers	Fighters
Nietzsche	Appollonians	Dionysians
Schiller	Sentimentals	Naifs
Poincare	Intuitives (Geometrical)	Logicians (Analytical)
Lippman	Gnostics	Technics
Pascal	Refined minded	Geometrically minded
Duhem	Abstractionists	Concretionists to

One has to be familiar with the philosophy or psychology of each of these authors to be able to see finally if we agree with their scheme or not. We shall not undertake this almost impossible task here. We do note, however, that all of them reduce types into two reciprocally conceived pairs, and that we are able to discover through their variety, a common principle running through them, based on horizontal variations of subjectivity or objectivity or variations of positive or negative states of consciousness on what we have called a vertical scale. To extract the broad outline from all these notions of type, let us content ourselves with quoting from some well-known authorities, just to make it clear that the scheme of correlation that we have systematically kept in mind throughout this Manifesto holds good in this domain of type psychology also. When types are thus unitively understood, the basis for comparing stages of adjustment in the educand and the kind of education most suited to each stage also become clear.

Jung defines the meaning of his terms 'extroversion' and 'introversion' as follows: "We should say there is extroversion wherever we find that it is to the outer world, to the object, that the individual gives his fundamental interest . . . There is introversion, on the contrary, when the objective world undergoes a kind of degradation or a lower estimation to the advantage of his own self. . . . This concentration on thought, that is to say, onto the inner world, is nothing other than introversion."[27] Quotations could be endlessly multiplied to show that the two lines of correlation could be used with validity even when we try to follow types mentioned by other writers such as Hinkle, Max Freyd, Jaspers, Kretschmer, Pende Klages, McDougall and others.

Dr. H. Wallon, who traces the neurological components of character, recognizes the principle of ambivalence which, he says, "plays in conduct the role of a stimulant or a reactive factor." He further introduces the expression "**surcompensation**" which is a factor which intervenes by its plus or minus in the behaviour of the subject.

The psycho-dynamism involved in types of educands follows the broadlines of what we have accepted as the basis of the **personal factor** even from Part I of this Manifesto. The following paragraph taken from Dr. Adolphe Ferriere's book, *Type Psychology*[28] must suffice to give us a fairly complete though somewhat imaginative picture of the dynamism involved here:

> A particular rhythm for each individual carries him at a certain time to the front, towards the future to be conquered; at other times to the rear, towards the past, with which it is necessary to conserve its contact. The future often represents effort and risk, or in any case the unknown, the past appears in general as repose and security, the known world in which one lived and which one had left. Certain pupils have the taste for taking risks and their nature tends towards progress; certain others who might be sickly or hereditarily enfeebled, or more simply speaking, gifted with a lesser vitality, remain infantile and take refuge, so to say, in the past; it is said of these pupils that they hang on to the apron strings of their mothers. The majority, however, oscillate between the two poles, the efforts for constructing the future being followed by periods of repose, where infantilism once again predominantes. This is normal. One should not be surprised provided one of these phases does not predominate too long over the other, for the effort continued too long leads to nervous strain and the breaking away from the healthy elements belonging to the past; and the infantilism that is too prolonged engenders stagnation and misoneism (fear of the new).

The psycho-dynamics of character and type, whether in its more fixed, or still flexible aspects, thus may be seen to follow the general lines of the **personal factor** that we have integrated in revalued terms so far in this Manifesto.[29]

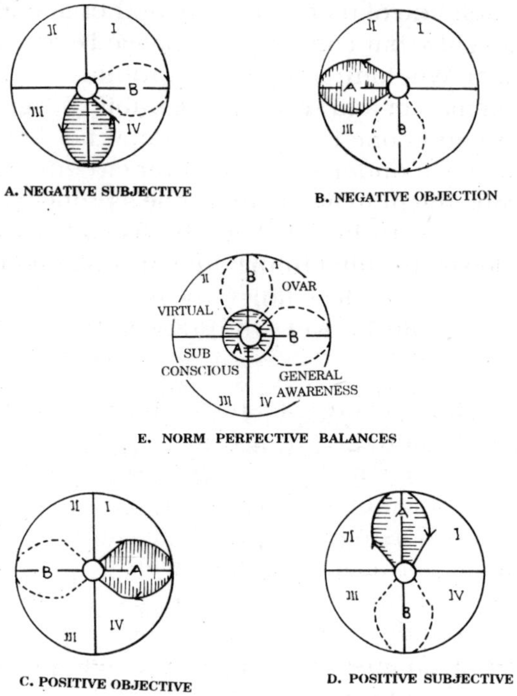

fig. 14.7

Explanation of Figure 14.7 : In each case the striped zone marked A is the dominant, while the dotted zone marked B is recessive. These are not to be confused with 'innate' or 'superficial' aspects, which have to be determined by reference to the four quadrants of I — overt, II — virtual, III — subconscious, and IV — general awareness, as marked on the central figure which represent the Norm (and in *fig.* 14.4). Figure A, the Negative-Subjective, represents innocent introverts and infantile types; Figure B, day-dreaming Calibans, Athelstanes or sleeping Kumbhakarṇas or opium eaters; figure C, extroverts, fighters, pugilists, war-mongers, desperate killers or bandit chiefs; and Figure D, contemplatives, in agony or ecstasy of oversensitivity (e.g. Keats, Amiel).

The Available Opportunities and Ready-made Patterns of Behaviour

The 'harsh otherness' of the world of objective humanity, into which each one of us has to fit, whether one likes it or not, is a fact of life that cannot be by-passed except by Absolute dialectical Wisdom. The incompatibility of husband and wife, or of master and servant, one's ability of gifts within and the occupation one is forced to adopt, not being able to be true to oneself under stress of outer circumstances, to be a monstrous misfit in life, to miss one's proper vocation, to be frustrated and to be let down by friends, to find love not responded to, to suffer from boredom, dishonour or self-pity, to be caught in restless toil — these are all due to some sort of incompatibility between the outer and the inner tendencies of life.

Young lovers enter on suicide pacts, a majority of them as has been noted, with joy on their faces, because what would unite them in death tends to separate them cruelly in actual life. Incompatibility of outside and inside is the tragedy here. Positively adjusted rich personalities are prone to this kind of tragedy, and untoward death is their normal fate. It is the penalty they pay for an over-developed aspect of the personality. Those whom the gods love, die young. Hamlet has an absolute conscience which could not live in a relativist outer world. Likewise Macbeth, Othello and King Lear had their price to pay to the tragic factor called the "harsh otherness", both within them as also outside. The choice of a right profession for a young man or woman calls for a morality based on Absolute Wisdom, which the science of dialectics alone gives. All else is fraught with great fear, as the *Bhagavad Gītā* would put it.

Even when we have been quite right with the educand in giving him due importance and respecting all his interests as they unfold in him, there remains the problem of fitting him into the mould available to him in the actual world. Actuality is rigid and cannot be changed overnight. Take it or leave it is the condition prevailing in the world of opportunities for good life. The dreamy contemplative must pay his rent or coal bills in time in a cold country, if he is to survive even one winter, and in warmer climes, the choice of employment, though not so rigid, is there with a general economic drought which one has to survive as an honourable human. Poverty and indolence are the enemies here. As a result, much laziness and hypocrisy passes for holiness in India, though in the name of contemplation, much is worth saving in spite of all. Climate again can kill contemplation both by favour as by cruelty.

Society is not so simple as it used to be, and the range of professions with their exactingly precise requirements, involving being 'laid off', retrenched or 'fired' at short notice, is ever staring in the face of young job-hunters, who have to go from one bureau of employment to another in mad competitive haste, which is enough to stifle all quieter, contemplative attitudes in them. Rules and paper formalities are on the increase, and civilization may be seen to be at the brink of some precipice. Wrought with fear and mistrust, interested propaganda, prevailing suspicion, with spy hunting, the electric chair for not keeping one's own secrets, besides frontier, passport and paper difficulties preventing man from living simply, the problems that education may soon have to solve, may become too much for us. Before a young man actually appears for an interview for a job, the whole complexion of a chance might change in such a way as to defeat the best efforts of a decade. As Rousseau puts it graphically, it is not enough for an artist to be expert with his brush; he has to take a cab and go from door to door before he could be a success through his vocation as a painter. Education as a preparation for life is fraught more and more with uncertainties, and what was preparation a month ago, might go against the person one month later.

If wisdom of a higher order is to help us even here, let us listen again to the voice of contemplation, though it is a voice lost in the wilderness, and still 'small' in character. The noisy world cannot be tranquil enough to listen to it, but it is yet there for us to hearken unto.

The High and the Low Roads

Rousseau's *Emile* stopped abruptly with the happy marriage of Emile and Sophie, but Rousseau had reserved the tragic aspects of the story for continuation in the novel he began but never completed, called *Emile and Sophie* or *The Solitary Ones*. Their natures separate them, and Emile has to wander about seeking jobs in various places. The solitary wanderings are full of suffering, whose counterpart was also in Sophie, who suffered because of her infidelity. Rousseau makes Emile earn a living by the very honest trade that he once apprenticed him for and, instead of widening the tragedy, Rousseau's idea in the projected novel was to reunite them, reconciled with happy reminiscence of their early love, once again, after years of cruel separation. The life tendencies which became horizontalised through the agency of the 'harsh otherness' of actuality, is vanquished and won over in their model cases, by the triumph of the tender, unitive, reconciliating way of Wisdom. Rousseau here wants to indicate that contemplation can triumph, given human **understanding in the light of dialectical wisdom**.

Wisdom is the foster-mother who consoles Boethius desponding in prison. This foster-mother called contemplative wisdom is still waiting for humanity to look up to her face, to hear the words of consolation. She can still speak to humanity if it would only listen.

In the interests of the world's proletariat, the commercial class, the daring conqueror of space and the seeker after contemplative quite, there are still legitimate opportunities for life expression. For each one of them there is a pattern of behaviour that would fit, if only contemplation could be brought to bear on the chaotic world situation.

Conclusion

Rousseau called himself "Citizen of Geneva" while he conformed to a quiet contemplative pattern of behaviour rather than to one of a man of action. The *Bhagavad Gītā* holds up before us these two patterns of behaviour as counterparts in the Kṛṣṇa who is the *Yōgeśvara* (Lord of *Yoga*) and in the Arjuna of the last verse where he is portrayed beside Kṛṣṇa bearing the bow and arrow. In our days, contemplation itself has to be revalued and restated more unitively. Wisdom, which is the highest human value, need not support mere quietism, nor should it be expected to counter the menace of the atom bomb by a frontal attack. The truth that shall make us free is lodged in the human heart, and sound education has to bring it into open life expression. This calls for a supreme white heat of wholehearted earnestness within each, which should be reflected with similar intensity in the soul of humanity.

The "Citizen of Geneva" must be a "Citizen of the World" and one and the same personality must combine the possibilities in behaviour of a *gendarme* and a quiet contemplative. Arjuna was given the alternative but whether he chose it or not is not stated. Emile and Sophie were tearfully reconciled, but no more of the story has been written.

The suicide pact of youthful lovers is the way that romance reaches tragic levels, which still indicates the starting point of Absolutism, where no consideration is greater. God, referred to as the fifth factor above the four factors in the *Gītā* (XVIII.14), these being the Basis (*adhiṣṭhānam*), the Actor (*kartā*), the Instruments (*karaṇam*) and varied Possibilities of Action (*prithagvidham-vividhas-ceṣṭāḥ*) has Himself to be included on revised and revalued terms, with a fully scientific status given to Him without which all our calculations must go wrong. A scientifically conceived God ought to be acceptable even to so-called 'materialists' and 'atheists', and if not, so much the worse for them! Pervert orthodoxy may likewise be ignored.

Rousseau was obsessed by the thought of his enemies who would slander him even after his death, and Kṛṣṇa, in many parts of the *Gītā*, complains of the disadoption and mistrust of his high teaching. The views set forth in this Manifesto, we feel, may be considered too good to be true. Humanity, who must have profited by the sacrifices of great souls like Socrates, Jesus, Joan of Arc and Hypatia, may be expected to have become more sobered now in this matter of throwing stones or slinging mud. With all its faults or imperfections, this Manifesto thus goes out to serve at least as a basis for the discussion, if not for the revision on drastic lines, of World Education.

—

Notes

1. p. 2, *Educational Abstracts*, Sept. 1956, Vol. VIII, No. 7.
2. p. 166, *L'Evolution Creative*, Payot, Paris.
3. *Śāṅkara Bhāṣya*, II.10.
4. ***See also*** the commentary on the *Bhagavad Gītā* by the present author.
5. ***see*** *Gītā*, XVI.16, 21.
6. For a complete and correct exposition of 'The Personal Factor in Educative Process', see the work so entitled, submitted as a thesis at the Sorbonne by the present writer in 1933, which was very honourably mentioned by the syndicate of the University.
7. *Emile*, Book I.
8. *Ibid.*
9. *Ibid.*, Book IV.
10. *Ibid.*, Book V.
11. *L'Evolution, Creative*, p. 109.
12. 3rd Edition, London, p. 486.
13. Vrin, Paris, 1933.
14. *How We Think*, Heath, New York, p. 79.
15. *Essay on Passions*, Alcan, Paris, 1923, p. 179.
16. *Emile*, Book I.
17. Cf. *Les Character et l' Education Morale*: Queyrat, Paris, pp. 122-25.
18. E.g. Achelle-Delmas and Marcel Boll, in their work with this title, Paris, 1922.
19. **See**, *Man the Unknown*, by Dr. Alexis Carrel.
20. **See**, *Listener*, London, Nov. 29, 1956.
21. **See** article on 'Theory of Knowledge' in *Encyclopaedia Brittanica.*
22. *The Sources of a Science of Education*, New York, 1929, pp. 67-68.
23. *Le Facteur Personal dans le Processus Educative*, Vrin Paris, 1932.
24. In the old edition of *Emile.*
25. *School and Society*, University of Chicago Press, p. 3.
26. *Ibid*, p. 15.
27. Cf. Claparede, p. 232.
28. p. 30, Geneva.
29. For fuller justification of this claim see the main work on the subject by the present writer, already cited .

Part IV

Religion and Ethics

15

One Religion

WHEN people are seen to be bound together by common articles of faith or by patterns of behaviour in group life, we recognize what we call religion, to which the belief and the behaviour belong together. To give an example, if some people go to church on Sundays, while others do not do so but prefer to go to their churches on Saturday, we are at once able to say that there is some difference in their religious behaviour. We could question them after observing this difference, to find if there are other specific characteristics by which we could classify their adherence to one or other various religious groups. We have no right to attribute to them characteristics that are neither observed in their behaviour nor known to form a body of beliefs belonging to such a group. Thus, Trinitarians will tell you that they believe in three aspects of divine manifestation. Unitarians will deny that, but would prefer to represent themselves as believing only in one aspect of divinity. We would be perfectly justified in not mixing these sects, and in treating them as belonging to distinct religious groupings.

One has either to be objective or subjective in fixing the specific characteristics of any religious expression. If one should say, "I beileve in Christ, but I neither go to church nor behave in any way which is in conformity with this belief", we cannot classify him at all. We can at best recognize in him a pseudo-religionist.

Classification of Religious Groups

Keeping in mind this method of diagnosing and classifying visible religious formations or believers in doctrines about some spiritual value dear to each religion, if we should look round and try to recognize the religious groups in this world, we could at once make the most striking of classifications of all religious people into two broad groups. There is no religion which does not offer some consolation or happiness to its followers. In other words, unhappiness cannot be held out as an ideal or end to be attained by any religion at all. Nobody aspires for unhappiness. It is impossible to think of such a negative value as motivating any serious group of religionists. We could of course find freaks who might insist on saying that they are aspiring for unhappiness. If we should admit happiness to be the common ideal or end in view motivating any religion whatsoever, it would only be deriving a corollary from this general statement to say that every religion has got some high human value on which it pins its faith. The Buddhist speaks in terms of *nirvāṇa*, and the Christian in terms of a life eternal where one could be as perfect as the Father in heaven is perfect. Hindu salvation consists of escaping rebirth altogether, and the true believer in Islam wants to obey the will of Allah, the Most High, so that on the Day of Judgment Allah should be pleased with him instead of being angry. Jehovah and Jupiter or Zeus are also Most High Gods of other prophetic religions. The Prophetic religions are those that are concerned with an event in the future called the Day of Judgment, on which they have to face God and give a good account of themselves. There are religions which have got this apocalyptic touch more pronounced than others.

When this futuristic orientation is weak, we begin to recognize certain religious formations whose unity lies in merely following past habits and conventions. Members of such groups are often referred to as 'pagans' or 'un-believers', fit to be treated contemptuously by the groups who claim to be true believers.

Thus, we begin to recognize in religious life two dominant groups: those who believe in the Day of Judgment, and those who do not give importance to that event in the future. These are characterized by the terms 'prophetic' and 'pagan' respectively.

Further Differentiations

After making this initial distinction between prophetic and non-prophetic or pagan religions, we could examine other items of belief or patterns of behaviour as implying some value conducive to the happiness of the group in question. Viewed in this way, we could distinguish other so-called pagans who do not believe in a God representing the side of light or intelligence, but who tend to substitute material objects or elementals in the place of the highest of intelligent principles. They go under the name of animists or materialists. The Ionian and Eleatic philosophers of pre-Socratic times belong to such a group. Pythagoras himself was not recognized by Athenians, and was treated contemptuously because of his glorification of mere mathematical entities or values. There were also those who were nearer to the side of matter than to the side of the spirit, who were classified philosophically as hylozoists. The values that they attached importance to in regulating their lives were not spiritual entities at all, but tended to glorify matter as against spirit. From Thales through Heraclitus to Empedocles of Agrigentum, we have a whole hierarchy of such animists or hylozoists who were essentially materialists, and who are thus to be ranged on the opposite side of what was respectable in the eyes of philosophers such as Plato and Aristotle. Thomism and Augustinianism had their origins in Dionysius the Areopagite, as also in Plotinus of the Alexandrian Neo-Platonist context. Abraham, the common ancestor of Christianity and Islam, laid down that idolatry was completely reprehensible — even as bad as stealing or murder. Hindus would certainly stand condemned completely in the light of such an uncompromisingly prophetic attitude. Unbelievers could be trampled under elephants' feet in the eyes of the teaching of the *Quran* understood in such a light. Many events in the history of India could be cited as examples of this kind of one-sided fervour. Hinduism, however, is not without its insistence on a God representing light or wisdom rather than the forces of darkness.

Scepticism and Belief

Now, if we turn our eyes in the opposite direction and see what the scientific attitude has meant in the realm of religious belief, we can easily concede that there have been many martyrs on the side of scepticism, as well as on that of belief. Giordano Bruno and Galileo Galilei were martyrs to science as against the early Christians persecuted by Romans, who were martyrs to belief. If it is possible for martyrdom to exist on both the sides of scepticism and belief, we can easily see how they form a part of a human nature which accommodates them both together in accentuated forms in the same phenotype called *homo sapiens*.

Buddhism is a religion which is essentially not theological, but this does not mean that rational or ethical values are not glorified and held up as absolute values, as dear to the believers in them as any other theological divinity could be. In other words, it is a high value conducive to happiness that is to be found within the essential content of any religion, whether theological or rational.

Each religion wants to avoid suffering and to promise happiness through some belief or behaviour. Seen from this perspective, even communism could be said to be a religion, or at least a surrogate of religion — only it promises, instead of heaven, a classless society or a dictatorship of the proletariat. It is possible in this way to compare all religions whether known as sceptic, rational, or as based on a belief in God.

All religions must have a norm in which an absolute value is held up as the most important one within its system of reference. If this structural norm common to all religions, whether orthodox or heterodox, could be visualized in a true scientific spirit of open and objective criticism, it would be possible for us to establish a comparative study of all expressions involving a high value to which both sceptics and believers might happen to be equally attached. Religion would thus include all possible surrogates of religion, and even what passes for scepticism (which, as we have seen, claims its own martyrs). Scepticism is a form of negative belief which can be as intensely fanatic as any other so-called belief, which mere label should not mislead us. There are believers who pass for sceptics, and *vice versa*.

Underlying Structural Unity

When we are able to take a normalized position between the extremes of the two major tendencies which the *Bhagavad Gītā* calls the black and the white courses, distinguishing the two rival paths in spiritual progress throughout the long course of human history, we shall be able to see that every religion has at its core a promised value for which one avoids what is taboo and adopts what is recommended. What is profane in one religion need not correspond to what is taboo in another. To a Mohammedan eating pork is taboo, but to a Sikh it can be a qualification of some sort at least. Long hair is likewise laudable for a Sikh to wear, while shaving one's head is orthodox to the other of the two rival faiths, historically developing like bodies and antibodies in bacteriology. The same historical conditions can produce both the body and the antibody. Accentuating one tendency can result in sowing the seeds of another. Thus, idolatrous and iconoclastic tendencies add vim and vigour to each other, and fan feuds by ambivalent exaggerations when overstressed.

What we wish to achieve by these varied examples is merely to point to a way in religious life which avoids unilateral exaggerations or excesses. Pontius Pilate said, "What is Truth?" Truth is not even a two-sided affair, but its polyvalence conforms to at least a four-dimensional quaternian structural pattern. All religions have premonitions of this verity distinguishable in one passage or another of their revealed or sacred books, which could be brought into view through the study of comparative religions. Modern science has brought us to the same structural pattern seen in terms of the four-dimensional universe which is at present being accepted from the side of physics. Even from the side of metaphysics, the same fourfold structural pattern prevails. A normative Integrated Science of the Absolute can alone fully reveal the common structural features underlying all religions, so that the believer in one religious formation could see eye to eye with his rival in the opposite camp, even as the blind men in the fable could reach agreement only when they could examine the totality of the elephant about which each of them had known only some particular aspect.

It is the total structure of the absolute value of Happiness implied in all religions — at least in structural outline — that can save the situation, avoiding by such Unitive Understanding all conflicts in the name of a high spiritual value representing the common aspirations of all human beings, however different they might be in temperament.

Viewed in this light, humanity can belong to only **one religion**, which is that of **Absolute Happiness through an absolutist way of life**. When the underlying unity of all religions is thus made evident to all intelligent men, holy wars will become outmoded as not in keeping with the dignity of the human race, which biology itself qualifies as being endowed with understanding by the term *homo sapiens*.

16

Ethics Normalized

ETHICS concerns good behaviour. Beside oneself, there is the other man who is also involved in the same picture. One is asked to be good to oneself and to somebody else at one and the same time. This is the dialectical basis of all ethics. Sometimes this other man or woman involved in one's ethics could be a father, a mother or a wife, or all of humanity treated as brothers in the eye of God. One is called upon to behave rightly towards his religion, or even towards the state treated as a personification either legal, moral or spiritual according to the intensity or seriousness of the relationship within a utilitarian or idealistic frame of reference. The welfare state calls for its own particular code of ethics or morals, while monarchical loyalties could attain to fanatic fervour.

To bring this subject into the scope of a universal and most generalized outlook from a global standpoint, **the first desideratum** of good ethics would be the breaking through of parochial or closed, cribbed and confined limitations or stultifying frontiers which, through egocentricity, persons or groups of persons are likely to create between themselves and the other man whom we have tried to distinguish above.

Duality in interests between oneself and the other man is the fecund cause of all violations of ethics. Good ethics therefore consists in a way of life in which oneself and the other man, thus understood as dialectical counterparts, are made to belong together to a unified or unitive context in such a way that conflict between them would become impossible. It is a unilateral or horizontal treatment of counterparts that can spell disasters big or small in life, thus tending to shock rudely the norm of all ethics, which is the Absolute Self, common to the two abstracted and generalized personalities to be first distinguished for any systematic principles of ethics to be developed in the interests of both of them at once. In other words, unilateral ethics spells disaster, and unitive ethics is the only ethics worth the name.

A mother tells her child to be good, but the child cannot visualize clearly what the mother means by 'good'. In the church, the mother herself hears the same talk of goodness that she cannot understand either, with the added prospect of going to heaven dangling before her eyes. Torrents of human tears have drenched the soil from the eyes of children both at home and in the classroom, as well as in the Sunday school, for which no one is responsible—especially not the child. The responsibility is rather to be located with the large number of ethical theories presented to a confused humanity ever since such a subject began to be formulated in various textbooks of the world.

We learn in college textbooks of Platonic, Nichomachean, Machiavellian and Utilitarian ethical principles, to name but a few, having notions such as "the greatest good of the greatest number" or freedom as motivating ideals. The "Golden Mean" of Aristotle is a vertical way of life recommended by him. In the world of political ethics, we have a galaxy of other names from Hobbes and Rousseau to Tolstoy, Emerson and Gandhi. The textbooks of ethics such as that of Sedgewick are increasing in size regularly, and new chairs for Ethics and Religion are being instituted in universities the world over. The ramifications into which this subject has now expanded have become so great that college student is unable to answer the simplest basic questions on such an important subject touching the welfare of humanity. This is due to the endless compartmentalization and specialization of disciplines prevalent today, stressing the varieties of a subject rather than its unitive aspects.

India has got here again a vast store-house of wisdom that could help toward the reintegration of such value-based objects as ethics, aesthetics and education. Economics is also of the same group of subjects concerned directly with human values. Sanskrit literature contains valuable hints on how to treat these apparently different academic disciplines under the aegis of one integrating Science of all sciences, having human life significance in the most general of terms.

The Normative Notion

Ethics has to have a normative reference in the Self of man. Take away the Self from the total ground of ethics, and what could be imagined as the end result of Ethics would at once evaporate and disappear. The benefits of ethics must necessarily have a beneficiary. Putting these two sides together is the secret of the unitive contemplative approach to ethics, so well-known to the Upaniṣadic *ṛṣis* (seers). As Yājñavalkya puts it in the famous passage from the *Bṛhadāraṇyaka Upaniṣad*, "It is not for the sake of the wife that the wife is dear, but for the sake of the self that she is dear" — and so in every case where two counterparts, one belonging to the self and the other belonging to the non-self, are involved. These two sides have to be properly distinguished as the two sides of a reversible equation involved together in the same context of the Absolute Self. To recognize the counterparts properly and to treat them as interacting unitively without horizontal interests creating conflicts is the way of correct ethics, to whatever department it might happen to relate, public or domestic.

What is good for oneself has also to be good for the other man: this is the basic formula to be followed in all ethics, when boiled down to its basic elements. Narayana Guru has put his finger correctly on some of these ethical principles, viewed in terms of such a bipolar dialectical dynamism, in some of the verses of his *Ātmopadeśa Śatakam*, by quoting which we shall have said what is basically necessary in respect of this very important subject. Such an approach might not seem to have academic dignity, but it surely brings us nearer to a clear view of the problems involved in the subject.

> Interestedness is but of one kind, but puzzlement
> Prevails variously with regard to objects of interest, such as
> What is dear to me, what is dear to you and what is dear to another;
> What is dear to oneself, do realize to be dear to another too
>
> (v. 21)

> The other man's interest, that is even mine; what to oneself
> Is beneficial is so for the other man also; such is the course of
> Discrete conduct. All acts aiming each man's Self-happiness
> Must spell at once the happiness of the other fellow-man.
>
> (v. 22)

> For the sake of fellow-man, unceasing, day and night,
> Unstinting strives a kindly man;
> The niggard, lying prone, what frustration's toil undertakes,
> That is for his own sake alone.
>
> (v. 23)

> What here we view as this man or that,
> Reflection reveals to be the Self's prime form;
> That conduct adopted for one's Self-happiness,
> Another's happiness must also secure at once.
>
> (v. 24)

> What spells beneift to one, while to another disaster brings,
> Such conduct is one that violates the Self; beware!
> Those who cause intense grief to another,
> Into inferno's ocean they fall, there to burn in flames.
>
> (v. 25)

Ethics is not to be conceived as depending on the conduct of a good man taken by himself; it is to be understood as a double-edged situation cutting both ways. It has to be conceived not as a lame or one-sided affair, but as a process in which donor and beneficiary belong to a unitive and universal context. Violation of the unitive Self-hood on the one side is equated here (v. 25) with its dialectical counterpart of a general fire of inferno, for which the spark of pain given to a single individual could be the partial stimulus to create a wholesale reaction. Just as intense pain on the tip of one's toe would suffice to upset the balance of the whole person in suffering, so the subtle reciprocity implied here, when the slightest discrimination is made between favourites and enemies, brings unforeseen quantitative or qualitative effects. Consequences flare up into a general conflagration. The sum total of human suffering consists of small sparks of partiality by men somewhere or other at one time or another. The general cause of war should be thought of in this way. Like one spark setting fire to the neighbouring faggot, the continuity of the process of evil effects is to be imagined as operating ceaslessly in the world of human relations. Clashes of clan, time-old feuds, racial, national or other rivalries and preferential pacts, all work together to keep the flames of inferno constantly fed with fuel, and burning incessantly.

When the dualistic attitude has once been abolished and generosity spreads evenly like sunlight without distinction on all human beings, even on the publican and the sinner, that kind of generosity belongs to the context of the absolutist way of life and is one that, in the context of Self-realization, is very important to keep in mind. The self can itself become the worst enemy of the self. This has been brought out with the full force of delicate dialectics in the *Bhagavad Gītā* (VI.6).

In short, one has to learn to live and let live, and to be more concerned in the happiness of the other fellow man, without imposing false frontiers or artificial barriers between man and fellow man. A dynamic, generous and open attitude is to be recommended if frontiers are to be abolished as they must be, and we are to be correctly dedicated to the cause of peace.

Part V

Unified Science

17

Integration of all Sciences

THE need for integrating the vast body of knowledge that men have been able to accumulate into a coherent whole is a subject that has begun to engage the serious attention of educators. Practical aspects of knowledge are now being stressed at the expense of the purer branches. Advanced studies now refer mostly to technological subjects. The universities turn out more and more experts or specialists. As a result, those aspects of higher knowledge which were covered by the term 'humanities' have been by-passed and left behind.

Except in a few places such as the College de France, the Institute for Advanced Studies of Princeton, or perhaps also in the recently started Committee on Social Thought under the University of Chicago, attempts at any serious integration of courses seem inadequate and negligible.

There is however at the present time, a growing feeling for a fresh synthesis of knowledge, so that the sterility of over-departmentalization and consequent lack of the human touch in education may be effectively stemmed. Specialization at least must not be for its own sake, but must serve some tangible end to produce a better-educated man.

Besides the UNESCO which may be looked upon as an expression of the desire for a revised impetus to culture and science on a world-wide scale, there are at present many private foundations both in the East and the West standing for the same ideal. They adhere to varied programmes, some being overtly scientific and others relying more on esoteric cultural values. A particular cosmology or a tacit dogmatic theology can be seen to be implied in many of them. Even the theory of evolution itself is being treated by some of them as an article of faith. They often become thus open to the objection that they tend to be dogmatic, sentimental or religiously pre-disposed. They would fall short of the requirement that any modern attempt at an integration of knowledge should be conceived on more positive or scientific lines.

No Common Intellectual Formation

Although senior professors of univerisites who may be in charge of admission of students for the higher courses may be heard to refer to what they call 'intellectual formation' as a necessary prerequisite for following a certain specialized course, this expression remains still a very vague one. What precisely the expression is intended to convey may not be clear even as between one professor of a certain department and another, who might belong to the same university. The expression as applied to inter-university standards generally becomes still more vague, because cultural backgrounds differ widely, not only between univerisities of the Old and the New Worlds, but even between universities of the same continent or even country.

Eastern and Western cultural standards may be said still to lie poles apart. German universities have each an academic reputation and tradition all their own, and certain universities specialize only in select branches. Even in England, an Oxonian is expected to have a formation different from that of a graduate of Cambridge. In France, although the situation has been somewhat mitigated by the existence of the centuries old foundation of the College de France, the 'intellectual formation' demanded by a certain professor even in the department of letters, may differ from the one required by another.

In India, which has no university tradition to call its own, but tries to graft Oriental culture on to the stem of Occidental classical tradition, the case for a preliminary intellectual formation for higher studies is in a sad state indeed. The influence, in itself not salubrious, of the non-idealistic and pragmatic tendency of the United States, that prevails in the cultural world, as in many other departments of life at the present-day, is tending further to lower standards in cultural education. Measurement is being given primacy, and everything that does not lend itself to a brass or electronic instrument experimentation or testing, is tending to be discredited.

This influence, which is itself enough to dampen intellectual and moral enthusiasm for culture, works hand in hand at the present-day with that other tendency to be noticed in India, which gives primacy to localized cultural values. Linguistic preferences in the name of a pseudo-nationalism which encourage parochial loyalties and closed orthodoxies of different shades, are being allowed to compromise more or less completely the cause of an open and universal outlook in favour of any integrated education worth the name. In this connection it has been interesting to note that a group of Indian university vice-chancellors have recently been touring the United States of America seeking a formula for integrated education. From the report of their impressions, it would appear that nothing striking was discovered for adoption in India. In the United States themselves, we find a dissatisfaction which is expressing itself in the form of sporadic revolt by youth.

Unitive Approach Needed

Whether we are concerned with 'basic' or 'fundamental' education for the emancipation, social or cultural, of the masses of the world, or think in terms of higher cultural values of an idealistic non-utilitarian programme in education for the select few, it is highly necessary at the present time to visualize the scope and methods of integrated education more clearly than hitherto. We have to be able to think of common human values in the global context of one solid humanity.

There should no longer be cultural preserves or prerogatives which try to divide humanity into sheep or goats. The myth of the primitive or inferior man has to be abandoned. The orthodox and heterodox, the conservative and the liberal, the rightist and the leftist, must be able to meet in the endeavour to preserve the best human heritage that belongs to all. A common cultural language which would enable these precious values to be referred to, irrespective of linguistic or traditional barriers, has to be evolved. Such a mathematically precise language would pave the way for the formulation of a regular science. Values preserved through humanistic studies could then be effectively cultivated without the arbitrary and sentimental barriers that history or geography might interpose between people. An open, dynamic and positive scientific attitude must invade the closed, static and private preserves in which higher human values have hitherto remained enclosed.

In other words, the challenge involved here is to bring back the humanities and human values involved therein, into line with the other scientific values which, for no just reason, have in recent years tended to be considered as if divorced or disjunct from the former.

The Science of Sciences

In the days of Aristotle all wisdom disciplines were more unitively understood than at the present-day. The term 'science' covered equally the whole range of subjects, starting from physics and natural history (or, rather, natural philosophy), to metaphysics, ethics, economics and politics. The Doctrine of the Mean which was Aristotle's contribution to thought, was a subtle underlying unitive principle which strung together branches of knowledge that have now come to be considered as different or disjunct from one another.

From the time when writers like Mill began to arrange cultural or economic notions on a less idealistic and more 'utilitarian' basis, the firm hand of classical unitive thinking based on such bold dicta as "It is in ourselves that we are thus or thus", and the singleness of human end or purpose in life, gave way to the hesitant and wavering attitude implied in such expressions as "Not expecting more from life than it is capable of bestowing". Unitive values began to be confused with non-unitive ones. The right regulative or normative principle that related ends with means through deliberation, began to be compromised. Horizontal or "here-and-now" values of an ontological nature were stressed at the expense of idealistic, teleological or vertical ones. The intuitive understanding of the Doctrine of the Mean was lost for ever, and thus cultural enthusiasm began to flag.

If we could again think of science as including both moral and physical sciences, the task of finding a basis for integrated education could be more easily accomplished. Knowledge can direct its search outward from the seat of the mind or soul within us. The "eye of the soul", to use Aristotle's expression, can look 'positively' and 'objectively' into the world of the 'knowables' or subjectively or introspectively into values or virtues within the personality of man.

The latter has been known as the negative way which, by the eye of the soul directed inwardly, can still conduct 'auto-experimentation' by comparing common human experience of the *a priori* order. While the positive sciences are *a posteriori* and actually objective, this negative science could still be 'objective' in discipline in a virtual or conceptual sense. The strictness of scientific exactitude in thinking need not necessarily suffer in the latter case. When proper terms have been fixed to refer to aspects of knowledge, the whole range of knowledge can be made to come under one science which could be called the Science of sciences. In fact this is what the Science of the Absolute (or *brahma-vidyā* as such is called in India) claims to be. 'Knowledge' (*jñānam*) and "the knowable" (*jñeyam*) are here to be distinguished, the first as negative and the second as positive. An epistemology and methodology based on a correct contemplative scale of values is here implied.

Descending Dialectics

Some recent attempts at integration of knowledge have proceeded from the variety of specialized analytic knowledge towards their synthesis. Thus there is the famous instance in which the top-ranking nuclear physicist Schroedinger makes a serious attempt to relate biology with chemistry and physics. In his booklet entitled *What is Life?* an attempt has been made to bridge the gap between inanimate and living matter. Later writers such as Andrew A Cochran* have availed themselves of the quantum theory to establish a link between life and matter. Such attempts may be said to travel from the positive and overt aspects of reality towards the innate and subtle aspects, or from the positive pole to the negative.

Distinct Value Worlds

Even while we speak in terms of poles, we have to distinguish two sets of poles as belonging to two distinct aspects of values or interests in life.

Reality, it must be remembered, is to be studied for the human interest in it rather than just for its own sake without reference to human interests or values. All attempts at integration are for man, and not for knowledge itself. When we visualize the world of values correctly, we will be able to see a vertical series of values in which the positive pole is the world of pure reason or that of the Platonic Intelligibles. The negative pole of vertical values will be in the **prime means** to the **supreme end** of attaining to the world of the Intelligibles when understood unitively and synthetically. Thus there is a vertical world of pure values, and a horizontal world of material values.

---

*Mr. Cochran writes a very interesting and well-documented article on "The Quantum Physical Basis of Life", postulating a basic hylozoism with the 'wave' phenomena as the conscious aspect of matter, in the May 1957 issue of *Main Currents in Modern Thought* (Journal of the Foundation for Integrated Education). Mr. Cochran is attached to the US. Bureau of Mines.

The building up of a cultural life in a person means the recognition of both these sets, while the Doctrine of the Mean must constantly convert knowledge in favour of virtues. As we have elsewhere tried to devlop it is possible to bring Gold, Goodness and God to be comprised within the amplitude of a personal scale of values between the poles of which the life of man may be said to oscillate. The science of things taken in themselves, and considered without their fundamental value-import for man, is like to magnetic field secondary to the main current along which life flows. This latter may be said to be along the vertical axis of pure deliberative values, by means of which man decides to affiliate himself to a good life. Actual physical life is of the nature merely of an epiphenomenon to the real life interests normal and legitimate to man as Man.

The Key to Integration

It is a recognized fact tacitly understood already in the East as well as in the West, that man himself is the subject of proper study. *Ātmavidyā* (Self-knowledge) in India has been treated as the same as *Brahma-vidyā* (Wisdom of the Absolute). *Ānanda* (Happiness) as a Supreme End or Value in life, has also been treated as, in effect, the same as the Self or the Absolute. Thus the key for integration of knowledge of wisdom is to be found in the human personality itself, where the subtlest aspects of wisdom find a natural home. The Self is the most precious of values for man, and the *mahāvākyas* (Great Dicta) such as "Thou art That" signify this supreme point of culmination of all integrated wisdom.

With such as the target before them, it is encouraging to note even physicists like Schroedinger have made some first efforts to bring these divergent aspects of human knowledge into integrated relationship. A contemplative Science of the Absolute conceived in terms of Self-knowledge could include the **Chief End** or the **Final Good** on the one hand, and the negative or prime counterparts of the same in actual life, within the range of an integrated Science of sciences combining ontological and teleological values. Aristotle's Doctrine of the Mean could then be understood in terms of *sāmya* (sameness) which is the central doctrine of such Eastern texts as the *Bhagavad Gītā*.

When both are properly grasped without prejudice, culture would tend to be integrated and understood in unitive and universal terms.

18

Integration of Elements of Thought in view of a Language of Unified Science

Division I : Observational

THIS study is devoted to explore the possibility of a scientific language. To think of the whole range of science as one integrated unity is itself a task that has engaged great minds from antiquity to recent times, without much definitive result. The approach so far has been more speculative than scientific in its full sense. A language that would have such character as to serve effectively as a common basis for the whole range of sciences, experimental or normative, physical or 'metaphysical', as we ought to understand by the term "Unified Science", is not easy to conceive. Of all the names of thinkers of old who had the ambition of accomplishing this impossible-seeming task, that of Leibniz stands out as that of one who came nearest to laying the philosophical, logical and mathematical foundations of a "universal language".[1] This was to counteract the confusion of vernacular tongues.

Even he did not live to see the great ambition of his youthful days accomplished.

In spite of the apparent difficulty and enormity of the task, it is our contention in this study that a simple approach is still possible along the lines that Leibniz indicated. Here we are thinking in terms of normalization and 're-normalization' of what constitutes a 'unitive' approach to linguistic activity understood in the context to which it has properly to belong.

A scientific language that is all ready-made for use is not our aim in this study nor even a scheme that has been worked out in detail to be considered as a blue-print for a universal language that could be adopted without further pains. This study is merely a contribution to a more fruitful discussion of this subject on which there is much interest shown both by qualified and unqualified persons. Over-speculative unscientific and pseudo-scientific attitudes in this alluring field have to be discountenanced.

A scientific language, in order to be truly so, must, firstly, be one that itself can claim scientific validity. It must not disrespect the requirements of a correct epistemology and methodology. Both science and philosophy seek truth behind appearance: both aim at serving humanity by the serious pursuit of worthwhile interests. What gives unity to science in this inclusive sense is the common human purpose that runs through its methodology, epistemology and axiology. Language lives and moves in that axis which is concerned with reasoning which links visible realities with the rational, intelligible or the calculable, or what lies beyond its scope, understood by such terms as the 'Absolute'. Although the absolutist way of thinking does not at present enjoy much recognition by strict scientific thinkers, an expression that has necessarily to depend on this notion is taking a large place in recent scientific literature, viz., **Relativity**. Side-by-side with those who denounce 'metaphysics' whatever they understand by it as 'non-sense', opposite trends are also becoming more and more evident.[2]

Secondly, a scientific language must be suitable for communicating to others whether scientists or common men, truthful information about the problems, methods and results of valid and precise knowledge of the required degree of certitude. It should not itself tend to become a closed and static jargon understood only by specialists of the same group. A certain public character and openness tend to make ordinary language more scientific. Universal communicability across geographic and linguistic frontiers is a necessary condition that should distinguish scientific language.

Thirdly, scientific language cannot afford to be merely a symbolic language of logical or mathematical abstractions. Unilaterally applied symbolism makes language a puzzle to solve as in the schoolboy riddle of *A* being the brother of *B* but *B* not being so. The fact that *A* and *B* are of two sexes is not revealed by symbolism as directly as in common language. The 'meta-language' that some propose for a scientific language has innate defects of this kind. We shall examine the case of symbolic logic in this connection.. Here we indicate in advance that as when we name an object and call a spade a 'spade' there must be two sides that must come together and fuse before meaning can emerge. The actual thing determined by its properties like form and its name which is a conceptual factor, come together to result in a meaningful event in consciousness. The elements of a symbolic meta-language have to be put in relationship with what we could with equal justice call a proto-language with validity and legitimacy to result in a naturally meaningful language. The apodictic or other certitude on which scientific language has to be dependent, could result only when name meets form.

The three desiderata of a scientific language are thus that it should be a language **of** science, **for** science and **through** science.

Broad Aspects of Thought and Corresponding Language

Language tallies with thought and the requirements of thinking or reasoning in turn determine the nature of any language. Science and philosophy have much common ground between them. Instead of scientists trying in vain to banish metaphysics as non-sense and philosophers excluding the matter-of-fact and considering science with mistrust, the language of unified science must try and adapt itself to the requirements of science and philosophy. There could be scientific philosophy as well as philosophical science just as there could be psycho-physics and physiological psychology. All science being an experimental discipline must have much of the matter-of-fact entering into its composition, while its inductive aspects may be said to be more philosophical in character. Thus we could think serially of three kinds of subject-matter comprised within what is scientific; viz.: scientific philosophy, science of science, and philosophical science. Linguistically speaking the first mentioned group relies on proto-scientific aspects which call for no proof, the second group hardly depends on inference except the most direct ones as when we say the colours of the spectrum is due to the breaking up of white light, and in the third group its apodictic quality is derived from some meta-scientific theory as that accepted for the purposes of quantum mechanics. We should thus be justified in referring to scientific language correspondingly to its subject-matter as proto-linguistic, normal or formal, or meta-linguistic in character. That apodictic certitude with which a man calls a spade a 'spade' and that down-to-earth certitude with which human children take for granted (whether by *a priori* or *a posteriori* reasoning) that 2+2 = 4, come together in a certain manner of independence and interdependence to result in the meaning certitude of scientific language. This subtle double or as we shall clarify later, fourfold origin of language, forms the theoretical basis of this study which it is our task to elaborate and clarify further in the pages that follow.

The Validity of a Language

Why a rose is called a 'rose' or by its corresponding term in any particular language does not call for any proof. In like manner, the relation that is implied in the linguistic context between what we have tried to distinguish as the **proto** and the **meta** aspects of any language, on which the structure of language itself is based, does not call for any proof in the usual sense. Validity is not to be sought through inference as is usual in syllogistic reasoning. A certain non-arbitrariness and intrinsic compatibility when respected shows itself directly, and conviction is already there immediately before forms of mediate inference could operate. It is to the credit of L. Wittgenstein to have worked out the implications of this statement in recent years. What he states in the context of logic and philosophy becomes all the more true in the context of the structure of linguistic thought:

> 4⁰121. Propositions cannot represent the logical form: this mirrors itself in the propositions.
>
> That which mirrors **itself** in language, language cannot represent.
>
> That which expresses **itself** in language, **we** cannot express by language.
> The propositions **show** the logical form of reality.
>
> They exhibit it.[3]

Language must correspond to the form of the thought that is implied in its expression.[4] We suggest here that the validity of the impression aspect of language, as distinct from its overt expression, lies deep in human consciousness where axiomatic laws of thought, on which all thinking itself has finally to rely without room for contradiction, but, as it were, tautologically and always with sufficient reason, are found.

The Archetypal Model of Linguistic Structure

In the familar linguistic context of the class-room the schoolmaster might put a dot on the black-board and call it, with maximum non-arbitrariness and sense of correctness possible by the letter *p* (or any other corresponding initial of the language he is employing). A student who would stand up and ask for the proof of it would be making a fool of himself. Although the selection of the name is arbitrary a maximum possible attempt has been made, without disrespecting any law of thought hitherto recognized, in the direction of non-arbitrariness. If he had used a letter of the Greek alphabet instead of a vernacular one, it would perhaps have been more scientific in that there was a greater effort at de-Babelization. Sanskrit letters could have been used for indicating levels of contemplative consciousness with equal justice. Somehow a meta-linguistic aspect and a proto-linguistic aspect have to come together for a precise meaningful situation to emerge. What is important for us to note at this stage of our study is, that in the most primary of linguistic situations in view of a scientific language already in vogue in the scholastic world, we have a visible or perceptual aspect brought into contact with a conceptual aspect of the same reality. In the mathematics class the school-boy might come to know, in a limited context, the meeting of algebra and geometry in the use of the language of Cartesian co-ordinates. School-room mathematics now comprises such notions as the group, the field, the vector space, homomorphism, isomorphism etc.[5] Starting from naming a point to communication through vectors, scalars and tensors the requirements of scientific language ranges between micro- and macro-cosms, analytic and synthetic thought.

Two Sets of Thought Elements Enter into Scientific Language

Ordinary everyday language has to do mainly with observables. Linguists have used the expression 'thing-language' and the language of 'handling action' in referring to this ordinary work-a-day world in which linguistic intercourse among humans thrives. Then there is the world of the 'calculables' which has a more theoretical or a non-physical reference or status in reality. In the latest mathematical language these two aspects have been referred to as **proper** and **improper** elements.[6] Whatever be the full implications of this kind of mathematical language which is still in the process of being perfected by those who want to use it for scientific purposes, such as that of the relativity theory and of quantum mechanics, all we want to derive for the purposes of our study here, is that science is the resultant of the summation or the multiplied product as between proper and improper elements and what emerges finally out of science generally, is something that could be stated, either in correct ordinary language of everyday life or else in terms of a verticalized version of the same which refer to improper elements. Hume as we shall see presently would refer to these aspects as quantity and number.[7] Just as the sum and product of mathematical elements could be said to have independence and interdependence at the same time the two aspects of thought enter into the composition of scientific language. Three kinds of connections between ideas have been recognised by Hume when he says: "To me there appear to be only three principles of connection among ideas, namely **Resemblance, Contiguity** in time or place and **Cause** or **Effect.**[8] If we add to this analysis of association of ideas of Hume what is more fundamental, which, as he himself said, pertains to either quanatity or number, we shall be able with these factors in mind, to re-construct for ourselves a schematic and proto-linguistic pattern of the global unit of integrated thought. This we shall attempt to do progressively after other epistemological and methodological aspects have been discussed. Here we have to note in passing that out of the four relational factors above two could apply to the proper and improper aspects of ideas. There could be innate causes and effects as well as causes and effects that belong to the existent experimental aspect. Scientific language thrives in the meeting place of the experimental and the theoretical, corresponding to quantity and number, respectively. Resemblance of past memory with future imagination would belong to contiguity of time rather than of place. The provability of the completeness of this enumeration was doubted by Hume himself, but with the help of a schematic proto-language, the validity of the list of factors becomes at least more certain.[9]

A Primitive Scientific Activity and Its Linguistic Scheme

Bertrand Russell writing on the importance of logical form in *The Encyclopaedia of Unified Science* says: "The old view that measurement is of the essence of science would therefore seem to be erroneous."[10] This revision of an old view he arrives at because as he points out, 'It follows that the laws of macroscopic physics are topological laws, and that the introduction of number through co-ordinates is only a practical convenience.'[11] What we should note here is that mathematics has arrived at topology after many vertical stages of abstraction and generalisation and just as the general theory of Einstein does not contradict but includes the special theory, so the idea of mathematical intrapolation and extrapolation could enable us to see that scientific activity could be understood schematically at different levels of abstraction or generalization or both and that the old notion that science is measurement is fundamentally not true when quantitative as well as qualitative aspects of number are admitted into the scheme.

The primitive pattern of a simple but typical scientific activity could be derived from a simple class-room example. The length, breadth and height of a table determined with the help of an arbitrarily fixed unit of length results in ordinary initial knowledge about it for practical purposes of classification or communication. Here the table itself is an 'observable' and the measurement especially with arbitrary units, in spite of a rod of platinum existing in Paris or London, is a speculative theoretical and non-empirical operation. Language may be said to participate on one said with brute actualities and on the other with elements opposed to perception diametrically, or at least by a vectorial angle of 90^0. Whether with or without measurement or reliance on number quantitatively, the principle of what number represents as an 'improper' element and what in principle again the actual table represents more 'properly', yield that apodictic certitude that belongs intrinsically to scientific language. Between **observables** and **calculables** conceived as pure mathematical elements all scientific activity is thus comprised.

The Languages of Apodictic and Probable Certitudes in Science

From the simple instance of measuring a table we could pass on to other examples of a graded order in which the two elements that we have tried to distinguish enter into combinations of different degrees or proportions with modalities entering in as a distinct factor. If we should take the case of the spectrum we know that it is, in the first instance, to be understood as equated to white light. It is as good for science to say that white light is formed from spectral colours as conversely to say that spectral colours form white light. As knowledge there is reversibility, but experimental reversal implies different experimental arrangements. Here the white light and the colours belong to the same grade of psycho-physical abstraction while if we should say that each colour of the spectrum has its wave-length of radiation, indicated by different numbers, the relation is between a set of obserables and a set of calculables. There was no proof needed in the conviction that white light was the same as spectral colours and **vice-versa**, when stated in language, but the apodictic nature of this direct conviction becomes overlaid by more complicated experimental and inferential steps in order to be able to equate and understand each colour in relation to its wave length. The inductive and deductive abstractions as between observables and calculables becomes more complex but retains its structural identity of form. In calculated predictions, later proved experimentally, we have probabilities that sometimes tally with possibilities. Except in axiomatically valid laws, observables and calculables can enter into the fabric of the language of science, giving threadbare or one-sided theories or hypotheses which later get revised or revalued with more calculable or observable inventions or discoveries. The falling of an apple in the garden was all the observable element on which Newton erected the theory of Universal Gravitation with calculations derived from the writings of Kepler, Copernicus and Galilee. In Darwin's Theory of Evolution we do not know whether it is life or organism that evolves. He never claims to have observed a monkey changing into a man nor has he been able to show the process experimentally with any direct evidence other than to give instances which resemble natural selection, struggle for existence and survival of the fittest under artificial conditions, and the rest of the evidence consists of museum specimens studied in the light of the theory. As there are rival theories by scientific men like Lamarck and Russell and rival philosophical versions of evolution in the Creative Evolution of Bergson besides the parallel evolution theory, the scientific status of Darwinism is not at all on very firm grounds. As it presents a picture of change quite on other lines from that contained in the scriptural version in the *Genesis*, evolutionism has attained in the popular mind, the status of an anti-religious doctrine of scientism. There is a just proportion in which the observables could be mixed in science with calculables, and when the balance is lost one gets pseudo-scientific literature between whose non-sensical verbalisms and the verbalisms attributed to classical metaphysics there would not be much to choose. Promiscuous mixing of the observable and the calculable elements in scientific language leads to absurdities of which Eddington gives a striking example:

> I am standing on a threshold about to enter a room. It is a complicated business. In the first place, I must shove against an atmosphere pressing with a force of fourteen pounds on every square inch of my body. I must make sure of landing on a plank travelling at twenty miles a second round the sun — a fraction of a second too early or too late, the plank would be miles away . . . . . These are some of the minor difficulties. I ought really to look at the problem four-dimensionally as concerning the intersection of my world line with that of the plank. Then again it is necessary to determine in which direction the entropy of the world is increasing in order to make sure that my passage is an entrance, not an exit.[12]

It is easy to see from this extract that between the rival claims of science and common sense, instead of certitude of any kind, puzzlement results, which defeats the purpose of scientific language altogether. We have to beware as much of the false shadows of science, to use the expression of Dr. Holton cited above, as of the false doctrines of metaphysicians.

Renormalization

The Pythagoras theorem could be proved either theoretically or practically. Mixed methods could perhaps to devised by those who know how to play with mathematical axioms and postulates and rules of inference, but the mixing of methods leads to various grades of pseudo or non-science. In such matters as determining the specific gravity of bodies, it is a relation that is established, of the form of an equation, based on experimental data which gain primacy, while in formulating the law regulating the increase or decrease of the entropy of the universe, the languages of science and philosophy are indistinguishable. The canons of Mill based on agreements and differences, agreement and difference treated together with residual and concomitant variations seem to refer to subtle laws of reasoning which give proportion, balance or harmony as between the two aspects of reality based on the observables and the calculables that we have distinguished. For the purposes of this study we prefer to think in terms of normalization and **re-normalization**[13] instead of thinking in terms of the canons of Mill which might be intended for the same purpose. Normalizations would presuppose the notion of a normative factor which it is the aim of this study to postulate in connection with a scientific language as we understand it here.

A Central Normative Notion Necessary for Scientific Language

Just as in biology plants or animals are classified and named by their characteristics that are primary or secondary with reference to some central representative of a family, genus or phylum, so scientific language would require that a central neutral and normative principle or notion should be postulated, balancing justly the two factors that we have seen enter into the composition of scientific thinking. Language has to concern itself with the mind and matter with which science itself is concerned and the normative principle has to be neutral as between the mental and the material, the 'psychic' or 'physical'.

We know in recent times, of the school of scientific philosophers who called themselves Logical Atomists. Influenced perhaps by the monadology of Leibniz, atomism postulated a unit entity as a basis for their discussions of questions of mathematical, logical or philosophical import. Precise notions about it have to be derived from the *Principia Mathematica* of Russell and Whitehead which deals with Logic and Mathematics as having the same principles. Logical atomism speaks of the distinction between 'atomic sentences' and 'molecular sentences' which result from the union of a unit atomic sentence. Earlier, Wittgenstein, while still under the influence of Russell, put more order into the concept of logical atomism when he said:

> 1°13 The facts in logical space are the world.
>
> 2 What is the case, the fact, is the existence of atomic facts.
>
> 2°01 An atomic fact is a combination of objects (entities, things)[14]

The unit of logical thought is an atomic sentence round which philosophy and logic was built. James and Russell also agreed in calling themselves 'Neutral-monists' which was neither mental nor material, thus attempting to formulate a normative notion for their philosophy.[15]

The very reference by Wittgenstein above to 'logical space' postulates a psycho-physical entity in which logical activity could have its being. That the concept is not totally without reference to the bodily aspect and the purely metaphysical, is clear from the fact that it belongs to the context of logical empiricism. This double expression is expressly meant to stand for that union of the two aspects which are the same as in the expression 'neutral-monism' which we have just examined. The psycho-physical character of this entity is evident from Russell's own words when he writes:

> Thus from both ends physics and psychology have been approaching each other and making more and more possible the doctrine of 'neutral-monism'

suggested by William James's criticism of consciousness.

He goes on to make the position of this school of thought clearer than ever when he adds in the same paragraph,

> I think that both mind and matter are merely convenient ways of grouping events. Some single events, I should admit, belong only to material groups, but others belong to both kind of groups, and are therefore at once mental and material. This doctrine effects a great simplification in our picture of the structure of the world.[16]

Although presented in the usual dogmatic form after the manner of older metaphysicians without reference to any experimental evidence, it is possible for us to see that logical empiricists generally are already committed to the recognition of a neutral entity which is a kind of absolutist abstraction, neither belonging wholly to any one of the two rival worlds of physics or metaphysics. While this view simplifies matters, it is still open to the charges of *a priorism*, solipsicsm and arbitrariness insofar that it is a doctrine that is asserted. Logical or linguistic structure generally could be examined more scientifically through observational situations of experimental status such as those we are outlining below.

Introspective Observations for the Study of Linguistic Structure

If the indirect evidences of pointer readings are acceptable in scientific experiments proper (which themselves depend on evidence many degrees removed from the direct observation of events), we may ask legitimately why introspective experimental situations could not be relied on to give us the same degree of scientific certitude that differentiates science from speculation. If a certain botanic specimen is available as a weed it is not necessary to grow it in a special herbarium. In common human life there are common human linguistic situations which have experimental value if the method of experimentation could be applied to them even introspectively.

Scientific philosophers like Bergson have relied both on the schematic proto-language as understood in this study and also have made use of the study of experimental situations to give validity to the discussion of factors of psycho-physical import. He puts the question: "*'j'écoute deux personnes converser dans une langue inconnue. Cela suffit-il pour que je les entende? Les vibrations qui m'arrivent sont les mêmes qui frappent leurs oreilles. Poutant je ne perçcoit qu'un bruit confus ou tous les sons se ressemblent. Je ne distingue rien et ne pourrait rien répéter. Dans cette même masse sonore, au contraire, les deux interlocuteurs démêlent des consonnes, voyelles et syllabes qui ne se ressemblent guère, enfin des mots distincts. Entre eux et moi, où est la différence?*" After tracing minutely and in detail the insurmountable difficulties that intervene between the physical fact of sound impressions and their understanding as language Bergson states: "*Ainsi se déroulerait dans notre conscience, sous forme de sensations musculaire naissantes, ce que nous appellerons le schème moteur de la parole entendue.*"[17] Thus we see already strict scientific philosophers employing a new kind of introspective experimentation which must be considered at least as valid as the indirect evidence of pointer readings in physical laboratories.

Introspective Psycho-physical Observations of Experimental Status

Russell's norm of logical atomism belonging to the philosophy of neutral-monism as he calls it, and Bergson's effort to establish a *schème moteur* in the context of his philosophy of change and becoming of the *élan vital*, are recent attempts on the part of philosophers who are fully scientific in their outlook, to arrive at a normative notion that would be free from the one-sided epistemological reference of classical speculations. Why should we not improve on this kind of approach by accentuating the experimental character more consciously and with greater scientific exactitude? By way of showing the possibilities that lie in this direction and since language itself thrives where mind and matter meet, we shall give here an outline of experimental situations which would yield us a greater degree of certitude than hitherto possible about the structure of linguistic consciousness. In doing so we shall try to keep as close to that fully scientific but as yet little favoured branch of knowledge called psycho-physics into whose domain both the logical atom and the *élan vital* should belong. We shall divide our experimental situation into two phases for making two sets of observations that properly belong to the observable and calculable worlds which meet in a unitively conceived psycho-physical event in terms of common human consciousness:

(i) *First Phase*

Think of two persons in a dark room.[18] Let us call them A and B. A says to B' 'Who is there?' B retorts with the same question, 'Who are **you** there?' The possible basic response of either of them or both of them would be contained in the common personal pronoun **'I'** which could equally apply to **anyone**.

The important condition here to note is that all visual and other impressions are meant to be eliminated except the auditory linguistic link. The observables are eliminated here by the condition of darkness and the calculables which have their roots in the sense of hearing which leads to meanings of a conceptual order which refer to central as against the peripheral objective realities, are isolated for epistemological analysis so as to arrive at a complete scheme of the structure of the thinking process that is to be understood as implied in language.

It is true that the voice of the two persons who communicate without visual impressions might contain certain physiological elements related to past habits or tendencies of the person giving him a certain individuality related to his memory aspect. The memory of the past might be said to determine in some indirect way the future conduct and the imaginative side of that person giving him imaginative or futuristic orientation of the normative entity, whatever it might be called. This aspect could also give personality or individuality to A as distinct from B. But the intention of the experiment is to give primacy to the central invisible subjective aspect of the personality. Peripheral or marginal factors which belong to the visible are meant to be eliminated in this phase of the experiment. Between the persons A and B, as they carry on conversation, different grades of pure or practical memory or imaginative factors might enter into the common consciousness of both. The ideas may be said to move in a trans-subjective axis which for taxonomic purposes (which we shall justify more fully later), we shall call the vertical axis.

(ii) ***Second Phase***

Now let us change the conditions of the experimental observational situation. A neutral observer or witness 0 may be thought of as switching on a light in the same dark room. The visible aspect of the reality of the situation now becomes added to the auditory which had a content belonging to the world of the calculables. The auditory content is not abolished but a new dimension depending on the perceptual, peripheral or more 'objective' is imposed on the original stem of the trans-subjective aspect while the trans-subjective remains intact like stars during day-time. The physical peculiarities of A and B gain primacy and prominence and sex complexion, stature and other particularities that are specific and empirical in content emerge into the situation. One could examine the finger prints of A or B to accentuate the individuality to its limits. Here the specific factors happen to be overt and not innate. They may in a sense be called outer ones as opposed to the innate or subjective ones of the first phase. This we shall refer to as the inter-physical. To put the line of demarcation between the two aspects would take much more discussion than what we might at first think. We could think of different grades of conceptual, perceptual or actual factors claiming primacy in consciousness at a given time. It would be impossible to isolate them and study their characteristics and modes of combination without going still one step into the implications of this second phase of our experimental situation. Let us suppose now that A or B or both are using telescopes or microscopes to aid their vision and are interested in the outer limits of space or the microscopic structure of matter as we can know it. They speak about what they are interested in to the neutral observer or witness 0. Now we are ready to extract the linguistic situation implied. In the consciousness of the neutral observer, language makes certain impressions which are events of a psycho-physical order of reality reduced into abstractions of a linguistic order.[19] It is not the actuality that matters any more but the conceptual aspect only. Between the trans-subjective concepts of the first phase and the inter-physical concepts of the second phase there is linguistic **parity** vertically and a '**strangeness**' if we may use a term borrowed from particle physics to express tentatively what we mean. Both these have the same status linguistically in the consciousness of the neutral observer. The inter-physical aspect thus isolated without full justification, which is to follow, we shall call the horizontal axis.

Further Implications of the Psycho-Physical Linguistic Situation

On the light being switched on the specifically overt or the objectively perceptual aspects of A and B stand revealed. Their memories and imaginations give them a trans-subjective dimension and their physical powers of seeing objects as such, in true or false light, is an inter-physical or horizontal dimension, measuring along its axis tendencies to day-dreaming or eidetic peculiarities such as exaggerated colour vision as when under the influence of drugs or ducts, colour blindness. The subjective 'I' may be said to converge into the common unity of the vertical self at its negative levels while the arrow pointing horizontally and perceptively towards the object may be said to diverge into the plurality of conscious units, each with its specific as against the generic characteristics of the former.

If we now think that one of the persons A or B suffered from a tooth-ache or a stomach-ache, the facts could have been communicated in words with lights out, and with facial or other expressions or contortions of the body when lights are on. If, as an alternative case one of them said, "I have a heavy burden on my head which makes me groan under its weight", the linguistic link in a dark room would give less certitude than when the load is seen and its weight, whether bearable or not, is appraised by the observer-witness. Between suffering from the weight of a load and that of a stomach-ache there is a change in the vertical scale as between the overt and the innate aspects. A sleep walker or a day-dreamer could have his mind at different points in the horizontal scale. When overt and innate factors enter into the situation, both vertically and horizontally without any regulating principle involved, we have an absurd linguistic situation. All we have to note at this stage is that physical and mental factors could enter positively or negatively into the dimensions that we have distinguished.

Neutral Normative Appraisal of the Two Main Types of Linguistic Events

If we think of the neutral 'observer-witness' 0 of the above experimental situation that we have examined, and appraise the content of his consciousness with a view to arriving at primitive, atomic or elementary, simple happenings therein we could think of two typical movements which would act as references for all possible events in consciousness. The inter-physical reference may be said to move within the horizontal range of phenomenologically represented objects or interests whether subjective or objective in origin. An atomic sentence representing this horizontal movement in consciousness could be the thoughts implied in the sentence of the model: 'This is a pot' where the word 'This' would correspond to the negative horizontal aspect, tending to virtuality and to general vagueness that is non-specific in character, while the word 'pot' would stand for a more specific actuality. Reversibility and irreversibility could both apply to the process or modality which depends on the degree of attention implied in each mode of thought. Likewise in the sentence 'This is Reason' we have the typical case of a vertical movement in thought, the word 'This' standing for understandable items of thought in general, implicitly understood, and 'Reason' would represent an element in thought which is more explicit in its content though still of the order of pure thoughts. Much concentrated direction of the inner power of attention is needed before one could think of the specific content of reason. It could therefore be called a vertical positive element in molecular thought consisting of atomic thought-events represented by the first instance.

The verb **to-be** is the link corresponding to the activity in consciousness which relates mental attention or relaxation in one sense or the other.

If we should now remember further that the neutral observer-witness in the imaginary situation does not enter into direct non-linguistic relation with either objects or with specific factors of elements of pure items in consciousness, we have within the schematically conceived and globally or unitively understood personal consciousness, all the possible combinations, characteristics and modalities in which thoughts integrate themselves to form normative linguistic units. Based on such units an over-all norm is also possible to conceive.

Division II : Experimental

In the previous division we have confined our remarks to the study of the linguistic structure of thought from the point of view of what can be described as scientific philosophy. Intrinsic forms of thought, axiomatically given in the laws of thought, were taken to be our point of departure. Science in the popular mind is associated with a laboratory where brass instruments record pointer-readings to reveal verities that are unquestionable. Instead of theological belief we have now truth told us by apparatus or appliances. These appliances verify equations experimentally. People are convinced more readily when we say that a cardiograph or encephalograph tells us the story directly or indirectly through automatic recordings of some sort. The chain of inferences and the indirectness of the observations are easily excused. After what we have said in the previous division it is hardly necessary for us to look for further proof. Still, out of respect for the popular temper of our times in such matters in this division, we are going to examine the merits of a certain number of evidences throwing light on the structure of thought whether of direct value or only of indirect significance. The normative notion of integrated thought that we have arrived at in the last part of the previous division, if kept in mind, and if the experimental evidence presented in the present division is closely examined, the resulting validity of the structure of thought will surely be enhanced, though certitude may not be totally based on them. As we have to think about thought in this division we can call this division as one belonging to a science of sciences. Observables and calculables come very close together here, one lending certitude to the other. Negative evidence becomes as significant as the positive.

Light on the Innate Structure of Thought from the EEG

That the activity called thinking has implied within it two different kinds of processes has been amply made evident by investigations conducted with the help of the recently invented Electro-Encephalograph (EEG). There is in the first place what is taken to be the normal activity of the brain which produces rhythmic oscillations which have been distinguished and named as **alpha** rhythms. The strange phenomenon noticed with regard to the activity of the brain is that these electric rhythms tend to disappear instead of getting augmented, as we should expect, when we know by other evidences that the brain is engaged in thinking or is really active in respect of some problem to be solved. Relaxing and shutting the eyes brings alpha rhythms into evidence normally, but with certain other types of persons they continue when eyes are open and some persons are without these rhythms altogether. These paradoxical effects seem to depend on deep-seated factors independent of anything physiological. Changes in the degree of attention or relaxation contribute to the appearance or disappearance of alpha rhythms depending on the psycho-physical personality of the individual in question rather than on any physiological factor. Prof. W. Grey Walter of the Burden Neurological Institute said recently in connection with the findings of the EEG as follows:

> One of the most sobering, even humiliating facts of the whole of brain physiology is that scarcely a single phenomenon discovered by the study of electrical activity of the brain — the EEG — was foreseen or predicted by physiologists. . .[20]

According to the same authority, not only are the evidences of brain activity independent of physiological foundations as taken for granted hitherto by empirical scientists, but there are deep-seated factors contributing by their elusive paradoxical expression through the language of the EEG which are of such an indeterminate nature as to indicate what may be called personality traits. He continues in the same talk as follows:

> The confusing thing is that even when the eyes are opened, or the person thinks hard the (alpha) rhythms may disappear. Unfortunately for our understanding of this effect, not everyone shows alpha rhythms, even with the eyes shut, and in some people the rhythms persist even with the eyes open, so we are faced with an objective sign of a mystery that we accept and delight in, in everyday life and find hard to fit into scientific analysis — that is human personality.[21]

Thus for the first time the notion of a human personality independently of physiological factors enters into the experimental domain of science. This fact suffices to give to the normative notion that we have outlined in the previous section sufficient status as a scientific fact for the purposes of this study.

Prof. Grey Walter has approached the same problem from another end and, when his findings in respect of brain activity are put side by side with the story that EEG has to tell, tends to make clear that there are two distinct kinds of thinking or brain activities going on alternately. Prof. Walter points out firstly that brain is 'a problem-solving organ' essentially. In solving problems a mental model that is either pictorial or verbal is involved. Actual seeing and visual imagination are activities that are different and even opposed by their effects. When mentally solving a problem, if the kind of model that the subject uses, happens to be one of the usual variety of imagaination (not vision) the alpha rhythms show a tendency to stop as seen through the EEG recordings. The brain mechanism has thus two different reactions: the first is the kind that resembles the movement of the eye-balls when looking at an actual sight and the second is when visual imagination operates at a deeper level of consciousness. The former tends to retain alpha oscillations while the latter tends to suppress them. Looking at a whole page in reading a book is a visual activity in which 'the sweep of electrical activity has implicit in it' as Prof. Walter puts it 'a sort of scanning process'. Scanning is different from looking at the whole page, in that 'one sees the words on it one after the other'. One changes the steady shape of the printed lines into a 'series of visual signals spread out in time'. In other words, scanning means 'turning spatial patterns into time ones'. Brain models have also been devised which have helped to reveal that they react as if they had the faculty of memory where the time factor rather than space factor counts. The relation between the scanning process of brain and the stoppage of the alpha rhythms which refer to the deeper or, as we might say, vertical activity of brain as opposed to its mere spatial (horizontal) functioning, is sufficiently clear from what Prof. Walter has to say on the matter:

> When one reads a page of print one's eyes scan it systematically line by line. The page is there all the time, but one sees the words on it one after the other. This means that one changes the steady shape of the printed lines into a series of visual signals spread out in time.

According to Prof. Walter again, scanning comes into evidence when a person looks for a word in the dictionary and finds it interesting. We can see his eyes stop moving. The Prof. suggests his theory when he puts the question: 'Is the sort of thing that is going on in the brain when the alpha rhythm stops as a person thinks?"[22]

EEG and Brain Model evidences put together thus lend much experimental support to the space-time correlation of mental activities which fall into two interdependent though independent classes.

Direct Evidence of a Psycho-physical Axis Afforded Between Aphasia and Apraxia

Various troubles connected with speech with which doctors have had to deal and which have been the subject of detailed experimental research in clinics and psycho-pathological laboratories in various progressive countries have already a rich fund of accumulated data which afford us as conclusive evidence as possibly could be expected supporting the reality of a psycho-physical link along whose length various grades of speech troubles could be located as between the psycho-physical function pertaining to one pole of linguistic habit or the other. The evidence that is quite stricking and conclusive has been before the scientific world for more than half a century now but the inferences that could have been made for the service of scientific knowledge about human faculties in general have not, for some reason, received the attention or been given the importance they deserve. It is to the credit of the intuitive intelligence of Bergson to have tried to enrich metaphysics with the minute details of speech troubles and to make valuable inferences based on the evidence they present.

It is not necessary for us to go into all the cases that have been passed in review by Bergson over several pages with full documentation in his fully scientific study, *Matière et Memoire: Essai sur la relation du corps a l'ésprit*, but scientism has, as we have said, its own prejudices imagining so to say that the soul if real should be found at the tip of the scalpel. Bergson's fully scientific inferences have been mixed up with other verbose speculations of no value perhaps because of the lack of a fully developed epistemology or methodology pertaining to science as such.

We need only two or three typical cases cited by Bergson[23] for the purposes of this study to see that understood in terms of the *schèma moteur*[24] that Bergson has developed elsewhere in his studies of *élan vital* and provided that scientific physicalism is not an end in itself, that there is sufficient evidence for inferring the reality of a schematically conceived axis that is mathematically and logically valid and which would help us to get a clear idea of the structure of thought that must be at the basis of linguistic expression. Bergon writes:

> *Ainsi, dans un cas observé par Lichtheim lui-même, le sujet a la suite d'un chute, avait perdu la mémoire de l'articulation des mots et par conséquent la faculté de parler spontanément; il répétait portant avec le plus grande correction ce qu'on lui disait. D'autre part où la parole spontanée est intacte, mais où la surdité verbale est absolue, le malade ne comprenant plus rien de ce qu'on lui dit, la faculté de répéter la parole d'autrui peut encore être entièrement conservé.*

After giving due consideration to all the theories that have been put forward by authorities like Bastian, Romberg, Bateman, Winslow, Kussmaul Arnaud besides considering the dozens of varieties of Aphasia studied by Lichtheim himself (Brain, Jan 1885, p. 447) and others Bergson is able to reduce the phenomena in terms of the *schèma moteur* with the help of which he is able to solve the mystery. He concludes by saying:

> *La vérité parait être intermédiaire entre ces deux hypothèses: il y a, dans ces divers phénomènes plus que des actions absolument méchanigues, mais moins qu'un appel à la mémoire voluntaire; ils témoignent d'une tendence des impressions verbales auditives à se prolonger en mouvements d'articulation, tendence qui n'échappe surement pas au contrôle habituel de notre volonté, qui implique même peut-être un discernement rudimentaire, et qui se traduit, á l'état normal par une répetition intérieure des traits sailants de la parole entendue. Or, notre schèma moteur n'est autre chose.*[25]

Bergson's schematic representation of a psycho-physical unit of consciousness involved in language function is seen to emerge in clear outline in his analysis of verbalistic troubles known to medical science. That he has kept it strictly within the pragmatic frame does not affect the intrinsic and valid character of the scheme which we can take as applicable to a more general philosophical context by extrapolation. Other cases of a related psycho-pathological order have also been studied and recorded such as the case of a virtuoso who had lost in some way his material technique of external expression in music while his thoughts and understanding of music remained intact, as opposed to that of an eminent medical man who had retained all his knowledge about anatomy and pathology who lost his power of fixing his will on one act that was pertinent to a situation and instead found himself helplessly cutting paper into bits, punching holes or tearing up books for some days.[26] As between neurological and psychiatric troubles there is a psycho-physical polarity which would justify our suggestion just made that the whole series of troubles whether strictly related to Aphasia or Apraxia or even *dyslexie*[27] can be fitted into a common scheme with the help of intrapolation or extrapolation as known to mathematical thinking.

Evidence of Psycho-Pathology

That a psycho-physical normative unit whether called by the names of libido, persona, psyche or self, has a distinct and non-metaphysical reality is brought out strinkingly by a case that Prof. Pierre Janet of the Collège de France has recorded in his lectures on 'La Force et Faiblesse Psychologiques'. He refers to a surprising instance of loss of speech. This loss of speech was due to a certain degree of negative withdrawal into oneself rather than the result of anything that had a physical cause in the physico-pathological sense. As one whose authority is high in such matters and one fully appraised of the latest development of this subject, both practical and theoretical, his estimate of the above case would help us to clarify the scientifically valid normative notion for the purposes of our study. We shall quote from

Janet a case in which it is neither a case of aphasia, apraxia nor dyslexia but one of general mutism and functional hybernation or inactivity:

> *Je racontais autrefois l'histoire d'un étrange malade; soignée dans une maison de santé, qui pendent trois ans entiers était restée sans consentir à manger un aliment et sans prononcer une seule mot . . . Après trois ans, un printemps cette malade se dresse sur son lit et se met à dire à la garde la phrase suivante: "Ah ça! on ne déjeune pas ici?*[28]

One would be fully justified in inferring from such cases that there is at least a real psycho-physical entity understandable as a mathematical unity at least, which is neither body nor mind but something intermediate between the two. When psycho-pathologists say that a certain state is opposed to certain others, as they often do as in the case of the troubles connected with the will above, or when they oppose or contrast cases of neurasthenia and psychasthesia or reduce both more simply into asthenia as Pierre Janet prefers to do[29] there is in their minds a vaguely conceived scheme of interrelation of psycho-pathological conditions.

Pierre Janet further suggests that mental cases which he classifies under '*Les délires*' could all be thought of as pertaining to degrees in a heirarchic scale of over-estimation and under-estimation of the self with reference to speech. He says:

> *Examinez les délires et même tous les toubles de la croyance, quels qu'ils soient, vous pourrez toujours les résumer par l'une de ces formules: le délirant est un individu qui place mal sa parole dans la hiérarchié des degrés de réalité.*[30]

Certain other writers on personality problems like F. Achelle-Delmas and Marcel Boll go as far as to suggest the methods of interpolation and its inverse procedure of extrapolation which latter he considers misleading in the cases of dementation. He also says:

> *D'une mannière genérals, nous nous efforcerons d'appliquer ce qu'on nomme après Stuart Mill, la methodes des variations concomitantes, qui est le véritable centre de toute raisonnement inductif.*[31]

The systematic classification and nomenclature according to a correct taxonomy becomes full of problems in this domain of psycho-pathology. If a central normative notion is supplied we could imagine how the vast amount of literature at present of a psudo-scientific or even non-scientific status could be normalized so as to standardize language generally. What the difference between the **libido** and the **sub-liminal-self** amounts to in precise terms, cannot even be discussed at present without taking sides with one school of thought as against another. The classification of mental troubles is at present a fecund field of unscientific statements which however pass for science. Normalization with reference to a norm conceived synthetically and re-normalization of terms that have tended to diverge into too many specific analytic sub-divisions of the same fundamental phenomenon, with which they may happen to be basically related, could be accomplished for the language of science, only when the neutral norm has been given an integrated status in respect of possible modalities, combinations and characteristics of thought and corresponding language elements.

Normalization of Pedagogic Thought

Psycho-pedagogy, as it is practised experimentally in modern times, is another department of knowledge from which we could derive some useful directives in regard to the normalization of scientific language. Teaching and learning involve that bipolar relationship in which a constant interchange of thought is taking place, like a subtle process of osmosis. 'Education' itself is an expression that is full of ambiguity and vagueness. Personal relations between the pupil and teacher are becoming recognized more and more as desirable in the process. The philosophical bases of education could be **negatively** conceived as with Rousseau, **naturalistically** conceived as with Spencer, **pragmatically** conceived as with Dewey and also **idealistically** or dialectically conceived as with Pythagoreans, Platonists, Neo-Platonists or their continuators in modern times like Whitehead or Royce. Whether a stimulus-response psychology, behaviourism or adjustments to the needs of man-making or character-building are to be given primacy as against adjustment to social or citizenship needs are all questions on which educational literature can differ widely. Normalization in this domain so full of possible differences of attitude can only be expected when the norm of the persons involved in the bi-polar process is scientifically postulated mathematically, logically, biologically or psycho-physically as the common personal factor at the basis of the process that is to take place. Verbose volumes are at present extant which are a hot-bed of confusions and this must be reflected in the language used. We cannot do better here than to quote from the writings of one whose scientific training and acquaintance with scientific problems cannot be questioned. Dr. Alexis Carrel writes:

> The tests applied to school-children and students by inexperienced psychologists have no great significance. They give an illusive confidence to those unacquainted with psychology. In fact, they should be accorded less importance. Psychology is not yet a science. Today individuality and its potentialities are not measurable. But a wise observer, trained in the study of human beings, is sometimes capable of discovering the future in the present characteristics of the given individual.[32]

Having in the year 1932 submitted a thesis myself to the University of Paris entitled '*Le Facteur Personnel dans le Processus Educatif*' and in view of the fact that my work fully answers the question of how normalization of personal relations with a central notion of the persons involved in an educational situation, as between teacher and pupil, it might be permissible in this section to pass over aspects of educational problems covered in detail and with ample documentation in that study. Since those days, however, some interesting developments have taken place in the educational world which deserve to be noticed here especially as they tend to confirm the schematic norm that we have in mind in the present study. On page 25 of that thesis I had given a schematic representation combining and correlating scientifically certain of the important aspects of educational psychology that have direct bearing on the development of the personality of the child. As most of what is represented there already is still to be considered valid and as by no means out-dated, and encouraged by the fact that it has passed already through the scrutiny of an academic body, the schema has been reproduced on page 193 above (*fig.* 14.3) whih when examined and read side by side with the concluding findings in the thesis also given as the foot-note below, would give us here, for the present, a rough idea of what we mean by normalization in the domain of psycho-pedagogics.[33]

Recent Psycho-pedagogic Evidence

Of the names that have made outstanding contributions of an experimental nature to the most recent developments in Pedagogics that of Prof. Jean Piaget may be mentioned as perhaps the most significant for us in this study. From the year 1921 he has been contributing serious works supported by experiments in every case on such subjects beginning with 'Une forme verbale de la comparison chez l'enfant' (1921) through one concerning 'Le langage et la pensée ches l'enfant (1928), and leading up to 'la Naissance de l'intelligence (1932) and 'le Formation du Symbole (1945). His latest publication in collaboration with Inhelder is devoted to the "development of two kinds of operational behaviour which are **calssification** and **seriation** which intervene in the formation of a large number of psychological and pedagogical notions".[34] Running through the whole series of works is his most important contribution of a vertical series of stages which he calls *paliers* described by him as a special type of thinking pertaining to child psychology. In the last of his works there is a reference to "the development of classification and that of seriation" which constitute "two unified and synchronous processes". Further there are said to be two factors whose co-ordination assures the reversibility of the operations which are called **retro-action** and **anticipation**. The overall explanation is based on the notion of **equilibrium**.[35] It is not possible nor necessary for us here to discuss the merits of these findings. All we have to note is that they do fit into the scheme that we have so far outlined in which mental activity takes two different directions, one that could be called spatial, and the other connected with the time axis, in which anticipation and retro-action with an overall notion of equilibrium marking the centre of the scheme. Expressions such a '**Correspondence topologique bi-univoque et bi-continue**'[36] which Piaget uses make it unmistakably evident that a mathematical structure is to be understood in the scientific nature of his writings. The new kind of language with latest terms, with a schematic pattern underlying it, can be discerned from the following summary of the import of Piaget's contributions from the pen of another contemporary authority in scientific pedagogy, Dr. H. Wallon of the Collège de France:

> *Les expériences ingénieuses de Piaget pour connaître comment l'enfant acquiert les notions de nombre et de quantité montrent en détail à quelles contradictions il peut se heurter dans son cheminement pour se débarasser des apparences purement sensibles, elles-mêmes contradictoires, et pour les résoudre en invariants auxquels il faudra que se superpose une vision opératoire . . . C'est par une suite d'échelons progressifs que le dynamismé des impressions et des réactions concrètes se fige en invariants auxquels doit se superposer un acte unificateur qui lui-même se fige en système stable de symboles. Et les symboles, prenant graduellement la place des éléments perceptifs, auxquels ils se substituent dans la mesure ou ils en experiment mieux qu'eux mêmes les rapports de co-existence et de devenir deviennent chacun à son tour les éléments d'une progression nouvelle dans la réduction de l'être à la connaissance.*[37]

Elsewhere in the same work Prof. Wallon speaks of three 'moments' which come into opposition in knowledge. The first he describes as having '*Irréversibilié absolue de l' empiricism brut*'; the second '*Reversibilité totale de l'acte intellectuel*' and thirdly, '*reduction d'un irréversible en réversible*.[38]

The number of scientific terms that have been used in the above paragraphs to represent something that could be intuitively understood immediately with the help of a schematic representation and the difficulty for the reader to follow the trend of the transformation that takes place in the child-mind through such words as belong to a sort of meta-language of science, should be sufficient recommendation for us to think of something simpler and of the nature of a proto- rather than a meta-language which would show these thoughts more directly. Such a language could be no other than the one that can establish a direct link between these two aspects of language. How such a relation could be established in a valid and workable manner is what we have still to make clear in the remainder of this study.

Thought Structure Examined from the Psycho-physical Standpoint

That branch of science known as Psycho-physics may be said to take its position between what is called physiological psychology and psycho-physiology. Physiological psychology and psycho-pathology as practised in clinics may be said to be on the side of physiology rather than on that of psychology. As our purpose is to discover the structure of thought just at the point where it gets inserted into matter, psycho-physics and its findings have special interest for us in this study. We shall therefore fix our attention on certain aspects of this branch of science which is based on simple stimuli and responses. Besides the study of relations which might be greater, equal or less than either stimulus or response, we have to have in this branch of knowledge what is called the threshold or limen. Sub-liminal responses both positive and negative ones and threshold or liminal ones are likely to give different laws such as the different laws of psycho-physics attributed to different experimenters like Weber, Fechner, Delboeuf, Breton and others. Each of them had his own mathematical formula expressing the relation between stimulus and response by which the body was to be understood in terms of mind and the mind in terms of the body. Some used logarithmic language while others used the idea of geometric or arithmetic progression to relate the bodily and mental factors. Merkel's law was seen to go against the validity of the Weber formulation of the relation. It states that within the limits of the threshold, there is a simple equality of proportion between stimulus and response. If we should think of the human organism as a whole in the light of these rival and different theories called laws it would not be difficult for us to see that the innate global structure of the psycho-physical entity involved is what is at the origin of the different partial experimental findings. The limen is a notion that touches that zone of the psycho-physical entity which is nearest to null or zero point. Stimulus must be said to be quantitative as it is actually physical and measurable as such and response which varies geometrically or logarithmically or according to more complicated mathematical laws may be more simply looked upon by us as a qualitative factor. It is because even such terms as qualitative are used in different contexts by different philosophers and thus tend to produce ambiguities that the need of a schematic language such as what we are proposing in this study, becomes a necessity. According to what we propose, the outline of which has already emerged from our discussion so far, we could call the response aspects which are of the order of calculables rather than observables, as pertaining to the qualitative or vertical axis of reference. The stimulus aspects would legitimately belong to the quantitative or horizontal axis of reference. By using these vectorial terms of projective geometry in a certain sense that is to be understood as belonging to the context of analytical geometry and topology at once as Spearman has already begun and as known to what is called vectorial psychology we have the unique advantage of a language for which the languages of the various particular branches of science become merely particular instances. It is in this sense that semeotics could be made a veritable organon for all sciences.[39]

Sir Russell Brain, President of the Royal College of Physicians, London, author of the *Perception and Science* in a recent pronouncement pertinently puts the question: "If we become aware of the colour solely as a result of changes occurring in the brain, which is inside the skull, how do we come to locate the red in the book which is lying on the table?"[40] If this book gets its colour from inside the skull and not from any primary quality in the book itself, we are witnessing in such a question put by a scientific authority a complete change of reference for science as a whole, which, from the days of Heisenberg's Uncertainty and the Relativism of Einstein has been shifting its accent from the observed to the observer. While we are still on the subject of psycho-physical light on the schema we are developing, we could also refer to certain findings that have had a well recognized place in science since many years such as the phenomenon called 'retinal rivalry' which records the peculiarity of colour on form of vision by which if the two eyes are stimulated by different colours or forms at the same time there is an element of intelligence that enters the situation by which the eyes together see only one colour alternately after another. The spatial rivalry is replaced by the mind or some inner factor which insists on seeing one at a time without rivalry. The very term 'retinal rivalry' retains the old prejudice in favour of physiology as against psychology within psycho-physics which ought strictly give equal importance to both aspects. A more correct description of the phenomenon would be to ask how the conceptual factor solves the duality of perceptions. Sir Russell Brain refers to the phenomenon of 'referred pain' which is not actually in the part to which it is attributed by the sufferer. He explains: 'many people who have had a limb amputated say that for a time it feels as though it were still there'.[41] Examples of this kind could be multiplied to show that even experimentally, mind and matter meet neutrally in psycho-physics.

The sensation of pain depends on its continuity or intensity while that of a 'just noticeable difference' of colour is more related to instant space than to duration. The saturation of hues and the brilliance or darkness of colour shades and the 'just noticeability' resemble modes of intensity and charactreristics of elements of thought. If we should add to these the notion of the peculiarities of combinations in which elements of colour integrate themselves we arrive at the well-known 'colour solid'. The taxonomy derived from this is now adopted by the American Standards Association and is the accepted language of colour for use by many manufacturers of paints and other products demanding a simple and accurate method of referring to colours and its innumerable shades.[42] Vectorial space and Cartesian correlation put together into the idea of the colour solid with whose help scientific precision is given to the confusion of the names of colours and their possible varieties, introduces for the first time a public and universally understandable language, at least with respect to one domain of language where ambiguity is most possible, whether between one vernacular and another, or even as between those who happen to be using the same language. The vertical axis is here represented by the central achromatic scale ranging from black through grey to white at the top. The spectral colours are related according to hue, light and shade, or degree of saturation, with three distinct integrating characteristic, combinatorial or modal dimensions or factors which though understood at present only in the psycho-physical context could well apply to integration of thought and language in general in an extended or extrapolated sense.

The Validity of Psycho-Physical Space

If in logical atomism it is permitted for us to think of logical space as a distinct entity, the non-arbitrary status of the colour solid must even by those who call themselves 'logical empiricists' be considered beyond any question in respect of its validity. Even when a modern physicist refers to space, there are two aspects of the notion of space that meet in it which have to be distinguished. Conceptual and perceptual spaces are put together by him consciously or unconsciously. It is a sort of neutral space that is involved as between actual space enclosed in a bell-jar in the laboratory if a perfect vacuum is possible and a space conceived by the mind as a metaphysical abstraction that has been defined by Aristotle as: "That without which bodies could not exist, but itself continuing to exist when bodies cease to exist". Space possesses magnitude or extension, though itself not a body for 'in case it were a body then two bodies would exist in the same place' (Aristotle, *Physics*, Book IV). Colours looked at in the light of Sir Russell Brain's recent words would themselves be within the skull rather than in the object. Putting this fact together with the structure of the colour solid with a vectorial psycho-physics to support it and understood as having dimensions which schematically represent tendencies in consciousness treated topologically we have arrived for our purposes at a rough idea of a unit integrated norm of thought elements. In order that the full implications of the structure of thought revealed by this analogy may be clear we are reproducing below its meaning with a full discussion of its possible grades of meaning. By the method of intrapolation and extrapolation we are expected to carry the pure schematic content revealed here to other departments of thought with the confidence that not only is this method non-arbitrary and justified but that it could claim to have that degree of apodictic or actual certitude which as we said is the criterion of science in general.

In passing it might be permitted to note here the slight difference that exists between this and the idea postulated by Ludwig Wittgenstein in his *Tractatus Logico-Philosophicus*.[43] The following is characteristic of his normative notion of logical space:

1°13 The facts in logical space are the world.
2°01231 In order to know an object, I must know not its external but its internal qualities.
2°0232 Roughly speaking objects are colourless.

The logico-philosophic world of Wittgenstein like the Monad of Leibniz suffers from a slight accentuation of the vertical as opposed to horizontal aspect of the global totality of reality with which a scientific language has to cope with. Colour is not to be excluded by us from our world of scientific language for otherwise it should become suitable merely for equations.

Integrated Norm of Thought Viewed Schematically

At this stage we are almost in a position to outline some of the more important ideas of import in this study, ideas which we were unable to clarify at the beginning. We used the expressions 'proto-language' and 'meta-language' and said that these have to come together to result in a 'scientific language' of universal understandability, utility and validity. We have also used the expression 'normalization' and 're-normalization' which require to be clarified. The three types of languages and the normalization which is important have to be conceived in terms of a normative notion which must be sufficiently easy for the human mind to grasp intellectually. What is more, it must have the advantage of easy communicability whether through speech or writing. It has to be proof against the gradual encroachment of vernacularisms or *patois* which may be called broad, low or parochial. It must have an innate stability depending on its intrinsic character. The very validity of the normative notion must be its recommendation, and the spread and acceptance of this norm must not call for any movement to propagate it as with closed religious groups. Its open scientific status must be the basis of whatever utility or interest it might have. As its soundness shows itself, it must get a reputation depending on its own merits private or public. To have all these conditions fulfilled naturally it is best that it agrees with nature both human and what belongs to the environment. Physics and psychology, as Bertrand Russell[44] said, have been approaching from both sides to meet in what he called 'neutral monism'. This process of mutal rapproachment of two natural aspects of human thinking as represented respectively by what we call physics and metaphysics, if it has been taking place, must be intelligently made all the more till these aspects of thought fuse into a normative basis both physical and metaphysical. Mind and matter, spirit and body, physics and psychology, geometry and algebra and many other pairs of words refer to the same schematically understandable aspects of human thinking. In the world of science we have already referred to them tentatively as the observables and the calculables. The distinction itself is a vertical rather than a horizontal one to use here in advance the terminology we are still in the process of justifying. Language itself can emerge only where it could be meaningful.

If observables refer backwards to an archetypal pattern of language within the mind of man naturally, resembling geometry as Pascal and Bergson[45] not to speak of Descartes and later Cartesians have intuitively known and have pointed out in their writings, the calculables would also be symbolic in the sense that algebra is. Algebra by its symbolism refers to the Platonic world of the intelligibles like numbers, as opposed to quantity. It may be said to be a language that refers forwards and upwards to abstraction of ideas. Symbolic logic which depends on algebra has already been named a **meta-language**. By this very token it is that we have here referred to the other anterior aspect of the structure of linguistic thought as referring to a **proto-language**. We have to visualize the whole matter schematically in order to follow the stages by which we could pass on from what we have called the normalization of scientific thought to what we are going to clarify as the re-normalization of the same.

The Colour-Solid of Psycho-Physics as Model of Proto-Language

The blue of the sky, the mirage, the sky-blossom and the gleaming sky-reflection of the mirage surface, have been used by Sanskrit philosophers in speaking up of the phenomenal aspect of reality as superimposed as a passing show or appearance hiding reality which is behind. Without lapsing into oriental contemplative ways of philosophising or promoting wisdom through mere *a priori* solipcism, pantheism or syncretism, we could in a very matter-of-fact sense still assert with justice here that the colour-solid could be availed of as a model at least for representing in tangible form what we have called the proto-linguistic pattern of archetypal thinking.

If the question is put: 'What is colour' it could be answered in different languages, in the same tongue. We could say as the dictionary first puts it: Red of the blood, the blue of the sky, the green of grass are colours. Here definition is by mere arbitrary juxtaposition of name and form or colour aspects and nothing more. The helplessness of the lexiconist is evident. Ordinary expression in any tongue has to have this form for the sake of apodictic certitude of the resulting knowledge and no one says 'prove it'. The second meaning goes further from just juxtaposing the observable or the nameable, thinkable or calculable which are, in principle, the same as that number which Pythagoras said was the secret of the universe. We have distinguished it as the vertical. When the vertical aspect of language is admitted into the meaning a second degree certitude results which is not derived from the horizontal axis of reference but from the vertical. 2 + 2 = 4 is an apodictic certitude that the human child learns and accepts quickly when normal. As Piaget would say, "Seriation and classification spatially and in time" are simultaneous operations the child is capable of through stages of its mental development.[46] In a higher stage of the education of the child it will be able to grasp the second dictionary meaning of 'What is colour'. This time the meaning will be put as in Webster's *New International Dictionary* under second meaning as follows: "A sensation evoked as a specific response to stimulation of the eye and its attached nervous mechanisms by radiant energy of certain wavelengths and intensities." We have already here two grades of language: one of the first degree common sense language belonging to what Carnap would call the Protocol language dimension and level, and another which a secondary school-boy is taught to understand in the class-room. Both of them are scientific. In fact the common sense language being the result of the closest union of the observables and the calculables is valid without the intervention of syllogisms or pointer readings which only make scientific knowledge less apodictic or certain.

The second meaning in the dictionary under the word colour' is less scientific in one sense and more scientific in the other. The common vernacular is easily understood by the closed group which pertains to the vernacular tongue and the certitude has that horizontal quality in which the thought moves between very real or certain factors whether actual or virtual. In the statement 'the sky is red' the word 'sky' is an observable and 'red' is a name and thus of a conceptual order to be counted as belonging to the calculables. The mental status of the colour sensation which is becoming more confirmed as we have seen from the findings of Sir Russell Brain above justifies our assigning a virtual status to it which could be described as eidetic in the terminology of Rorschach's psychology. Colour vision has its cause within the skull and not in the object outside but the name by which a certain colour is recognised through ordinary language in any vernacular, belongs to the metaphysical context rather than the physical one. A concomitant correlation between two postulated points in the positive and the negative sides of the horizontal axis would thus characterise the nature of the common sense language. In the terminology developed in the Carnap school[47] this would correspond to the axis in which the pragmatic 'handling action' language,[48] the semeotic dimension of thing-language and the protocol language may be said to move. We shall be considering these terms presently in their proper contexts. For the present it would suffice to recognize that within the amplitude of actuality and virtuality which the mind is capable of in its alternating perceptual or conceptual activity there is always a concomitant variation as between points that we could mark in the positive limb of the horizontal and its own negative limb.

The second meaning is removed from the protocol language by its participating in less actual and more calculable aspects of knowledge which function simultaneously to create the phenomenon of meaning in consciousness. Since the vibrations that corresponds to colour and sensations are both physical facts one treated perceptually and not actually and the other treated conceptually and not virtually, we have to select the points of concomitant variation involved here very cautiously without violating methodological, epistemological or axiological factors which enter into the consideration of the particular language that science might employ systematically for some utilitarian or idealistic end to which the science is to be said correctly to belong. The person responsible for the discovery of the relation between vibrations and colour may also have to be taken into consideration for determining precisely the points of concomitant variations, agreements, differences or both that may belong to the four limbs of the vertico-horizontal frame of reference that we have outlined. Experts of the department of knowledge might have to have their say to be finalized by an expert commitee who understand what normalization means. One thing can be said at once. While in the first common sense meaning the two points were located apart in the total range of the amplitude, here they have to be brought together. If the knowledge is for merely serving curiosity about colours the branch of science is to be placed neutrally, and instinctive dispositions involved in curiosity and its intellectual counterpart have to determine where two other points have to be placed in the vertical axis. Instincts are retrospective in reference and therefore negative while the interests of scientific progress involved must find a degree marked on the positive side of the vertical axis. The relational picture involved here is quite different from that of the actual and virtual colours that were placed on the horizontal axis to begin with. The mystical joy, if any, involved in the first meaning must also be marked, if necessary on the vertical axis, to the extent that it is considered positive or negative in tone. The second case being relationally of another epistemological context, the curiosity satisfied is a more scientific one. Any number of other fractional or multiplied dimensions, qualitative or quantitative, could be added to analyse the proto-linguistic implications.

Normalization of Scientific Language

Out of the two ways of giving meanings to the question 'What is colour' we have so far discussed two varieties, one conforming to common sense requirements and the other with a more scientific purpose. The vertical component of the psycho-physical entity which gives us the satisfaction of knowing what colour is, has been slightly accentuated in the second instance when vibrations were equated with the name symbols standing for the different colours of the spectrum. If a colour manufacturer interested in actual colours and not in science for its own sake was thinking of vibrations with relation to colours these two factors would have to be put in the horizontal axis. For a pure scientist in the class-room thinking of the subject for its pure knowledge a symbolic equation treating colour by letter in the abstract and vibration grades by number would bring them both into the vertical. When the relation is still of a hypothetical status the vertical and horizontal may be put together tentatively in view of apodictic certitude when it will be vertical, horizontal or both. What is positive horizontal might have to be put on the negative side and primacy given to what appears otherwise. Normalization thus has its rules derived from epistemology and methodology with an axiological purpose as an over-all consideration. Symbolic logic can deal only with the verticalised aspects and can therefore have no utility except in steps of mathematical inference involved. We shall be returning to this question later. All that we wish to stress at this stage is that normalization is not easy and as we have said already in page (280 above) promiscuous mixing up of aspects in violation of the innate structure of thought makes the language absurd. If metaphysics is non-sense we could retaliate and say pseudo-science lends to the point of absurdity.

What Normalization Can Do to the Language of Science

When the vertical and the horizontal aspects of language are juxtaposed a certain system is put into language and it gains an apodictic character without further demonstration or syllogistic steps of inference. No better example for this could be found than the case of the colour solid. The colour solid is able to circumvent the difficulties of vernacular confusions of tongues and in one domain at least succeeds in creating the possibility of a standard universal language that is scientifically valid. From it we are able to derive the theoretical basis of a universal language for all sciences if the integration of all branches of knowledge would be possible. The over-all integration of the whole range of sciences and philosophies could be undertaken with the same model of the structure of thought. In branches like sound or heat or the sensation of taste we could adopt the same model so that the monadic units and the monad-of-monads unit conceived on an absolute basis could all adhere and organically cling together. The rough possibility of a language for unified science based on a scheme of integration for each minute branch of science having the same proto-linguistic elements as the over-all scheme thus comes into view.

How to Adapt the Structure of Colours to Linguistic Purposes

Again let us put to ourselves the question 'What is colour?' A complete scientific answer is found in the second half of its second meaning of it as given in Webster's *New International Dictionary*[49] which fortunately gives us within as short a span as possible the full psycho-physical and categorical implications: We shall take the liberty of extracting from it here expressing our gratitude to the author of the same:

> Colour may be regarded as a psychological category; it can be described and specified in terms derivable from introspective analysis, without any reference whatever to wave lengths, to energy or to any physical category; but it is also possible to state the physical correlates of the psychologically determined attributes of colour and to draw up some psycho-physical relations between them. All colours are divisible into two classes, the *chromatic* colours, as reds, greens, purples, browns and pinks, and the *achromatic* or *neutral* colours, including black, white and the intermediate series of greys. The latter are found to differ from each other only in their degree of resemblance to, or difference from black (or white), and with each other, grey differing from its intermediate neighbours by equal sense of differences.

This series can be made into a scale by assigning an ordinal number to each grey either ascending towards the lighter greys from black as zero or ascending with positive numbers or descending with negative numbers from median grey as zero. That attribute which thus measures the variation of the greys is called **brilliance**; dark greys have low, median grey has medium and light greys have high brilliance. Chromatic colours differ from each other not only in brilliance, but also in hue and saturation. **Hue** is that attribute in respect to which colours may be described as red, yellow, green or blue, or as intermediate between two of these. Hues form a natural **cyclic** series (**hue cycle**, **colour cycle** or **colour gamut**). Colours of the same hue and equal brilliance may differ from each other in **saturation**, that is in vividness of hue or in degree of difference from grey. In terms of these three attributes, colours may be arranged in a symbolic tri-dimensional space (**colour solid**) having the grey series as axis, with median grey at the centre and black and white at the extremities; (*fig.* 18.1). Corresponding to each grey is a plane perpendicular to the axis, in which lie the points representing all colours of equal brilliance. In each plane hue is represented cyclically in the order of the hue cycle; and saturation is represented radially with the axial points (greys) as reference points of zero saturation. Thus any colour can be specified by giving three ordinal numbers (colour constants or dimensions) which are co-ordinates of the corresponding point in the colour solid. By establishing arbitrary division points on the scales ofbrilliance and saturation any colour can be described as having very low, low, medium high or very high position in these scales. . . . . . . By the establishing of arbitrary points of division on the hue cycle, hues can be classified as yellowish-red, reddish-red-yellow, red-yellow, etc. . . . . . All principal definitions in this dictionary are in introspective terms like the following: **bay** a colour red-yellow in hue, of low saturation and of low brilliance; **carmine** a colour red in hue, of high saturation and low brilliance.

We can see here that hue is a factor that could be correlated to the horizontal axis of the scheme we have been developing in this Part and that brilliance belongs to the vertical axis. Saturation is a third radial reference depending on the degree of centralization. This last could be described as representing the combinatorial mode in terms of thought while the other two dimensions determine the two main categories into which characteristics of thought could exist negatively or positively in the schematic linguistic space of human consciousness. A normative proto-linguistic basis for the correlation of thought characteristics and modes of combination has been outlined on an experimental basis so far and we pass on to the re-normalization of meta-linguistic aspects in the next division of the study.

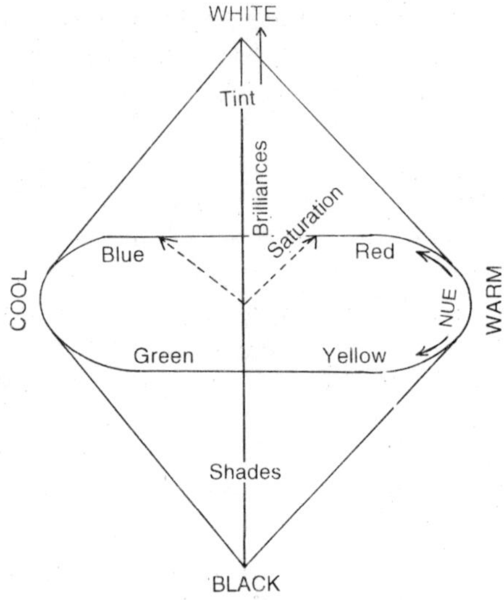

fig. 18.1: Figure of Colour Solid treated as a non-arbitrary basis for thought integration.[50]

Division III : Theoretical Considerations

As we are leaving behind with the present Division our discussion of a language for unified science from a strictly experimental point of view into the present one which relies on purer linguistics, logic, mathematics and more philosophical or 'meta-physical' aspects of reality it becomes necessary to preface it with certain preliminary remarks of methodological, epistemological and axiological import. Scientific validity depends on the apodictic certitude resulting from a methodic treatment of items of knowledge which have sufficient significance in human life. Far off ends and means dualistically conceived would be less scientific to the extent that the verity in question is not certain. Too many indirect pointer readings of observables and too many steps of inference intervening in calculables detract to that extent from the degree of certitude of scientific findings.

As we are here concerned not merely with scientific certitude but also with the language that can express this certitude derived from the various aspects of reality correctly put together to result in conviction and as language itself is an activity belonging to a neutral trans-subjective and inter-physical order, as we have already explained, that language which is most suitable for the scientific purposes of scientists for their own sake, for the expert outside public and for the common man's edification or education has to follow the broad lines of the structure of thought as it exists anteriorly as it were in the proto-physical as well as the metaphysical-aspects of thought. Linguistic consciousness may be said to have a stratum that is anterior and one that is posterior. The latter is more overt than innate. Corresponding to the innate and overt levels there should be an accordance or agreement reflected in the language employed. Mathematical, symbolic or logical language outside geometrical thinking which though mathematical belongs to a proto-linguistic order, leads us upward as it were, into the proper domain of the meta-language relying more on the **name** aspect than the actuality of **form**.

This study is based on certain fundamental notions out of which we have to keep in mind a few leading notions so that details may not confuse the reader. Firstly there is the notion of the unitive norm as neutral between physics and meta-physics. Proto-language and meta-language must refer to this norm from both sides. The meaning that emerges like all the varieties of colours in the colour solid that we have examined in detail at the end of the previous division could be treated globally or item by item to reveal the combinations, modes and characteristics of language. Normalized meaning would be understandable to experts, the intelligent public or to the common man, just as the definitions colours (as explained in the last Division) in the dictionary are meant to be understood by all who are capable of using a dictionary meant for common use. A standard terminology could be developed as it has been done in respect of various shades and intensities of colour. Normalization takes place in two opposing senses; one in which proto-language lends certitude to language which is from the negative to the positive direction in the vertical axis. We have called this process 'normalization' because this process should be first understood before the downward or negative normalization of the over-specific aspects of thought can be clearly visualized. As in psycho-physics and in the colour solid to which we have referred, psychology and physics meet neutrally with perfect legitimacy and validity without contradicting any epistemological, logical, mathematical or linguistic thoughts. The author of the dictionary article on the colour solid has stressed the physical side of its reality as against the aspect of science which depends on calculables. If the measurements of a table could be said to be arbitrary the geometrical language used in integrating colours schematically would be arbitrary. As we have explained at the beginning, if a school-master puts a dot on the black-board and called it *p* he is as non-arbitrary as language could ever permit. As the question is of an epistemological order we are justifying the objection recorded in the footnote there in this general section where we are considering neutrally and normatively the status of the scheme even as a psycho-physical scheme which has its reality at the meeting point of introspection and open-eyed observation. Instead of algebra and geometry meeting in analytical geometry the observables and the calculabes meet on neutral ground in the schema built on the analogy of the colour solid. We claim for it full scientific status, in the name of the common epistemology which must be implied in any integrated or unified science.

Other Equally Valid Schematic Representations

In Eddington's *Space, Time and Gravitation* there is an imaginary conversation between a relativist and a mathematician in which the latter admits that pure mathematician is not concerned with the truth of his propositions and the Relativist replies:

> *Je pense que dans l'Univers réel il doit exister un groupe d'entités liées les unes aux autres dans un ordre quadridimensionnel bien defini et qu'elles sont les bases de l'univers que nous percevons aussi loin*

> *que la physique nous a permis de l'explorer. Les lignes droit dans l'espace à trois dimensions forment groupe quadridimentionnel d'entités, autrement dit elles ont un ordre quadruple. On ne peut donc pas prévoir le nombre ultime des dimensions de l'univers si toutefois le mot dimensions est applicable.*

Earlier in the same conversation the distinction between a **variable** understood mathematically and a **dimension** understood relativistically was explained by the Relativist as follows:

> *Je crois qu'il-y-a une signification réelle attaché au temps consideré comme quatrième dimension, et non plus, simplement une quatrième variable, le terme 'dimension' me parait lié à une idée d'ordre. Mon opinion est que l'ordre des évenements dans la nature est un ordre quatri-dimensinnel indissoluble . . . .*[51]

Vectorial psychology uses the same scheme. Variables pertain to meta-language and dimensions to the proto-linguistic context. Valid science results by their fusion.

The Philosophical Basis of the Proto-Language

Besides Pascal and Bergson who have used the schematic proto-language like the Cartesians we have the case of Kant himself who was able to think of his categories in its primitive schematised form. The summary of his schematism is explained as follows:

> Now all the primary modes of the operations of the understanding, whereby objective unity is imparted to perceived matter may be reduced to one of these four quantity-quality, relation and modality. These with their subordinates Kant denominates categories after Aristotle, as determining in and by themselves, what in general and antecedentally (*à priori*) may be predicted of objects. The three categories of quantity are, unity, multitude and totality; those of quality, reality, negation and limitation. Those of relation are

> double and are paired together, as substance and accidents, cause and effect, action and reaction. Lastly the subordinates of modality are possibly existence and necessity.
>
> The process by which the categories or pure notions of the understanding are combined, with space and time, the pure intuitions of sensation, and thereby presented to knowledge, in their possible application to the objects of sense, Kant calls Schematism (schematismos). For instance the notion of substance is said to be schematized when it is not conceived of absolutely as a self-subsisting thing, but as one that persists in time and therefore as a constant and persisting substrate of certain variable qualities or determinations. Notions thus rendered sensible are called schematized in opposition to the pure categories.[52]

Descartes' great discovery contains the same elements of schematised correlates which belong to a proto-linguistic context. It constitutes a major event in the history of the development of scientific language.

Leibniz had a monadology constructed on the same schematic basis in which he tended to verticalize reality by abolishing the value of space. He used the expression 'meta-physical points and substantial forms' as applied to the 'prime absolute principles of all composite things which he ultimately resolved into them'.[53] The principle of occasionalism in Descartes was elaborated by Spinoza into his concept of the 'thinking substance' which was to be fitted into his double aspect theory or scheme which means:

> . . . that the mind and the body of an individual are two distinguishable but inseparable aspects of a single underlying substance or process. Spinoza as a consequence of his metaphysical doctrine that 'thinking substance and extended substance are one and the same thing' (*Ethics* Part I : Prop. 7) was committed to the two aspect theory of the body-mind relation.[54]

Scientific philosophers have always adhered to this proto-linguistic pattern of thinking. We have seen how Hume has no respect for anything but number or quantity (cf. p. 277 above) and even Locke, known for his dictum that mind is a clean slate, we find adhering to the following analysis of the content of consciousness. While his doctrine of signs might refer to the metalinguistic aspects, his analysis of basic aspects of knowledge is contained in his *Essay Concerning Human Understanding*. We read:

> Within the four sorts of agreement or disagreement is, I suppose contained all the knowledge we have, or are capable of: for all the inquiries that we can make concerning any of our ideas, all that we know and can affirm concerning them is, that it is, or is not, the same with some other; that it does or does not always co-exist with some other idea; or that it has a real existence without the mind.[55]

The categories of thought are here stated in such simplicity that a schematic representation becomes necessary even to say that we follow the classification.

The idea of the quaternion from which vectorial and projective geometrical ideas have developed is a very ancient one. We shall consider the mathematical and logical implications of this ancient idea separately. Before passing from this division we are tempted to quote two lines from Milton to show how the idea has persisted in literature from ancient times:

> Ye elements of the eldest birth
> Of Nature's womb that in *quaternion* run.

Proto-Linguistic Elements in Complex Numbers

Proto-linguistic elements are seen to be present in the structure of complex numbers. The imaginary number 'i' enters into the structure of complex numbers in which real and imaginary numbers enter into relations to be understood in terms of quaternions. Vectors, tensors and scalars are later outgrowths of the concept of quaternions.[56]

Proto-Linguistic Structure Implicit in Syllogistic Form

When Leibniz wrote, 'I hold that the invention of the form of syllogisms is one of the most beautiful that the human mind has made, and asserted that 'It is a kind of *universal mathematics* whose importance is not sufficiently known' he was undoubtedly thinking of the proto-linguistic elements that it represented. Continuing the same line of thought he wrote:

> Algebra itself is not the true characteristic of geometry, but quite another must be found, which I am certain will be more useful than algebra for the use of geometry in the mechanical sciences. And I wonder that this has hitherto been remarked by no one. For most of all men hold Algebra to be the true mathematical art of discovery and as long as they labour under this prejudice, they will never find the true characteristics of the other sciences.[57]

When he referred to the **alphabet of human thoughts** as also to *de Arte Combinatoria* and the *ars characteristica* and added that by the first he had found the "means of accomplishing in all sciences what Descartes and others

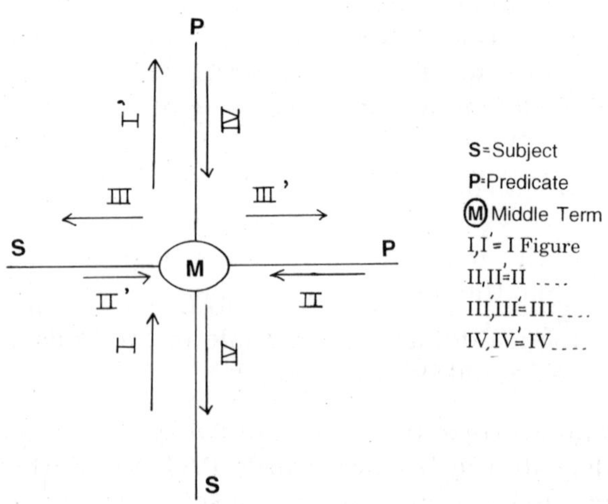

fig. 18.2

have done in Arithmetic and Geometry by algebra and analysis" it is not too difficult to guess what was in his mind. He had discovered a proto-linguistic element on which he could build his universal language. The fourfold structure of the form of syllogisms gave him the basis for the superstructure he was planning to erect. Syllogisms represent inferential movements in consciousness represented by the middle term which we might call zero point. Instead of subject and predicate we could have the signs (–) and (+). There are thus two sets of reversible movements involving the middle term. Schematically we could represent the syllogistic inferences as shown in *fig*. 18.2.

Un-normalized Use of the Schematic Proto-Language

The properties of a right angled triangle as revealed by the Pythagoras Theorem holds good in two ways referring to the two axes vertical or horizontal or both treated together. There is the practical verification that is possible as also the pure one through mathematical logic un-aided by experimental aspects. Thought or reasoning may be said to move along the two axes while the resultant conviction refers to a middle term which corresponds to the norm. Now that Euclidean space and Newtonian motion have been questioned other considerations have come in to distort the certitude. The three angles of a triangle do not amount to two right angles any more. Non-Euclidean geometry has displaced the Euclidean. Relativistic epistemology gives primacy to the observer and there are many right answers to the same question instead of a single right one. As Wittgenstein would put it,

> 2°03 In the atomic fact the objects hang one in another like the members of a chain.[58]

Speaking about Eddington's Principle in the *Philosophy of Science* Sir Edmund Whittaker said:

> Leibinz however initiated a new philosophical outlook: he advocated in his own words (Vol. VI, Mathesis Universalis) a subordination of a science of quantity to the science of quality — of a science that deals with

> numerical relations to that which treats of order and similarity. This is Eddingtonianism pure and simple.

Earlier in the same context he had said:

> Eddington's Principle depends on the distinction between what we have called quantitative and qualitative assertions; it may be stated thus: *All the quantitative propositions of physics, that is the exact value of the pure numbers that are constants of science may be deduced by logical reasoning from qualitative assertions without making any use of quantitative data derived from observation.*[59]

That geometrical representations were part of the programme that Eddington had in mind when influenced by Leibniz became evident when the work of Eddington was followed up by others like S.R. Milner F.R.S. after projective geometry was developed and adopted as a language for advanced science. It is interesting to follow Whittaker further to see with what hesitation the claims of a normal proto-language became tacitly adopted. He continues:

> The first progress in carrying out the Leibnizian programme was achieved in the field of geometry . . . The new projective geometry included old metrical geometry as a particular case, the qualitative concept of *order was shown to lead to a greater degree of power and generality than the quantitative* concept of *measurement.*[60]
>
> . . . . Eddington based his theory, so far as mathematics is concerned on what he called e-numbers. These are sixteen symbols on the foundations of which it is possible to construct a non-commutative algebra. . . . . Milner has now formed from them a class of expressions which he calls E- tensors which may be regarded as a new kind of tensors since they possess in common with tensors the linearity and the group property, but they are transformed by the rotations of the axes of space and time in a different way from

> ordinary tensors and thus he has created a new branch of tensor analysis, which he has used as the basis of new developments in theories of gravitation and electromagnetism.[61]

He consludes strikingly with reference to the **structure of the universe** which is to be understood in terms of number:

> . . . . I think we are compelled to believe that there is a number, at present of the order 10 raised to 78/1 which is fundamental in relation to the structure of the universe. The question is whether with Eddington we believe this number to be constant in time or whether with Dirac and Jordan, we believe it to be increasing.[62]

He alludes to the reciprocal interdependence between the amount of matter in the universe and the constant of gravitation. With the schema that we have developed in these pages it is not difficult even to see without entering into the specialized mathematics that is employed by Whittaker that gravitation qualitatively understood would correspond to our vertical axis and that numbers when referring to the quantitative aspect of the universe must be what we call horizontal. There is a slight touch of mysticism and theology when Sir Edmund concludes:

> We stand in awe before the thought that the intellectual framework of nature is prior to nature herself— that it existed before the material universe began its history—that the cosmos revealed to us by science is only one fragment in the plan of the eternal.[63]

It is not the mystic touch that we wish here to refer to as un-normalized use of the schematic proto-language. Leibniz minimised the importance of the horizontal aspects of reality and monads were like the chain links that Wittgenstein speaks about. A tendency to verticalization at the expense of the ill-understood pre-established harmony factor as Leibniz would say is what is not correct according to strict norms of epistemology.

Other Ways of Violating Normative Rules

Number and quantity as representing the vertical and the horizontal aspects of thought, meet in a certain way with Eddington and Leibniz. With both they tend to be verticalized and the harmony between the two axes of reference are to that extent marred by disproportion. The schematic language that Eddington uses to show the difference between the Absolutist pattern of thought and the Relativistic pattern which, according to him, should be four-dimensional as we saw above (p. 318). In discrediting the Absolutist version he gives a figure which we copy below from his *Nature of the Physical World* which affords an example of the use of a schematic language violating normative rules. The time element is reduced into a mere point and the unrealistic pattern of a plane geometrical model used while for the Relativist pattern he takes care to give duration a line rather than a point as here. The divergent lines are not justified when rational and axiological values are included. A present devoid of significance is what he represents. There are subtle violations of epistemological, methodological and axiological rules:[64]

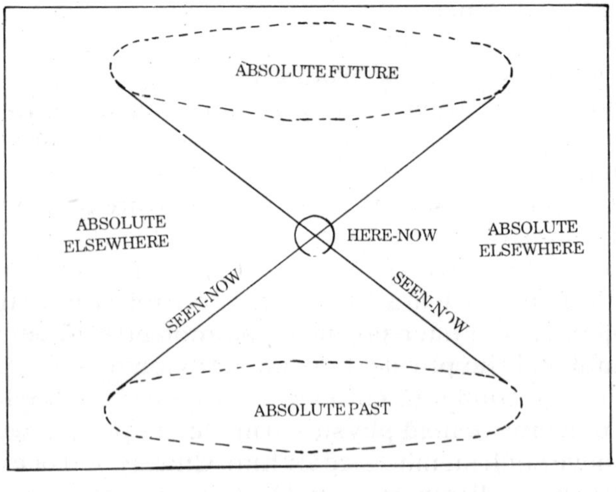

fig. 18.3

He explains in the text as follows:

> These hour glasses (drawn through each point of the world considered in turn as the Here-Now) embody what we know of the absolute structure of the world so far as space and time are concerned. They show how the grain of the world runs.

The arbitrariness with which he treats this schematic language which should be normalized, is admitted by Eddington when he continues:

> Father time has been pictured as an old man with a scythe and an hour-glass. We no longer permit him to mow instants through the world with his scythe; but we leave him his hour glass.

Bergson's Schematic Language of a Changing Reality

After examining Eddingtonian proto-language the philosophy of Bergson which is both scientific and intuitionist at once offers us a chance for making more explicit the use of the schematic proto-language in integrating different schools of philosophy. There is, as we said, a scientific philosophy, a scientific science and a philosophy of science based on whichever aspect of reality we consider primary, whether the vertical or the horizontal or both. Locke, Hume and Berkeley take their stand on values belonging to the first mentioned category. Eddington is a philosopher of science which is a recent development. In between we have philosophers or scientists or those who are both who speak of the subject and the object together. Psycho-physics is at the core of such a compact central group and language has its life in the vertical aspect of this core referring to the trans-subjective and inter-physical common ground between the mental and the physical. As an astronomer and a physicist Eddington thinks in numbers and quantities applicable to the universe of field physics. Time in its pure aspects does not have such significance for him. Change and becoming for Bergson are all important and he takes his position as it were

within reality rather than as a thinker **outside**. He refers to *éxpérience integrale* in contradistinction to a mere generalization of experience.[65]

Bergson mistrusted '*le rêve d'une mathématique universelle*' as a survival of Platonism, and continues:

> *Kant a pris pour une réalité ce rêve de quelque philosophes modernes: bien plus il a cru que toute connaissance scientifique n'était qu'un fragment détaché, ou plutôt une pierre d'attente de la mathematique universelle. Dès lors, la principale tâche de la Critique était de fonder cette mathematique, c'est-à-dire de determiner ce qui doit être l'intelligence et ce que doit être l'objet pour qu'une mathématique ininterompue puisse les relier l'un à l'autre.*[66]

Bergson's mistrust of an integrated understanding of reality through the symbolism of mathematics even when symbolism is made more universal was natural for his time because the latest developments of topology which belong to the proto-language aspect with its geometrical schemes is a new kind which had not attracted much attention at the time he wrote his best works. When we find that he himself uses such a proto-language in his writings this proves that the kind of mathematics involved in schematised explanations of reality synthetically understood was not repugnant to him. He should himself be classed as a psychologist rather than as a cosmologist. Just as the observer and the field of his observation went together in relativism as opposed to absolutism, so Bergson viewed the evolutionary process of reality as an inner witness rather than as an outer observer.

The proto-language employed by Bergson becomes clear to us from the following example:

> *D'où vient alors qu'une existence en dehors de la conscience nous paraît claire quand li s'agit des objets, obscure quand nous parlons du sujet? Nos perceptions, actulelles ey virtuelles, s'étendent le long de deux lignes, l'une horizontale AB, qui contienttous les objets simultanés dans l'espace,*

> *l'autre verticale CI, sur laquelle se disposent nos souvenirs successifs échelonnes dans le temps. Le point I, intersection des deux lignes, est qui soit donné actuellement à; notre conscience . . .*[67]

We are not concerned directly in this study with the philosophies of Kant or Bergson. It is not therefore the question here to decide whether Eddington or Bergson are nearer to reality. From the way they give coherence to their views through a proto-linguistic schema it is possible for us to take a position in the integrated whole which is the field of reasoning Bergson's philosophy may be said to derive its validity and value from, that zone where body and mind meet. What he calls his *schèma moteur* tallies on broad lines with our own except that its colouration with actuality is feeble. Its brilliance as referring to the vertical is high and realities that are peripheral or actual in an empirical sense do not count for much in his writings although colourlessly implied in the intensely active *élan vital.* A verticalized type of absolutist and living psychology could be the characterisation that we could make *grosso-modo* in a mixture of the common language with the schematic language developed here. Further precision will be attempted in the pages that remain.

If we add here that for Eddington, time was an abstraction and space more real while for Bergson it was the other way about, a fair comparative appraisal of the two philosophies would be seen as possible in the light of our scheme of integration.

The Light of Scientific Linguistics on Prime or Proto-Language

Other experts who have been engaged in linguistic research have at last discovered that it is useless to follow that hackneyed line of investigation which looks for the origin of language in the gestures and laconic grunts of savage people. This kind of theory which is based on a Darwinian evolutionist bias, hitherto affecting the thought of many branches of science, is more and more discredited at present. How far experts are turning their backs on this kind of approach is marked by the interdiction officially announced by the *Société Linguistique de Paris* who say : The society does not admit any communication concerning either the origin of language or the creation of a universal language.

In spite of this negative attitude to this aspect of the subject, however, interest in the origin of language, not necessarily evolutionist in the usual sense, has survived and progressed till modern times. Some attempts to reach backwards by extrapolation from the given in language has been undertaken both in the old and new worlds. Two theories stand out claiming our notice here: One is based on the lyric songs and dances of primitive peoples and the other is seeking the origin of language in verbal imperatives like 'kill', 'smash', 'help', 'strike', etc. of people of the area of the African Great Lakes. This last thesis is that, as with Dr. A.S. Diamond who published his *History and Origin of Language* in 1959, with imperative utterences like 'Help', 'Murder', etc. other parts of speech developed round the noun-verbs through accretion of necessary elaboration. John L.M. Trime who has traced these details in a recent talk on *Who Taught Me Language* explains:

> In all languages the stock of basic significant sound units (phonemes) is small . . . . Of these, certain types, plosives (p, t, k, b, d, g, etc.) and nasals (m, n, ng) are particularly common. Upon this narrow basis is constructed a large number of morphemes — simple words, roots and affixes.[68]

After thus probing to the very bottom of linguistic elements that combine to make language he refers to what he characteristically calls the **ascending heirarchy of units** which expression is of particular relevance in reference to our suggestion in this study that language belongs to the vertical axis. As what Mr. Trim says gives us the position of the latest of scientific linguists we reproduce here the paragraph that would give this study completeness in respect of linguistics approached from an angle that may be said to be our own.

> When subjected to proper methods of analysis, *the language of every community* investigated has proved

> to possess a fully developed '*regular structure*'. The types of structure encountered vary widely, but all share certain fundamental characteristics. All operate with a small repertory of basic sound units (phonemes) which are combined together in *set ways to form morphemes*, the basic meaningful *unit of language*, roots and affixes. These in turn are combined together in *set ways* to form an *ascending hierarchy of units* (such as 'word', 'clause', 'sentence') each having its own set pattern of subordinate units, each in turn larger and more complex and with a larger inventory. Above the word level the inventory is *too extensive* to list. Instead, statements of combinability are generalized in grammar. Above the sentence, permitted sentence is so free that no attempt is made to state the possibilities. Any substantial sequence of sentences will probably constitute a *unique utterence*. All languages are like this; the faculty of language consists simply in the ability to acquire and operate such a system, and all human beings possess it.[69]

We have quoted at some length from Mr. Trim and italicised those parts which concern this study closely to show that the general lines in which modern linguistics for all human beings is being developed has much that is in the spirit of the present study. 'Extension' and 'uniqueness' in the paragraph evidently suggest the two axes respectively, horizontal and vertical, the heirarchy itself being the active living and changing zone extending horizontally at its middle and re-uniting into uniquely significant speech at the top of the vertical axis. An electro-magnetic field may be said to present this kind of structure. In modern Particle Physics we have the structure of strangeness and parity with right-handed and left-handed spins which again suggest the same inner structure of the thought of man reflected in his language making him *Homo Sapiens* and *Homo Loquens* at once.

Our search so far has been into the domain of what we have tried to distinguish as proto-linguistics polarised as it were negatively at the bottom of the vertical axis of consciousness. Intellects that conform to what Pascal would call the *esprit géométrique*' are those best suited to an understanding of the structure of this aspect of language. The geometrical structure suggested is necessary to give to language its solid basis but this does not necessarily mean that a schematized reality is the best version of neutral normative reality understood philosophically which is quite another matter. The norm itself is somthing that is neither physical nor metaphysical. Between an epistemology that gives primacy to the physical aspect and the one that gives primacy to the metaphysical aspect there is a neutral ground in which the Absolute unitive norm is to be placed at the very core of our scheme. Language can result only by bringing together the proto or geometrical aspect in relation with the meta or algebraic aspect. If we have given importance to the geometrical aspect at this stage of our discussion it is for linguistic reasons and not for philosophical ones. These two aspects have to be kept apart in this study which is limited to the requirements of a scientific language. We pass on to the search for a meta-language in the next section.

The Difference Between Proto- and Meta-Language Aspects

Before we can pass from the discussion of the innate formal and schematized basis of language to the more open nominalistic and symbolically calculable terminal points of linguistic expression tending to what has been called babelization, we have to make this distinction more precise. Instead of entering into the merits of the three levels of semiotic (i.e., the general theory of signs) namely pragmatics, semantics and syntactics, for fear of getting lost in the tangle of theories and counter-theories about the subtler aspects of linguistics (e.g. as between leaders such as C.S. Peirce, Ogden and Richards, or by Morris and Carnap himself, who differ slightly or considerably between themselves in the matter of pragmatics and as between Aristotle's logical form, Euclidean axioms and Leibnizian calculi not to speak of Boole's logistic, Schroeder's higher functional calculus together with the contributions made to this body of mathematical, linguistic and logical thought in the recent years touching on the syntactical aspects and then entering into the various secondary grades of truth functions that belong to secondary aspects within the semantic level itself separating L-true or L-implicate or the F-false but L-true possibilities), we are concerned with seeing what kind of link there could be betwen what we have called proto- and meta-languages. The latter term has already received the recognition of Carnap who defines it as follows:

> Whenever an investigation is made about a language, we call this language the *object-language* of the investigation, and the language in which the results of the investigation are formulated, the *meta-language.*[70]

Even when a meta-language is employed to examine an object language the syntactical aspects which lie deep down the pragmatic level have to be studied by the same aspect in the meta-language leading to a linguistic indeterminacy due to the instrument of observation being more delicate or elusive than the object of investigation itself. Bertrand Russell writes about Carnap:

> Carnap advanced the theory that, when errors of syntax are avoided a philosophical problem is thereby either solved or shown to be insoluble. I think, and Carnap now agrees that this is an overstatement, but there can be no doubt that the utility of philosophical syntax in relation to traditional problems is very great.[71]

Besides Carnnap, Russell himself is the principal spokesman of the group of logical positivists who have behind them names with corresponding theories as between Morris and Bloomfield. Frege thought of logical rules without designata. Hilbert developed the axiomatic aspects with geometrical and symbolic calculi together.

The three vloumes of the *Principia Mathematica* jointly produced by Whitehead and Russell is the one work which brings to its culminating point this kind of logico-mathematico-philosophico-linguistic thought. The whole domain of investigation is capable of being characterised as bristling with hair-splitting if-s and but-s and tread certain grounds only when dealing with tautologies and contradictions analysed into numbered varieties of paradoxes. After looking at its pages full of symbols of which many other varieties exist adding to the confusion of tongues, one asks oneself 'what then' even supposing all this is true? Is this meant to serve human progress and in what respect?

The great Hume himself whose scepticism is referred to as the starting point for scientific philosophising remarked that it is clear definitions that count and not difficulties created by indeterminate meanings of words. 'Propositions are definitions' he states and continues, 'It is the same case with all those pretended syllogistical reasonings, which may be found in every other branch of learning except the sciences of quantity and number'.[72]

The attitude of Logical Empiricists in general is to give importance to signs and symbols as against schematic models or geometrical patterns. In other words they have a meta-linguistic prejudice. This is expressed by Carnap when he writes about attempts to make **intuitive** models by analogy with known **macro-processes**. Evidently, he is referring to schematic patterns such as what we have tried to present in this study. Carnap says:

> Many attempts have been made in this direction, but without satisfactory results. It is important to realize that the discovery of a model has no more than an aesthetic or didactic or at best a heuristic value, but is not at all essential for a successful application of a physical theory.[73]

Further on, he makes his attitude to proto-linguistic patterns clearer still when he states: "There the physicist could not tell us what he meant by the symbol 'E' in Maxwell's equations. Perhaps in order not to refuse an answer, he would tell us that 'E' designates the electric field-vector." Carnap concludes characteristically in a two-faced attitude: "An 'intuitive understanding' or a direct translation of 'E' into terms referring to observable properties is neither necessary nor possible."[74] The sour-grapism implied here is evident. The physicist is, generally speaking, not any better here.

Division IV : Logistic to Dialectic

The Attitude of Logical Empiricists

This makes of the language of symbolic logic, like that of higher mathematics suitable only in equating subtle epistemological or axiological counterparts, understood as it were in a dialectical context. While fighting *a priorism* and solipsism, the language preferred by empiricists, by a strange irony, fully admits these elements by the back door. The school-boy riddle about *A* being the brother of *B* but *B* **not** being the brother of *A* needs the horizontal observable aspect, the very aspect that symbolism misses totally. Physics above all other sciences to which the empiricist must give primacy, depending on field dimensions referring to quantitative, experimental and observable factors which are exactly what is omitted by the meta-language of signs and symbols. Even in the domain of calculables it takes three lines of formulae containing Greek letters with exponential signs and other special signs between them before proving as Wittgenstein points out,[75] that $2+2=4$. We cannot copy them here nor an ordinary printer print the three lines without having special types of innumerable varieties. This cannot be said to add to the simplicity of symbolic logical language for science. That it is not tenable for other intrinsic reasons of epistemology has been strikingly pointed out and not answered effectively by Russell himself for in Russell's own words in the Introduction to Wittgenstein's work:

> The essential business of language is to assert or deny facts. . . . In order that a certain sentence should assert a certain fact there must, however the language may be constructed, be something in common between the structure of the sentence and structure of the fact. This is perhaps the most fundamental thesis of Mr. Wittgenstein's theory. That which has to be in

> common between the structure of the sentence and the fact cannot, so he contends, be itself in turn *said* in language. It can, in his phraseology only be *shown*, not said, for whatever we may say will still need to have the same structure.[76]

To the syllogistic forms of Aristotle logistics have added their propositional calculus which instead of being based on middle term, subject or predicate have been further elaborated with the inclusion of words like 'is', 'are', 'not', 'and'. 'or', 'if'; 'any', 'some', 'every', 'all', which are said to correspond to signs of logic. The formalism of Aristotle is said to be superceded by the term syntactical structure. The meta-language must further have its preferred philosophical terms, replacing the more commonly understood ones. What contribution these make to an open and universal scientific language to be used by all, or by any at all is problematic. The airy verbosity in which semiosis has to thrive is evident from one more quotation we shall take, this time from C.W. Morris whose *Foundations of the Theory of Signs* offers as consistent a picture of the implications of the relation between signs and language as can be reasonably expected in any possible meta-language.

> Thus in Semiosis something takes account of something else mediately, i.e., by means of a third something. Semiosis is accordingly a mediated-taking-account-of. The mediators are *sign vehicles*, the taking-account-of are *interpretants*, the agents of the process are *interpreters*, what is taken-account-of are *designata*. There are several comments to be made of this formulation.[77]

The underlying credo of the school of linguistics is given in the following:

> . . . . it is necessary from the standpoint of behaviouristics to deny that such (*private*) experiences are of central importance, or that the fact of their existence makes the objective study of semiosis . . . impossible or even incomplete.[78]

Thus by being affiliated to one particular outlook and by reason of preferring meta-language as against any other possible or legitimate ones although such may be recognized as necessary as also by reason of the circumlocutory abstractions of the sign language which shuts out one whole aspect of truth from its purview and condemned anteriorly by Hume and posteriorly by Wittgenstein, the whole volume of effort in the direction of a language for unified science by logical empiricists seems to us to be heading towards an inevitable impasse. The later Wittgenstein has indicated roughly a way out of the blind alley which we shall presently examine linking it with the contributions of Leonard Bloomfield and Braithwaite's contributions to our correct understanding of what a scientific language should be.

The Inter-Physical and Trans-Subjective Structure of Language

At the beginning of this study we clarified the inter-physical and trans-subjective nature of linguistic events in the neutral consciousness of an observer-witness of a typical composite linguistic situation with four dimensions of two axes. Much experimental and theoretical evidences have been adduced to give this scheme its fullest possible status of non-arbitrariness and scientific, logical, mathematical and philosophical validity. More direct or indirect support will be derived in what we still have to say. Although avowedly affiliated to the context of Behaviourism C.W. Morris, in his efforts to delve into the syntactic structure of logical form depends more than perhaps he would admit on mental dimensions and subtle invisible processes. He uses expressions like the **dual control of linguistic structure** and is obliged to use such self-composed compound expressions 'mediated-taking-account-of' which are not fully made explicit. The later Wittgenstein may be said to step into the context at this point and his *Philosophical Investigations* contain an analysis of the subtler aspects of linguistic structure which is not given to the tough eye of mere behaviourists. Empiricism is only one degree removed from strict behaviourism and the pragmatists' approach is perhaps another degree. The behaviouristic aspect of language may be said to be the fraction of the ice-berg that is above water. Any linguistic that refuses to take account of the subtler explicit aspects unrecognized by behaviourism may to that extent be characterised as inadequate for arriving at a scientific language which combines observables and calculables together. The limitations under which a pragmatic linguist suffers have been put together by Leonard Bloomfield whose approach to linguistic problems is diametrically opposed to that of C. W. Morris. His linguistic credo is stated as follows:

> If language is taken into account, then we can distinguish science from other phases of human activity by agreeing that science shall deal only with events that are accessible in their time and place to any and all observers (strict *behaviourism*) or only with events that are placed in co-ordinates of time and space (*mechanism*), or that science shall employ only such initial statements and predictions as lead to definite handling operations (*operationalism*), or only terms such as are derivable by rigid definition from a set of every-day terms concerning physical happenings (*physicalism*).[79]

Bloomfield takes care to add soon after 'this delimitation does not restrict the subject-matter of science but rather characterises its method'.[80] How matter and method could be separated is not easy to understand, and if the limitations were strict the causes of negative hallucinations or pains or troubles like mutism and its etiology would be taboo to scientists. Such a closing of the frontiers of science is not in the interests of a unified science with a universal language.

Braithwaite of Cambridge has a more open attitude towards scientific language, as explained in his recent work to which Mr. B.C. Brookes refers in his article on the *Difficulty of Interpreting Science*.[81] Braithwaite distinguishes three levels of abstraction in a terminological hierarchy. The terms of the lowest level refer to simple observables. In the second level observables and theoretical terms are related and finally in the third level there are formulae (like Maxwell's hypothesis). These are formulae containing theoretical terms only which he distinguishes by the name Campbellian hypotheses. These include the highest and the most general laws. Mr. Brookes observes relevantly in this connection, 'Any actual science robbed of its most general hypotheses would, I believe, collapse under its own weight of detail.'

Terminological Hierarchies in Language

This terminalogical hierarchy with the first level lying at the meeting point of the vertical and the horizontal axes but referring only to the horizontal the second heirarchical level lying in the vertical but referring to the horizontal and the third lying wholly in the vertical and implying the horizontal, just as a magnetic field is implicit in electricity, could be very well appreciated by us in the light of the remarks and discussions above. Mr. Brookes concludes his article saying:

> . . . . any language . . . . in a literal sense is both the experience and the expression of it . . . . So those who ask for more and better interpretations of science can be wholly satisfied only if they join the scientist in his laboratory and learn how to share his scientific experience.[82]

The personality of the scientist as in the neutral witness observer '0' of our linguistic experimental situation is where, after all, scientific or any other language must be said to have its being.

The terminological hierarchy of Braithwaite is nothing other than the basis of the 'family resemblance' that Wittgenstein tries to reveal in his *Philosophical Investigations* through what he calls 'language games'. Linguistic space like logical, monadic, atomic or vectorical space is an abstraction where physics and metaphysics meet and fuse into unity. The unexpected puzzlements that are possible within this meeting point of the *logos* and the *nous* eludes strict scientific analysis. It can be looked upon as a mystery or a verbal oddity according to the temperaments ranging between the scepticism of a Hume or the belief of a Kierkegaard. This contains variables according to mathematicians or dimensions to relativists, and the principle of the quaternion runs through it. Such are some of the passing remarks we have to make before placing Wittgenstein rightly in the linguistic context of philosophical investigation. He may be said to mark an important stage in the understanding of the nature of language in its full philosophical light which is neither confined to observables nor calculables.

The Enigma of the Difference Between Earlier and Later Wittgenstein

Ever since the publication of the *Tractatus Logico-Philosophicus* of Wittgenstein a feeling of discomfort has been produced in the minds of philosophers who thought that factors like mind and self were so to be discovered by scientists at the tip of the scalpel or in the space within a bell-jar. Relativist and quantum mechanical ideas had opened a new vista for science, and empiricism and logic were put together. Mathematics and logic were married and logic was examined in a larger philosophical context. The laddar of logic itself was to be discarded and philosophers were asked to observe silence about matters that they did not fully understand as in the last saying of the earlier Wittgenstein which read:

> 6⁰54 My propositions are elucidatory in this way: he who understands me finally recognizes them as senseless, when he has climbed out through them, on them, over them. (He must so to speak throw away the ladder after he has climbed up on it.) He must surmount these propositions; then he sees the world rightly.
>
> 7 Where one cannot speak, thereof one must be silent.[83]

The content of this silence was meant perhaps to give the same subject a philosophical status. Philosophical puzzlement was such that language alone could finally penetrate into its secrets. Thus he called what he wrote *language games* instead of entering into proof, ontological or otherwise, about philosophical verities whether absolute or relative, pluralistic or monistic. Simple words were to divulge the subtle factors of philosophical puzzlement. The method was so novel and deturgent that intelligent thinkers in the West have not yet fully recovered from the effects of the sheer novelty of the approach to philosophy through language.

The language games devised by Wittgenstein amply make evident that the philosophical implications of language do not stop within the limits of physicalism, mechanism or operationism. It is not so simple as the handling action such as when someone said 'pass me an apple' and one was handy, one passed it and that was what covered the scope of all language as understood pragamatically by Bloomfield. The lyrical origin of words as Vico of Italy advocated and word-origin in verbal-noun imperatives like 'Help', 'Kill' as we have examined already, were not sufficient. The interconnections of the structure of language went in different dimensions or as between inner variables. Under item 67 of Wittgenstein's *Philosophical Investigations* we read:

> 67 . . . And we extend our concept of number as in spinning a thread we twist fibre on fibre. And the strength of the thread does not reside in the fact that some one fibre runs through the whole length, but in the over-lapping of many fibres.[84]

Just as the word games cover many kinds of games, number has kinds that have a family resemblance factor running through all of them. Here by the example of the fibres that go to give strength to the thread he wants to say that individual concepts have a dovetailing series of shades of meaning which make them hang together, with a subtle import running through their whole series giving them a vertical bond of unity.

Again under 284 we read:

> *Regardez une pierre et imaginez qu'elle ait des sensations. On se dit à soi même comment porrait —*

> *on en venir à cette idée d'attribuer une sensation à une chose? On pourrait aussi bien l'attribuer à une nombre! Et maintenant, regardez une mouche se tortiller; du coup la difficulté a disparu, et il semble que la douleur puisse s'attaquer là ou il n'y avait, pour ainsi dire, qu'un terrain trop lisse, trop uni pour elle et donc défavourable.*[85]

He then goes on to take the case of a dead body which would appear to be completely inaccessible to pain. The difference in attitude is not to be explained by saying that there is only difference of behaviour. He would rather say '*c'est là un cas de la transition de la quantité à la qualité*'.

He goes on to say under item 293 that an object could itself disappear out of account if put in a certain relation:

> *. . . si l'on construit la grammaire des expressions de la sensation d'aprés le modele "object et designation", l'objet même disparaît comme hors de propos.*[86]

In the example given of attributing sensation or pain to a stone above the psycho-physical or neutral status of language is brought out. Quality and quantity are treated on a par equitably as interchangeable trans-physically and inter-subjectively. The neutrality established between subject and 'designation' in the last quotation amounts linguistically to the abolition of the objective status of the thing to which the attribute is said to belong. Both the elements have to be on a par to be related at all.

The nature of the vertical relation that Wittgenstein takes all the trouble to explain, is strikingly brought out by another of his items of investigation. Under 77 he writes:

> . . . . the degree to which the sharp picture can resemble the blurred one depends on the latter's degree of vagueness . . . but if the colours in the original merge without a hint of any outline, won't it become a hopeless task to draw a sharp picture corresponding to a blurred one? — anything and nothing is right — and this is the position you are in

> if you look for definitions corresponding to our concepts in aesthetics and ethics.[87]

From the standpoint of a neutral-observer and witness which we have postulated earlier in this study, for experimental observations we could think of two situations arising as between the two persons in the dark room. Supposing that one had a tooth-ache or stomach-ache, to appreciate his pain it would be the same if the lights are on or out. If on the other hand the suffering was due to a heavy load that one carried it would be definitely better to have the lights on to measure the suffering involved. The age, stature, sex, complexion and other factors have to be appreciated by a **rapport** that is overt and inter-physical or to use our terminology, horizontal while the silent pain suffered without physical change in behaviour but possibly expressed in words would be activity that still remained within the limits of the vertical, at least from the linguistic standpoint.

After recommending silence in his earlier work at the end, Wittgenstein introduces us into the core of the philosophical sub-stratum of all language and thought in his later work.

In the last of the quotations above he hints that a vertical psycho-physical relationship between model and imitation is the way to axiology.

Pure Mathermatics and Dialectical Reasoning Fitted into the Scheme

Before we can treat of subjects like Aesthetics and Ethics which imply axiology we have to explain here a higher kind of reasoning which pure mathematics shares with what is vaguely understood in our times as Dialectics. Syllogistic propositions are the rungs of the ladder with which one attains to a-syllogistic reasoning. This ladder was what Wittgenstein asked the person who followed his propositions to discard in the last item of his *Tractatus*. When two pictures tallied with each other but differed in the degree of clarity of line, light or colour there is a maximum limit and a minimal limit within the amplitude of which such bi-polar relation could be recognized. Beyond these upper and lower limits as between tautology and contradiction in the propositional calculus of symbolic logic 'anything or nothing' is right. Ordinary syllogistic calculi refer more to the horizontal than the vertical movement of reasoning. The distinction drawn between fact truth and 'logic-truth', is that one is independent of the other. This verity is brought out strikingly by Wittgenstein when he states 'One can draw conclusions from a false proposition' (4°023).[88] Truth-functions and truth-grounds are distinguished under item 5°101 of the *Tractatus*, and a schematic representation of sixteen truth-possibilities in symbolic and ordinary language ranging from an upper limit of tautology and a lower limit of contradiction as between '*p*' and '*q*' which are related elements. The shortcomings of Frege's and Russell's way of looking at logic giving primacy to the horizontal aspect without recognizing the vertical principle running through the whole series are effectively pointed out in several places such as where he says: 'Laws of inference, which — as in Frege and Russell — are to justify the conclusions are senseless and would be superfluous.' (5°132)

In this vertical view of logic taken by Wittgenstein what is important for us in this study, is to note what he says in respect of relations between a theory of knowledge, a branch of natural science and philosophy conceived as an activity.

> '(The word philosophy must mean something which stands above or below, but not beside the natural sciences).' (4°111)
>
> 'Philosophy is not a theory but an activity' (4°112)
>
> 'The theory of knowledge is the philosophy of psychology' (4°1121)

Earlier he said: All philosophy is 'Critique of language" (4°0031)

Put together in the light of his later writings which go beyond the zone oı propositions into the domain of linguistic structure in a purer form irrespective of considerations of duality between '*p*' and '*q*' which is the subject of all the paradoxes of Russell, we have a modernized version of the age old dialectical method of reasoning dating from Parmenides and Zeno of pre-Socratic days. It represents according to the schematic terminology that we have developed in this study simply a vertical way of higher reasoning. A.C. Bradley in recent years devoted a whole volume to the demolition of conventional textbook logic and install, instead, the time honoured dialectical way of which Hegel in modern philosophy revived a version though vitiated by historical perspectives which were extraneous to pure dialectical thinking. A horizontal bias has been given to dialectics in the version which is known as dialectical materialism that is meant to support politics. What Bradley says in the context of double negation would be sufficient for us to quote here just to show that there are other modern writers who understood fully the implications and the differences as between horizontal and vertical reasoning:

> It is obvious that *duplex negatio affirmat.* To say 'It is false that A is *not* B is equivalent to the positive assertion 'A is B'. But this is not because the added negation barely negates the original judgment. For if that were all, we should be left with nothing. If mere not-A is simply zero, then not-not-A, is if possible less. We must not say that negation presupposes a positive judgment, which is left in possession when the negative is negated. For we saw before (Ch. III Sec. 4) that this positive judgment is not presu-pposed.[89]

What is important for us to gather here from the above is that logic like language is an activity that moves up or down a vertical scale as implied in the familiar terms still prevailing in academic circles from most ancient times: ascending and descending dialectics. Let us hear the words of Prof. Louis Lavelle of the Collège de France who summarising his course and said:

> . . . . *Enfin, la question se pose de savoir comment*

> *l'unité de l'esprit peut engendrer la multiplicité des idées. Et si l'on remonte facilement du monde à l'idée dans une dialectique ascendente, c'est la dialectique descendante qui est l'objet propre de la metaphysique. Platon ne l'a qu'esquissé.*
>
> *. . . . il s'agit surtout pour Aristote de montrer comment l'idée s'incarne, alors que pour Platon, il s'agissait au contraire de montrer comment elle se désincarne.*[90]

Bergson himself refers to the two functions of the intelligence in terms of what he calls a latent form of geometrical or spatial intuition that is latent at the basis of deduction and induction in reasoning which he qualifies as '*fonctions essentielles de l'intelligence.*'[91]

Even Charles Sanders Pierce could be quoted to support this vertical and active view that he evidently takes when even remaining a leader of pragmatic and pluralistic thought he says:

> When I just said that thought is an *action*, and that it consists of a *relation*, although a person performs an action and not a relation, which can only be the result of an action, yet there is no inconsistency in what I said, but only grammatical vagueness.[92]

It is not certain if the followers of Pierce would accept that he had consciously or unconsciously something of the old world way of dialectics in his mode of thinking but a close scrutiny of the distinction he makes is the same as what we want to make in this study as between the vertical and horizontal aspects of language and grammar respectively.

Pure mathematics which consists in equations especially in the statements of the principal findings of science, is a highly verticalised **version of** a common language which might be said to spread its ideas horizontally.

The quantum theory tends to abolish the concrete or the horizontal aspect of language in favour of a verticalized one. Eddington writing on this subject shows us how the new language of physics in the context of quantum mechanics speaks the symbolic and concrete language of co-ordinates.

> . . . if the quantum theory condemns these images as too concrete, and leaves us with no co-herent images at all, at least we have symbolic co-ordinates and momenta and Hamiltonian functions devoting themselves with single minded purpose to ensuring that qp-pq shall equal to $ih/2\,\pi$.[93]

Every equation may be said to imply dialectical reasoning because the contrete sensory aspect is absent and reasoning moves up or down inductively or deductively through an axis where all active thinking may be said to reside, to give clear ideas primacy over brute matter. Dialectical reasoning is most concerned with that third level of scientific terminological hierarchy that Braithwaite refers to as consisting of Campbellian hypotheses. Between what we have called the proto-linguistic and the meta-linguistic the former resembling geometry and the latter algebra there is a vertical line along which thought moves up and down to produce the language of Campbellian hypotheses. When translated into common language the same findings of science become expressed in a horizontal version of the same fact, truth or value content. All scientific language when properly normalized or re-normalized upward to the central norm or downward from the meta-linguistic side result in common language irrespective of the vernacular tongues. Such is the main line of thought that we have sustained throughout in the present study. That mathematics itself consists of an ascending or a descending hierarchy of linguistic elements is referred to graphically in the following quotation:

> All the lore of mathematics may be considered as stored in a tall building with many floors, each having spacious entrance hall, large rooms, closets and cupboards of every sort. The ground floor is devoted to arithemetic, the second floor to plane and solid geometry, the next to algebra, then come trigonometry and analytic geometry. Above this are successive floors devoted to calculus, differential equations,

probability, complex function theory, mathematical logic and so on.

There are many books in the different floors but 'Few of these books, however, provide easy transition between floors'.[94]

Ethics, Aesthetics and Mysticism Understood in Relation to the Scheme

Unified science conceived in its global totality and unity cannot afford to leave out any aspect of wisdom, science or knowledge that, when normatively ordered, could belong to it with legitimacy. We have in our days books devoted to what is called the science of emotions. We could have similarly a study of passions as Th. Ribot has done. Mathematics itself has its emotional repercussions and Eddington and others have treated of dry physical calculations and mysticism side by side as aspects of the totality of the human world of inner or outer values or interests. We can only refer to these aspects of the science of man in order just to assign them their positions in the scheme we have so far developed.

Personal taste and aesthetic appreciation go together. The creative artist stands before a painting and what he is capable of appreciating is just what corresponds to what is in him already. The self at the negative pole of the vertical enters into a bi-polar relation with its own non-self aspect and, projecting a world from within outwards is capable of seeing itself in terms of the object of art. Except in the appreciation to cheap multicoloured representations which can still remain in the horizontal, real art is where the self enters in relation with the non-self vertically. This applies to all other art based on other senses or activities than the visual.

Ethics depends on a sense of goodness or value which one admires in oneself as in others. Aristotle's Nichomachean ethics is based on this principle of being specifically oneself. There are other ethics like hedonistic where horizontal values enter.

Mystics are those who are said to cultivate the presence

of God. There are active and intellectual ones among them as also quietists who could be classed as belonging to one or other aspect of the normative scheme we have outlined. Any further elaboration of these aspects will take us beyond the limits of our present study. Whatever space remains we shall devote to applied aspects of the theory we have developed so far.

The Ordinary Language Plea and its Natural Norm

In a speech delivered before the British Academy as recently as the year 1956 the late Prof. J.L. Austin is reported to have had "his eye on the distant — the very distant — prospect of what he called 'a true science of Language', the joint offspring of philosophy, grammar, linguistics, logic and many other disciplines". He was reputed to be a person who advocated the adoption of the common language because he said, among other reasons for basing a scientific language on it "our common stock of words embodies all; the distinctions men have found worth drawing, and the connections they have found worth marking, in the life-times of many generations". Words moreover in the ordinary vocabulary of any language were numerous and already available material to work on. Instead of thinking up new expressions we have to take the given, and, if necessary with ordinary language as basis, improve on it. He thought it important that the tools that philosophers had to use should be clean ones, and words that were to be the tools of philosophers deserved to be treated not as mere facts or things but as representing entities of a subtler order. In thinking of a true science of language he thought in terms of detailed and patient 'anatomisation of attendant vocabularies'. When once asked if this kind of modest ambition would solve all problems, the remarkable philosopher who had devoted his long labours on this subject terminating by his death only this year (1960) is said to have replied characteristically 'No — or if you prefer it; alas, no'.[95]

We are referring here to the above report in order to indicate roughly the prevailing mood at the present moment in respect of the project such as ours in this study which follows roughly the same ambitions, and lines of thought as that of the professor of Oxford. It came to our hands at the moment of the same challenge of this difficult subject on which many noble minds have in the past exercised their superior intelligence in vain. We have taken care to indicate this at the very beginning so that anyone whose expectations were raised higher that what was possible would be intimated in advance. A **veritable science of language** and a **veritable language of science** are the obverse and the reverse of the same coin. In language we touch that central core of all science or wisdom in which philosophy and science meet differencelessly. The uncertainty principle applies here as between the horizontal and vertical aspects of science. The neutral consciousness is where both the axes meet.

This is the age of analysis for philosophy as some thinkers declare and among the analytic philosophers are included all those who do not pin much faith on the notion of the Absolute. Pragmatics and pluralism go together and all notions that seem to refer to the Absolute are not at all in favour with these philosophers who are classed together for some subtle reason as standing against any absolutism in style as in doctrine. Anti-absolutism and de-Hegelization as Morton White would call the attitude in general, characterise the philosophy of the analytical philosophers among whom we have names such as Pierce, Whitehead, James Dewey, Russell, Wittgenstein, Croce, Bergson, Sartre, Santayana and others.

The Decline and Fall of the Absolute

Whether Wittgenstein especially the later could be fitted into a common frame of philosophical reference with the others is itself doubtful. This has been expressed by Morton White himself who has grouped them together.[96] The words analytic and synthetic as applied to philosophies is perhaps the most misleading. An analytic judgment in Kant is not the same as used by Bradley and Bertrand Russell has his own connotation for it in the context of Logical Atomism. The very first chapter of the compilation of analytic philosophies is entitled *The Decline and Fall of the Absolute.* This distaste for anything that savours of Absolutism is a wave of vogue that affects the best of modern minds. Perhaps the bad taste for the word, otherwise a respectable and scientifically and epistemologically strict word, has something to do with the last World War and the bitter taste that some political absolutists left behind. Dialectics and absolutism go together in the sober philosophical context untainted by power politics, and there is no reason why it should not be re-instated after "its decline and fall". The indeterminate neutral world which we have had so often, indicated in this study, and without which a normative notion would be difficult and incorrect to postulate, is in fact tacitly accepted by the most extreme of pragmatists as can be proved from the examination of select paragraphs from their writings. In fact the notion of the Absolute is at the basis of philosophising and in thinking so we have the support of no less a philosopher than Bergson who is otherwise referred to as the greatest of the philosophers of action or pragmatism. Speaking of the extra-intellectual element that Kant introduced into philosophical thought Bergson writes:

> *. . . . Coincidant avec cette matière (extra-intellectuelle) adoptant le même rhythme et le même movement, la conscience, ne pourrait — elle pas, par deux efforts de direction inverse, se haussant et s'abissant tour à tour, saisir du dedans et non plus apercevoir du dehors les deux formes de la réalité, corps et esprit? Ce double effort ne nous ferait-il pas, dans la mesure du possible, revivre l'absolu? Comme d'ailleurs, au cours de cette operation, on verrait l'intelligence surgir d'elle même, se découper dans le tout de l'esprit, la connaissance intellectuelle apparaîtrait alors telle qu'elle est, limitée, mais non plus relative.*[97]

This dialectically revalued and revived notion of the absolute placed by intrapolation, as it were, into the context of the extra-intelligent factor which is the extrapolated factor of the same principle with the dichotomy or polarisation as between mind and body, is a complete schematic representation of what we have called the vertical axis of reference in different contexts in the course of this study. A scientific normatively understood notion of the Absolute placed at the core of life is one of the principal contributions we wish to make in the present study as necessary and inevitable for building round it a veritable science of language and thereby laying the foundations of a veritable language of science. Just as we have seen how elements of dialectical thought are implicit in philosophers who would disavow any such description of their philosophies the notion of the Absolute is still implicit in their writings.

The Prime Nuclear Pattern of Integrated Thought

The personal pronoun 'I' and the relative pronoun 'This', the one referring to the self and the other referring to the object give us the two primary directions that radiate outward from the central consciousness represented by the neutral Absolute. The horizontal may be said to refer to spatial and the vertical to time or duration in consciousness. We rely on Bergsonian Metaphysics to give the philosophical amplifications in these matters. Intelligence, innate instinctive dispositions and emotions could be referred to the vertical. The line that would demarcate the vertical from the horizontal would depend on the subject in which the norm is postulated. This is because, as Leibniz would put it, "The universe is in a manner multiplied as many times as there are substances".[98] Each monad is a world in itself, and, just as the political personality of a state is complete with ruler and all other aspects temporal or spiritual, so each branch of science of philosophy has its central norm and its other secondary aspects of the vertical and the horizontal. The unit of units is the Absolute Unit. Just as one salt crystal is the same as another in the same matrix, so normalized thought has the same type and form. The microscopic structure in particle physics with its 'parity' and 'strangeness' refer to the two axes within the branch of science of particle physics. The expanding universe with its cosmic rays and galaxies influencing across axes conform to the same model as in quantum physics. They resemble thoughts which, between them, have the same structure. This is what made Sir Edmund Whittaker say: "the intellectual framework of nature is prior to nature herself". We can imagine these nuclear patterns of unit or integrated thought themselves holding together in a pattern that is more general. Small salt crystals adhere to bigger ones with the same crysollographic form.

The Over-all Pattern and the Nuclear Structure

Whether big or small, unique or aggregate, a single over-all framework connects the core of the psycho-physically conceived human consciousness with which we are concerned when we use language scientifically as **of** science, **for** science and **through** science. To bring out the structure of this **frame of the universe** whether anteriorly within us or posteriorly in the visible universe of quantities or calculables resembling number we can think of no better single example than the theorem of Pythagoras. We could think of two right angled triangles with eyes shut or on paper, one of which would refer to the relations between three stars in the sky and the other existing as a familiar notion of its schematised properties in the mind derived from, say, earth measurement in an every-day sense. Divested of colour and form, except in the topological sense, we have a movement of reasoning or thought that could equate, with or without intermediate steps of a mathematico-logical or syllogistic order, the more familiar triangle with the less familiar one. This latter could be the object of investigation. These properties of right-angled triangles could be investigated horizontally in the way known in the class room by cutting out and fitting parts that correspond to the squares of the sides. Even if Euclidean space is not what is to be investigated, some normative over-all notion with two axes of reference could be called the over-all framework. Common sense science lives and moves in the horizontal while the scientist trained to use the concepts and arguments of theoretical mathematics or logic live and move in the vertical. Thus we are able in science to distinguish between two languages, one that is now called ordinary and the other which is called logistic. The controversy now at its zenith, perhaps, as between the choice of a common language or a symbolic language for science could be settled by saying that both have their uses. Scientific certitude is the resultant of the two ways of reasoning taking place simultaneously in the space of linguistic thought neutrally conceived in the context of the Absolute.

The Over-all Structure Applicable to Linguistic Levels

Conviction or certitude that is theoretically apodictic or practically verifiable is both admissible and at the core of the activity called scientific thought. The language of science and the science of language have their common origin in the degree of certitude which is of the essential value that science represents. This certitude can refer to existents like the earth that we measure with geometry or to topological triangles in the mind, leading reason through higher and higher stages. Just as the map and the turn we have to take at a certain crossing of roads in a big city has to be certain only when the roads and the map markings agree, so the central certitude that is a neutral value in science has to be translated into verticalized or horizontalized aspects before communicable common knowledge or calculable pure ideas could take place in the consciousness of man neutrally or norm-atively understood. Scientific language can result only when the structure and peculiarities of the norm of all thought are fully respected. A common man standing in the laboratory of a specialist might need an ordinary explanation of how pointer readings are related to facts or events in the ordinary way that a mechanic can repair a car without being an expert engineer. How they are or how they work is what matters here. If the common man is so interested he might need explanations about the steps of inference that the scientist might use sometimes with many black-boards on pulleys by means of which common sense language becomes more and more verticalized without reference to observables, and going past the point where calculables and observables are both understandable to the common man to the region of Campbellian hypotheses that we have referred to earlier. Thus the same vertico-horizontal structure has to be thought of as applicable at every stage of science. Indirect observables as with stellar spectra and bands that move showing a universe that expands or galaxies moving out peripherally in space and complicated calculables with E numbers thus get into the scope of what is called scientific language. For clarity and certitude that should result from the use of scientific language what is horizontal in content should not be mixed up with what is vertical except for the sake of a particular expert branch where one has to specialize. The dentist should not wait till he attains to the pinnacle of the theoretical secrets of the medical profession before he could ply his trade. That proportion of the calculables and observables that belong properly to an expert-specialist has to be put into an organic or global whole to serve the purposes of that central value that a scientific activity serves. A creative painter who might want to ply his trade can cut himself away from the theory and conventions of painting by imitating a Rembrandt or a Picasso. He would be having his own combination of vertico-horizontal elements that make him valuable or merely successful as a pavement artist. Language might have innumerable shades of possiblities as the colours that are imaginable or possible to make with paints.

Proto-Linguistic and Meta-Linguistic Levels in Scientific Language

Hume, when he asks us categorically to 'Commit it then to the flames' of a correctly conceived book neither containing **experimental reasoning concerning fact and existence** nor **reasoning concerning quantity or number**[99] has a certain conviction which is as it were at the back of his mind. Hume, as a sceptic and phenomenalist would not perhaps approve of the *a priori* as understood by scholastic speculations which he mistrusts strongly. In spite of this however it is certain that he is thinking in terms of certain categories which he wants to put as apodictically certain as possible. As a philosopher he is able to reach within himself, as it were, to this twofold conception which would give according to him any value at all to scientific or scientifically conceived literature of any kind. He may in short be said to have a proto-linguistic pattern in his mind. We have seen how Locke himself, in spite of his clean-slate doctrine of mind, had his categories which fitted into the same pattern. Berkeley differed from Locke and for doing so, while independent of accepting Locke's views he still accepted the same methodological and epistemological frame of reference. His theological affiliations as a dignitary of the church was kept apart perhaps for non-philosophical or unphilosophical reasons. As empiricists all three gave primacy to values said to originate outside or inside some sort of mental space which they never clearly explained. Their scepticism did not amount to disbelief in God but in the tangle of theological disputations about the nature of God. They sought a greater degree of certitude in speculative matters and mistrusing the meta-language of theology which had gone too far in the direction of over-speculativeness, they turned to other frames of reference on which they could feel as if standing on firmer ground. They had, in other words a proper proto-linguistic frame of reference scientifically conceived, for them to erect the superstructure of their philosophies. The result was that their philosophy had a scientific character.

To visualize the meta-linguistic aspect of scientific language we have to choose another example. The vast body of speculative literature giving primacy to names rather than forms could be included under the term. A school-boy who might be describing how a certain salt is to be obtained from an acid and a base might go into details that have nothing to do with the scientific problem, method or value involved. Rules of epistemology might be violated. If a stone hit the head of a boy in the playground he would have to adopt a common proto-language removed far from the meta-language of science. Weeping for it would not fit into the context of the science class or the laboratory. Thus within the limits of the proto- and meta-languages there are many vertico-horizontal systems proper for each level of language to adopt. In a psycho-pathological clinic even the emotional language that the boy might use might fit with more correctness or propriety. Language games refer to the possible levels and dimensions that one has to respect in speaking correctly or scientifically. Now that there is a whole volume of language games of philosophical, logical or linguistic import it is not necessary for us to multiply instances. We are referring here to the *Philosophical Investigations* of L. Wittgenstein published in translation at Oxford in 1953 posthumously.[100] The whole of that book may be treated as a meta-linguistic analysis of the science of linguistics. By normalizing common language on the basis of the implications understood in its complete setting from the point of view of every possible branch of scientific literature is the service that the *Philosophical Investigations* could render to the cause of a common scientific language for unified science.

Meta-language itself could be conceived at different levels in the vertical positive series. Thus we have the logistic formulation in the form of tabulated matrices to clarify the algebraic content of signs and symbols. The lines of the tabulation really belong to the proto-linguistic pole while the letters, symbols or signs used really pertain to the opposite pole. In other schematic representations of the sixteen possibilities of propositional calculus set out with truth or falsehood possibilities, with the truth, grounds which gives both to truth and falsehood possibilities and probabilities a common basis ranging between the limits of tautology vertically above and contradiction vertically at the zero point referring to the contradiction between '*p*' and '*q*', we have, strictly speaking a Platonic world of reasoning through dialectics implicitly contained vertically while syllogistic and Aristotelean horizontally. Aristotelean dialectics did not concern itself with the meta-language of ideas but was limited to the world where matter and form were the polarities involved. His was therefore more in the domain of probabilities rather than possibilities. From contradiction zero point as between '*p*' and '*q*' we could extend the reasoning by descending dialectics to another intuitive unity reaching down to the non-relativist notion of matter itself through such notions as the *prius nobis* that Aristotle uses along the lines suggested in the quotation from Bergson given above in this section.

Meta-language is thus what tends to stand apart from scientific language proper in order to examine it from apart just as proto-language is also meant to function from the negative pole of intelligence. We have by extrapolation and by intrapolation to visualize the three levels here involved: The meta-language above, the proto-language below and scientific language proper in the central zone of the vertical axis with the 'two efforts in inverse directions' that Bergson refers to above, we come to the emergence of scientific language. When correctly horizontalized at the point of intersection where contradiction is accpected as against mere sufficient reason we become able to interpret the purer language of any science into the scientifically correct ordinary or common language. Common language is thus to be understood as nothing but the horizontalized version of the pure language of science which tends to become a meta or proto-language in inverse senses.

Any number of compromises between the vertical series containing proto- or meta-elements of language would be possible, and experts in each science should decide for themselves where they want to fix the standard language in the scale of possible languages. They have to delimit its range and take account of overtness or innateness involved in each branch of science. Gestalt psychology may have to be given an inner zone while stimulus-response or behaviouristic psychology is like the colour that is less saturated. The analogy of the colour solid with which we terminated the first part of this study should be used here for further guidance.

Horizontal Implications of Scientific Language

Before passing on in the next section to the practical steps we have to take in the direction of making a language for unified science we have to mention where the colour solid analogy comes in as more useful than the mere vertico-horizontal correlation of plane geometry. The solid gives us a means of integrating all strictly 'objective' sciences such as heat, light, electricity, mechanics, etc. without any vertical depth involved in them. Here instead of an axis it would be better to think in terms of radii that diverge from zero vectorial point through the 360^0 and assign to each branch a well thought out number or letter or both to mark overtness or deflection from negative to positive.

Even in this strictly horizontal psycho-physical level

where body and mind meet it is possible to think of an axis of reference for linguistic purposes as valid as the words we use when we call a rose a 'rose'. Here we have to think of the distinction that Fechner makes between inner and outer psycho-physics and also of the primary and secondary qualities as known to Locke from the time of Democritus. A colour attributed to an object would have a primary status if treated as outside the mind and as colour vision could be accentuated by the drinking of drugs like mescaline and lysergic acid as Sir Russell Brain has pointed out. To the extent colour is virtual one has to take it to belong to the negative pole of the horizontal and when taken as 'outside the mind' (which possibility is questionable according to the epistemology at the basis of psycho-physics) we have to place the colour as belonging to a paint that we might be using to colour wash a wall as pertaining to the positive pole of the horizontal. The question of the delimitation of dimensions for each branch of science we shall consider in the next section. The Ladd-Franklin theory of colour vision might also help us to fix further points or degrees in the schematic analogy of the colour solid that we have adopted for correlating the structure of thought scientifically.

Misplaced Enthusiasm for a Scientific Language

A misplaced enthusiasm for a scientific language is sometimes worse than no enthusiasm at all. We have seen a sample copy of the *International Language Review* from the perusal of whose pages it is amply evident that there is a world-wide interest in this question. Esperanto and Sanskrit have merits which could be compared and pronounced by the touchstone of our scheme here as fitted for horizontal and vertical aspects of language communicability respectively. One is all roots and the other has no roots yet worth speaking about. Both root and branch aspects of a language have to be considered necessary. There are others who stifle their enthusiasm and fervour in such a way that hurts them making for martyrs in the cause of a universal language, the dream of humanity since the days of the Biblical episode of the Tower of Babel. From the start, in writing the foregiong pages we have had no illusions about the complexity and enormity of the task. But side by side with the sentiment, there has been the opposite feeling that even if the idea of a universal language and its accomplishment are to be separated by time and much effort there would be no harm still in exploring its avenues and possibilities. After having made as genuine an effort in this direction as perhaps it would be possible to make on the part of one individual isolated and not in contact with those who can really deliver the goods in such an undertaking, the following suggestions are made in the genuine hope that those who are placed in better positions of advantage may follow up further the lines on which this study has been undertaken and we only brought this up to a point on which more fruitful discussions could be based. Sobering though the effect has been of making an effort in the ambitious direction in which many minds have been frustrated, there is no cause still for any discouragement. Given the cooperation of cultural or scientific bodies who have an open and understanding mind in such matters, unlike some who believe in closing rather than broadening their frontiers of enquiry, there is hope that the idea of a language of science could be realized when approached with the proper attitude.

Division V : Retrospect; Present Position; Concrete Suggestions

Main Findings

The reader who has taken the trouble and had the patience to go through the foregoing pages, now that we are drawing close to the termination, may be expected to put the question: 'What then?' Is there anything that could result in tangible form as the upshot of the whole study? What is the practical value? We shall begin by summarising what we have tried to establish and then make the suggestions.

We have tried to supply a normative notion for a science of language. Such a norm has been approached both experimentally and merely normatively in the two parts of the study.

We have offered some methodological and epistemological clarifications leading up to the normative notion. The experimental discipline of science is based on observations and not primarily on inference. We have tried to show that observations could be made through the indirect evidence of pointer readings as well as by introspective experimental situations and we have tried to make clear that one kind of certitude is as good as the other.

We have supported the central notion of this study, which pertains to the reality that we have referred to as the vertical axis of thought as distinguished from its own horizontal counterpart, with evidence derived as far as could be from the electro-encephalograph. The study of psycho-pathology, psycho-pedagogics and psycho-physics in the light of our revised epistemology and methodology has brought us support of an experimental status to the central notion.

Colour solid has been given a central position as representing the two kinds of certitudes on which science has to depend, viz., the observables and the calculables. The visible and the thinkable come together as it were from both sides of physiology or of psychology so as to yield a model of the integration of thought — characteristics, combinations and modalities after the pattern of the colour solid. We could think of it with intrapolation or extrapolation in our minds so as to extend its applicability beyond the limits of the colour world to the larger scientific world where elements of thought have to be perceived and conceived as forming a global whole.

The abstract notion of the norm would have a neutral ground with the help of which what we have tried to distinguish as the proto- and meta-linguistic aspects to come together from opposite poles as it were to coalesce to result in a normalized common language.

Non-experimental but fully philosophical evidence of the use of a schematic proto-language by many philosophers already who may be called scientific to the extent they adhered to the normative principles implied therein was then discussed by us.

We then passed on to examine the claims of the logical-empiricists in the cause of a unified science and a language that would correspond to it. Their failure consisted in that they had a horizontal axis of reference instead of a vertical one whose importance was brought out by certain members of the group who had gone beyond their point of view and left the school of thought behind.

The investigations and interest in the dimensions and implications of simple everyday expressions have been examined and fitted into the frame of our scheme. Mathematics and dialectical reasonings which represent highly verticalized thought have much to do with scientific thought and reach beyond its ordinary limits to the domains of mysticism, aesthetics and ethics.

We have upheld the plea for a common or ordinary language for all science provided no methodological, epistemological or axiological rules, principles or laws are violated. Normalization ascends to the neutral, as it were, from below, and re-normalization descends to conform to the requirements of the neutral norm, as it were from above. At each level we have to delimit the vertical or horizontal factors that enter into the composition of a science as having a unitive value or significance. The notion of the modality is to be addded to the integration as a dimension to be understood after the analogy of the factor called saturation in the context of the colour solid. It could be stated meta-linguistically as that modal relation between subject and predicate referring to the degree of concreteness or apodictic certitude as between those that are hypothetical, theoretical or problematic.[101]

Normalization Calls for Cooperative Effort

The process of normalization within the limits of any particular branch of science has to be conceived in the light of concomitant variations on the vertical as well as the horizontal. The canons of Mill and many other epistemological and methodological requirements would be respected by this principle of paired limits to be fixed round a central normative notion of each branch of science. Botany will have an ideal plant or a cell depending on morphology or histology. Psychology would belong to the proper study of man both from bodily and mental sides. In mysticism the study of man has to have the vertical aspects pronounced as against the mechanized man who fits into a robot world. This work of finding the central normative value, fixing the vertical amplitude and concomitant positive or negative factors or the horizontal amplitude with its limits of agreement or disagreement with residual factors, is the task experts have to do sitting round a table collecting, collating and organically ordering data. Such work must proceed from two ends viz. normalization and re-normalization of the simplest elements of thought like words, and the normalization and re-normalization of whole branches such as psychology, sociology, economics etc. Then there is the overall normalization in more comprehensive absolutist terms. This has to be tackled with a plan commonly conceived by a group of persons sufficiently interested in one language for unified science. It is not in terms of an invention by one or two individuals that this aspect of the work is to be conceived. It has to be a combined and cooperative effort of an adventure that would take forward strides by discovery of new possibilities as the work goes on.

Inevitability of a Certain Vagueness in the Study

Looking retrospectively for a minute over what we have been able to express with any degree of definiteness we have to admit that in many parts, especially as we approach the middle of the study as a whole, there is a vagueness that belongs as much at least to the subject-matter as to the lack of power of expression on the part of the present writer. An uncertainty principle seems involved here, but this is not said for excuse for lack of clarity which we are conscious is there.

Vertico-Horizontal Mapping of Word Systems

Just as imaginary numbers could be arranged with reference to lines that resemble latitudes and longitudes[102] it is suggested here that the first bit of concrete work to be undertaken even if the above ideas are only tentatively accepted as a basis of discussion and prospective action, would naturally concern the systematic correlation of words into integrated systems conceived round the correlates. As a first step it would suffice to correlate the vertical and the horizontal aspects. The other variations based on the colour solid analogy would serve for the establishment of a hierarchy of concrete sciences. Heat, light, electricity etc. may be given radial positions round the base of the double cones that meet neutrally at the zone where spectral colours of medium brilliance are located. The 360 degrees of variation radially possible will give to librarians and others a way of classifying objective or positive physical sciences. Already there are two kinds of 'objectivity': one speaks of the real objectivity and the virtual objectivity often written within quotation marks.

Review of Recent Efforts

The confusion of tongues in the Bible and the great dream of Leibniz which seemed to come as an answer to need that humanity has felt for a universal scientific language have culminated in our own times in a concerted effort on the part of leading scientists to proclaim their solidarity and singleness of purpose as evidenced by the publication of an *International Encyclopaedia of Unified Science*. It is hard to say from a perusal of the leading articles in the first volume where the scope of the publication is indicated, whether this age old ambition that has persisted through the centuries is actually heading to a successful climax or a mere anticlimax. The cover itself by its blurb design shows that the integration that is intended in the publications is nothing more than that of a mosaic where black and white are put together according to some distant general or vaguely understood over-all design of a common plan. We read in the very first article by Otto Neurath that the ambition of an 'All-embracing vision and thought' is an 'old desire of humanity'; and that an 'empiristic mosaic' was the limit of the ambition of the compilers is stated as follows: "For, since one cannot compare the historically given science with 'the real science', the most one can achieve in integration of scientific work seems to be an encyclopaedia, constructed by scientists in cooperation."[103] In another context we read: "If one prefers a comprehensive scientific attitude, this encyclopaedia tries to show him the spectrum of scientific thinking".[104] We already notice a difference between a mere mosaic and a spectrum, the former being a more arbitatrary relation between colours than the scientific and neutral relation between spectral colours. Scientism and empiricism to which the group is committed in advance cannot evidently permit them to go any further. Bertrand Russell speaks of the principle of a dictionary and remarks: "Given two sets of propositions such that, by a suitable dictionary, any proposition of either set can be translated into a proposition of the other set, there is no effective difference between the two sets . . . ."[105] Such dictionaries, which can, as a rule only be constructed by the help of modern logic, suffice to dispose of a large number of metaphysical questions, and thus facilitate concentration upon genuine scientific problems. Niels Bohr takes the view that "science is, according to its aim of enlarging human understanding, essentially a unity". Extremes of materialism and mysticism are to be avoided as he says by a "never ending endeavour to balance analysis and synthesis".[106]

All the above writers are right to the extent that they think in terms of encyclopaedias and dictionaries and, what is more, there seems to be a strange undercurrent of agreement between the different contributors though this is not evident at the surface. In the light of what we have said in the present study the plan of Russell to two sets of propositions seems to suggest the same distinction as between the vertical and horizontal aspects of thinking or reasoning. Niels Bohr's vision like ours does not exclude mysticism from the scope of science and even in the very conservative looking attitude of Otto Neurath we notice that there is more than a mere mosaic to be understood by a non-pretentious encyclopaedia. The principle of unity or integration must be implicit rather than explicit. Thus we see that the dream of Leibniz who is still the inspirer of the unified science movement, is far from being abandoned by his followers although the warmth of the first enthusiasm seems to have sobered down a great deal.

Scientism has its own affiliations and loyalties to the exigencies of which all these writers seem to bow down too repectfully. A true scientist according to us should be free from all taint of 'isms' however justificable on their own merits. Only then could the cause of unified science and of a language that is its corollary be even viewed in its proper proportion and perspective. One has to be able to stand back and look at the whole form to see not only the mosaic and a spectrum but a psycho-physical totality which is no other than unified science. The language of unified science has to result from the meeting of two views from opposite sides.

Conclusion

It is not difficult to see from the few quotations that we have taken from the leaders of the logico-empiricist school who plan a unified science and a language to go with it, that the ideas of integration and the possibility of a language do not hold before us anything of the nature of a very encouraging prospect that could rouse our enthusiasm. What we have to suggest, after discussing the same subject from a more comprehensive and global point of view, is that integration in a more cohesive sense and what we have called a unitive attitude of non-duality between body and mind would be possible as soon as the partiality for empiricism is relaxed. One has to begin at the normative core which is neutral and which is the meeting point of the tendencies that radiate along the two axes in which scientific thought, reasoning or interest might be said to live and move. We can only hope to elaborate what we mean in the merest of outlines here because in an undertaking of this kind it is not the philosophy of one person that should count. At every step we take in the direction of the ambitious ideal that we set before ourselves we have to see that there is the greatest of consensus of intelligent opinion behind us.

In this connection the age old saying that the proper study of mankind is man would at least indicate where we have to begin. Cosmology puts the accent on the visible world and psychology refers to the world within as given to the shut eyes. We could take to begin with such pairs of names like

Descartes and Newton and think of them with reference to their contributions to cosmology and psychology. Voltaire has compared and contrasted these great personalities of science and philosophy. Before pronouncing any opinion on this, let us pass on to think of a pair of modern thinkers like Bergson and Eddington. How are we to give them their respective places in this psycho-physical or psycho-cosmological scheme? Eddington as a non-experimental scientist has to be given a place with thinkers who use the subtle dialectical language of mathematics. What is within himself when his eyes are shut he is able to equate with cosmological realities of the outer universe. Bergson being against mathematics and still essentially dialectical in his approach, and also because he affiliates himself to a world of living activity, must be located more towards the centre of the vertical axis. The man and the world that goes with him have to be put together before the process of hierarchisation of sciences could be thought of at all.

We have broadly referred to three divisions from the beginning of this study, viz. scientific philosophy, science of science and philosophical science. If we think of the trio of British empiricists Locke, Berkeley and Hume, as sceptics who gave primacy to the horizontal values in life, we could grade them roughly as follows: Locke should be placed at the extreme right or plus of the horizontal because he went so far as to say that things could exist outside mind. Concomitantly he made the mind blank like a clean slate. Berkeley would pertain to the negative end of the same axis and Hume as a phenomenologist who believed equally in number and quantity should occupy a central place. If we take the four rationalist philosophers from Descartes to Kant through Spinoza and Leibniz we could at once see that the Cartesian dictum 'cogito-ergo sum' gives the key to all of them. They fall in the vertical axis and the body-mind duality for which Descartes is often blamed is because his zone pertained to the central core of the psycho-physical norm in a very scientific or real sense. Occassionalism touched the neutral point of the vertical axis. Kant's 'thing-in-itself' and the noumenon was a full recognition of the vertical axis and its philosophical implications. Occassionalism, elaborated a little, gives us the thinking substance of Spinoza with its *natura naturans* and *natura naturata* which refer to the vertical and the horizontal respectively. The monad of Leibniz is nothing but a more elaborated version of the thinking substance with the accent on the vertical aspects and made into a hierarchical series. We too have put forward the view that there should be as many vertico-horizontal frames applied as many items of scientific reality there are to be dealt with by a scientific language.

Now if we pass on to phenomenologists, existentialists, hylozoists of the pre-Socratic times or even to the patristic and scholastic philosophers of various grades we have to think more in terms of a dialectics that is subtle and tends to be forgotten in modern times of mechanistic progress. Aristotelean dialectics moves only as between matter and form, while Platonic dialectics soars up and dowm at higher levels of the vertical axis. Existentialists especially when they discredit essence in favour of existence, and shut their eyes to the abstract notion of the Absolute, tend to place their interest at the bottom of the vertical scale of values. Post Hegelean phenomenologists have a dynamism where thoughts meet from opposite sides to constitute events in consciousness in which the equation of the self with the non-self is implied. This kind of equation is explicit in the philosophy of Fichte. Renouvier translates the same verticalized bi-polar relation into more personalistic terms. He could be placed high up in the vertical positive side of the scale.

We do not wish to tread on these grounds in any greater detail. In order to secure the greatest volume of support for this cause of unified science and its language we cannot do better than to follow the lead given by the scientific empiricists but on different lines. A vertico-horizontal mapping of word systems has first to be undertaken. The usual dictionary may be conceived more on the lines of a thesaurus like Roget's but with synonyms and antonyms of two sets, referring to the vertical and horizontal meanings. Word-system maps could be appended to usual dictionaries inspired by normalization and re-normalization.

If what we have very roughly indicated is understood at all, the rest of the work may be left to a committee of experts.

Notes

1. "Leibniz thought that a language could be constructed which would be much more efficient for reasoning and for communication than the vague, complicated and more or less parochial languages then available. This language would be completely universal in the sense that all scientific and philosophic concepts could be expressed in it, and also in that it would enable scholars in all countries to communicate over the barriers of their vernacular tongues." — P.P. Wiener, *Dictionary of Philosophy*, by D. Runes, Jaico Publishing, Bombay.

2. Dr. Holton, Prof. of Physics, Harvard University wtites: ". . . Science advances faster and faster everyday, widening the rift between science and culture.

   To restore them to some kind of reciprocal contact within the concerns of most men — to bring science into an orbit about us instead of letting it escape from the field of our common culture — that is the great challenge before intellectuals to-day. And nothing better illustrates the urgency and difficulty of this task than the false images prevailing about science." Cf., *Art, The False Images of Science*, The Saturday Evening Post, Jan. 9, 1960, p. 72.

   Earlier in the same he had point out: "Having destroyed absolute standards, it (science) puts nothing in their place." (*Ibid.*, p. 70)

3. *Tractatus Logico Philosophicus*, London, 1922, p. 79.

4. Leibniz himself had hinted at the importance of 'form' in logical or other reasoning when he wrote:

   "I hold that the invention of the form of syllogisms is one of most beautiful which the human mind has made, and even one of the most considerable. It is a kind of *universal mathematics* whose importance is not sufficiently known" Quoted from "New Essays", p. 559 in *Russell's Philosophy of Leibnitz* Camb. 1900, p. 282.

5. Cf. *The New Mathematics*, Irwing Adler, Day and Co. New York, 1958.

6. "Pour donner, dans tous les cas possible, une signification à la somme et au produit de deux éléments, on introduit deux éléments nouveaux: l' *élément zéro* V (ou absence de points, de droites et de plans) et l' *élément universel* U (ou totalité de ces éléments, c'est-à-dire l'espace). Par définition l'élément zéro V est contenu dans tout élémént et l'on convient qu'il a un nombre négatif — 1 de dimensions; par définition également, l'élément universel U contient tout élément et a trois dimensions. Ces deux éléments nouveaux sont appelés les *éléments impropres*, les autres sont les *éléments propres*. Supposons, maintenant, que A et B représentent par example, deux droites qui ne se rencontre pas dans l'espace; on

aura A + B = U et A.B. = V et on voit que la somme et le produit de deux éléments quelconques représentent toujours un élément soit propre, soit impropre." — Col. Ar. Colin, *Les Nombres et Les Espaces*, Gustave Verriest; Paris 1956, pp. 180-81.

7. "When we run over libraries . . . . what havoc must we make? If we take in our hand any volume, of divinity or school metaphysics for instance, let as ask, *Does it contain any abstract reasoning concerning quantity or number?* No. *Does it contain any experimental reasoning concerning matter of fact and existence?* No Commit it then to the flames; for it can contain nothing but sophistry and illusion." — Essays Routledge Lond. , pp. 384-85. Cf. Also *Ibid.*, p. 383 'It seems to me that the only objects of the abstract science or of demonstration are quantity and number . . . '
8. *Ibid.*, p. 321.
9. He adds : "But that this enumeration is complete, and that there are no other principles of association except these, may be difficult to prove to the satisfaction of the reader, or even to a man's own satisfaction." *Ibid.*, p. 321.
10. p. 41, Vol. I Chicago University, 1955.
11. *Ibid.*
12. *The Nature of the Physical World*, Dent. Lond. 1947, p. 328.
13. Speaking of Eddington's Principle on the Philosophy of Science Sir. Edmund Whittaker F.R.S. said: "The development of quantum electro-dynamics has, in fact shown the necessity for what is called *re-normalization* which is precisely a recognition of the difference between observed and theoretical values . . . etc." — Camb. Univ. Press 1951, p. 25.
14. *History of Western Philosophy*, London, 1946, p. 861.
15. *Tractatus Logico-Philosophicus*, London 1922, p. 31.
16. *History of Western Philosophy*, London, 1946, p. 861.
17. Bergson, *Oeuvres*; Centenary Edition, Paris 1959, pp. 254-55.
18. The initial idea of the scope of such 'experiments' in philosophy is found in the Verses 10 and 11 of the *Ātmopadeśa Śatakam* of Guru Narayana translated by me and commented. cf. *Life and Teachings of Narayana Guru*, East-West University, Fernhill, S. India, 1990, pp. 488-99.
19. "If S1 and S2 are different people, 'S1' s protocol language refers to the content of S1's experience. S2's . . . to the content of S2 . . . 'What can the inter-subjective physical language refer to?' The answer is it refers to the experiences of anyone you please." — A.J. Ayer, *The Problem of Knowledge*, London 1957, p. 211.
20. *The Listener*, London, Oct. 1, 1959, p. 521.
21. *Ibid.*
22. *Ibid.*, p. 522.
23. *Matiére et Memoire*, ed. by Skira; Geneva 1946, pp. 117, 130 ff.
24. Bergson, *Oeuvres*; Centenary edn. Paris 1959. pp. 254-55.
25. *Matiére et Memoire*, ed. by Skira; Geneva, 1946, p. 118.

26. *Psychoses et Névroses* by Henri Baruk, Paris 1946, pp. 5-6.
27. Bergson alludes to *Dyslexie* in connection with the two forms of memory that he distinguished to which he alludes as follows:

    'Ce souvenir spontané, qui se cache sans doute derriére la souvenir acquis peut se révéler par des éclairs brusques: mais il se dérobe, au moindre mouvement de la memoire. Si le sujet voit diaparatre la série de letters dont il croyait avoir retenu l'image, c' est surtout pendent qu'il commence a les répéter 'cet effort semble pousser le reste de l'image hors de la conscience.' He adds in a foot-note on the same page: 'Ne serait-ce pas quelque chose du même genre qui se passe dans cette affection que les auteurs allemends ont appelée *dyslexie*?' *Matiére et Memoire* Geneva 1946 pp. 89-90 and fn.
28. *La Force et Faiblesse Psychologiques*: Malone edn. Paris, 1932, p. 11.
29. Henri Baruk '*Psychoses et Névroses*, Paris 1946.
30. *Ibid.*, p. 25.
31. *La Personnalité Humaine; Son Analyse*, Delmas et Boll Flammarion Paris, 1930, p. 25.
32. *Man the Unknown*, Lond. 1956, p. 231.
33. Extract from the Conclusion of 'Le Facteur Personnel dans le Processus Educatif' by the present author of this study (Thesis for Univ. of Paris later published by Librarie Philosophique Vrin Paris 1932, out of print at present) page 171.

    Notre point de depart principal a été de considérer l' individu comme un tout, c'est-à-dire ayant une vie corporelle, avec ses comportements et ses emotions; doué d'une intelligence et d'un pouvoir de pensée réfléchie. Cet examen de l' inventaire de tout ce qui appartient à l' individu, nous a permis de parler de deux aspects de la personnalité: l'un qui envisage l'activité réceptive, représentative, symboliqu et *strictement individuelle*; l'autre, l'activité expressive, réelle, sociale, se conformant au monde objectif qui nous entoure. Ce qui ressort tout d'abord de cette distinction, c'est le fait que nous ne pouvons pas nous baser uniquement sur l'expression des capacités mentales de l'enfant, mais qu'en le jugeant nous devons tenir compte de l'arrière-plan de la personnalité de l'enfant. Cette distinction nous a amené aussi à considérer les types d'élèves comme les expressions asymétriques de ces deux aspects fondamentaux de la personnalité. En examinant ce processus d' éducation, nous avons constaté que les étapes de croissance de l'enfance á l'âge adulte présentaient des caractères qui correspondent en même temps, aux types que nous avons distingués: l'enfance, jusqu'á 8 ans environ, se présente sous ce que nous avons appelé le type négatif-subjectif, l'adulte, qui a passé la vingtaine, le type positif-subjectif; le type négatif-objectif et le type positif-objectif s'intercalant entre les deux âges mentionnés ci-dessus.

    Nous avons essayé de voir comment, en rapport avec chaque ètape et chaque type d'élève, le maître doit se représenter le type de son influence éducative: rétrospective, prospective, négative ou positive, suivant les cas.

Cette dernière nécessité implique une relation entre la maître et l'éléve, qui doit avoir un caractère bipolaire, remplissant les conditions exposées plus haut. Ainsi l' éducation doit être conçue comme un contact entre le maître et l' élève, dans un sens intime et personnel, ne pouvant en aucun cas, être remplacé par un systéme, par des régles, des programmes ou des méthodes élaborées.

Nous avons finalement examiné les théories existentes sur l'éducation et essayé d'en voir la relation avec les différentes étapes de l'adaptation personnelle. Dans l' étape négative, le maître a une influence de contrôle et de sélection, sur l'ambiance de l'enfance. Il n'est pas question de guider intellectuellement, mais d'établir des relations intimes entre le maître et l'élève. Dans l'étape moyenne de l'adaptation (c'est-à-dire entre 15 et 20 ans), l'enfant a besoin d'une activité sociale. La relation intime et personnelle n'est pas aussi nécessaire que dans la première et la derniére étape, comme nous l'avons dit. Dans la derniére étape, le maître devient à proprement parler un guide: il représente l'idéal subjectif qui est caché dans l'avenir. Ceci constitute l'étape idéaliste dernière dans le processus. L'idéal de vie, des attitudes mentales, les interêts dirigeants d'une personnalité plus évoluée sont, par une méditation constants de la part de l'élève, transférés ou greffés sur lui-même, lui donnant une vision plus profonde de la vie.

Nous avons examiné d'autre part quelques concepts de la pensée hindoue qui donne depuis des temps anciens une importance particulière aux relations personnelles entre le Gourou et l' élève. Nous avons pu d'ailleurs utiliser dans notre discussion quelques-uns des concepts spéciaux appartenant à la pédagogie hindoue, à propos surtout des étapes négatives et idéalistes de l'adaptation personnelle. Ils ont suffi à démontrer amplement que cette pédagogie, dans ce qu'elle a d'essentiel, est conforme au schéma du développement personnel et des relations éducatives que nous avons présenté dans cette étude.

34. *Child Psychology*: Neuchatel and Paris, 1959.

35. We are indebted to the review of Piaget's latest work appearing in the Bulletin of the International Bureau of Education 4th Quarter, 1959 for the resumé and quotations of the work. cf. p. 241.

36. *Les Notions de Mouvement et de Vitesse Chez l' enfant*: Paris, p. 273 fn.

37. *Les Origines de la Penséé Chez l'enfant*, Paris, 1947, p. 209.

38. *Ibid.*, p. 437.

39. C.W. Morris *International Cyclopedia of Unified Science*, Vol. I, Part I, Chicago, 1955, p. 134.

40. *The Listener*, London, March 10, 1960, p. 443.

41. *Ibid.*

42. The classification of colours on the basis of the colour solid as the introspective psycho-physical entity is now well-known as attributed to Albert H. Munsell (1858-1919) who, it is stated: 'Borrowing

from Helmholtz . . classified colours according to hue, lightness and saturation. The horizontal axis proceeds from the vertical black-grey-white. cf. *Colliers Encyclopaedia*, p. 485, Vol. 5, (More details below).

43. Kegan Paul London, 1922, pp. 31-35.
44. **See** pp. 280-81 above.
45. '. . . notre intelligence triomphe dans la géométrie, où se révèle la parehtéde la pensée logiqe avec la matiére inerte etc . .' Bergson; Ev. Cr. Cf. Pascal, *Pensées et Opuscules*: Lib. Hatier Paris, p. 13; 'de l'esprit géométrique; *Oeuvres*, Paris, 1959, p. 489.
46. **See** pp. 298-300 above.
47. Carnap's Article *Int. Ency. of Unif. Sc*, Vol. I Part II, pp. 143 ff.
48. Broomfield's article *Ibid.*, p. 219 ff and p. 88 Morris Sec 4 Language.
49. Unabridged Second Edition.
50. The characterisation of this scheme being intropective and arbitrary.
51. Quoted from *Panorama* Gallimard Paris, 1957 extracted from trad. Rossignol Hermann, p. 575.
52. *The English Cyclopaedia*, Vol. 3, London, 1856, p. 697.
53. Cf. Under Leibniz, *Ibid.*
54. *Dictionary of Philosophy*, Runes, Jaico Bombay, 1956.
55. Quoted from p. 132 *Philosophy Made Simple*, New York, 1958.
56. Cf. *Columbia Cyclopaedia* under Quaternions. (**See also** Note 7 above)
57. *A Critical Exposition of the Philosophy of Leibniz*. B. Russell, Camb. Univ. Press, 1900, p. 252 and 283-84 respectively.
58. *Tractatus*.
59. pp. 2 to 25 ff. Lecture Delivered 9th Aug. 1951, Camb. Univ. Press.
60. *Ibid.*, pp. 5-6.
61. *Ibid.*, pp. 14-15.
62. *Ibid.*, p. 29.
63. *Ibid.*, p. 31.
64. Copied from p. 57 *Nature of the Physical World*, Everyman, Lond. 1947.
65. *Oeuvres*, Centenary edn. Paris, 1959, p. 1432.
66. La Pensée et Mouvant, Ganéve, 1946, pp. 211-16.
67. *Oeuvres*: Centenary edn. Paris, 1959, pp. 284-85.
68. *The Listener*, Lond. Feb. 25, 1960.
69. *Ibid.*
70. *International Encyclopaedia of Unified Science*, Chicago, Vol. I Part I, p. 147.
71. *History of Western Philosophy*, Lond. 1946, p. 859.
72. Hume's *Essays*, Routledge, London, p. 383.
73. *International Encyclopaedia of Unified Science*: Vol. I, Part I, Chi-

cago, 1955, p. 210.

74. *Ibid.*
75. p. 173, item 6⁰241 : *Tractatus Logico-Philosophicus*, Kegan Paul, Lond. 1922.
76. *Ibid.*, p. 8.
77. *International Encyclopaedia of Unified Science*, Chicago, 1955, p. 82, Part I Vol. I.
78. *Ibid.*, p. 84.
79. *International Encyclopaedia of Unified Science*, Vol. I, Part I, p. 231.
80. *Ibid.*
81. *The Listener*, Lond. Oct. 1, 1959, p. 519.
82. *Ibid.*
83. *Tractatus*, Kegan Paul, Lond. 1922, p. 189.
84. *The Age of Analysis*, Mentor, New York, 1956 as quoted from *Philosophical Investigations*, Oxford, 1953, p. 231,
85. *Les Letters Nouvelles* : Nov. 25, 1959, p. 37, Julliard Paris, Tr. from German by Pierre Klossowski.
86. *Ibid.*, p. 39.
87. p. 235-6, *The Age of Analysis*, Mentor New York, 1956 as quoted from item 77 of *Philosophical Investigations* of Wittgenstein, Oxford, 1953.
88. The numbers in brackets in this chapter and previous chapters refer to items of Wittgenstein's *Tractatus*.
89. *Principles of Logic* : A.C. Bradley : Kegan Paul, London, 1883, p. 149.
90. *Annuaire du Collége de France*, 1948, p. 121.
91. *Oeuvres*, Centenary edn. Paris, 1959, p. 674.
92. *The Age of Analysis*, New York 1955, p. 144 quoting *Popular Science*, Monthly, Jan 1878.
93. *Nature of the Physical World*, Lond. 1947, p. 306.
94. *Mathematics for Science and Engineering*, Philip L. Alger, New York, 1957, p. vii.
95. The report above is from *The Listener*, London of April 7, 1960.
96. The passage below gives a glimpse of the contrast between the later Wittgenstein and all the three of the other 'analytic' philosophers represented in this volume : Carnap. Moore and Russell. In fact the contrast is great enough to warrant our not calling the later Wittgenstein as an analytic philosopher at all. — *The Age of Analysis*, New York 1956, p. 229.
97. Bergson, *Oeuvres*, Paris, 1959, p. 797.
98. Cf. *Encyclopaedia Britannica*, under *Theory of Knowledge*.
99. Hume's *Essays*, Routledge, London, pp. 384-85.
100. Blackwell, Oxford, Tr. G.E.M. Anscombe.
101. 'We may take for instance a content S-P, not yet asserted, and may claim for modality the power of affirming this content S-P unaltered and unqualified in several ways. S-P, it is supposed, may be

asserted, for instance either simply or problematically or apodictically and yet remain throughtout S-P; and thus, though the content is unmodified, the assertion is modal. — A.C. Bradley. *Principles of Logic*, p. 181 (London, 1883).

102. Explaining this method of longitude and latitude we read: 'Imaginary numbers are a particular case of what are called complex numbers, which consist of a real and an imaginary part . . . a so-called complex number is actually a pair of numbers, and if one thinks of it in that way the mystery vanishes.' — M.G. Kendall, Prof. Lond. Univ., cf. *The Listener*, Nov. 19, 1959.

103. *International Encyclopaedia of Unified Science*, Vol. I, Part I, pp. 12 and 20, Chicago, 1955.

104. *Ibid.* p. 23.

105. *Ibid.*, p. 41.

106. *Ibid.*, p. 28.

Index